LOVING
OURSELVES

LOVING OURSELVES

*The Gay and
Lesbian Guide
to Self-Esteem*

KIMERON N. HARDIN, *Ph. D.*
FOREWORD BY JOE KORT, *M.A., MSW, ACSW*

alyson books
NEW YORK

To Judith Leary, who raised five good kids into five wonderful people.
Thanks for sharing one of them with me.

Portions of this book were first published as *The Gay and Lesbian Self-Esteem Book: A Guide to Loving Ourselves* by New Harbinger Publications, Inc.

Manufactured in the United States of America

Published by Alyson Books
245 West 17th Street, New York, NY 10011

Distribution in the United Kingdom by Turnaround Publisher Services Ltd.
Unit 3, Olympia Trading Estate, Coburg Road, Wood Green
London N22 6TZ England

First Edition: March 2008

08 09 10 11 12 13 14 15 16 17 ▉ 10 9 8 7 6 5 4 3 2 1

ISBN: 1-59350-045-9
ISBN-13: 978-1-59350-045-0

Library of Congress Cataloging-in-Publication data are on file.

Cover design by Victor Mingovits
Interior design by Nicola Ferguson

CONTENTS

PART III: *Healing: Doing the Work*

PART IV: *Expressions: New Topics and Currents*

ACKNOWLEDGMENTS

Many thanks are due for help with this book, to Robert Allen, MD, Katherine Bowman, Ph.D., Greg Garavanian, Psy.D., Chad LeJeune, Ph.D., Jack Huntington, Psy.D., Jim Raines, Ph.D., Marny Hall, Ph.D., Betty Berzon, Ph.D., Mike Nadeau, Michelle Angello, Ph.D., Nancy Nangeroni, and Joe Kort, MA, MSW.

Thanks are also due my agent, Sorche Fairbank, who found a great home for this project at Alyson. Thanks also to Joe Pittman and the rest of the Alyson crew for making a place for this title.

I'd like to especially recognize the people in my life who have both supported me and taught me a few things along the way: Vera D. Hardin, Virginia Taylor, Tina Dawkins, Rob Allen, Mary Palmer, my brother Dale, and James E. Seegars, Jr., Ph.D., the psychologist who told me when I was seventeen that I was "okay."

Of course, I also have to thank my husband Bradford Leary, for everything he does to make me feel loved, to make me laugh, and to bring joy to my life.

FOREWORD

Would the small gay child you once were look up to the gay adult you are today? If not, then this book is for you.

When I was age 15, still in high school, I was seeing a straight male therapist who was trying to help me restore my "innate heterosexuality." His intentions were good, but the therapy program was anything but. Back then in the 1970s, therapists believed—and today, many still do—that adolescence offers a second chance at returning to one's innate biological heterosexual orientation. I wanted to believe my therapist, but privately, I knew he was wrong.

When I started college in 1981, there were few–if any–books on being gay. Taking classes in sociology, psychology, and social work, I would look in the indexes at the back of my textbooks, hoping to find useful information on homosexuality. I also visited the campus library, and went where no one would see me or discover my interest, and look in the card index for other books on homosexuality. My shame was intense, and often I worried that I'd been seen and identified as a "homosexual." When I finally did find something on the topic, it would likely be just a paragraph or—if I was lucky, one or two whole pages. They usually touched briefly on the etiology of homosexuality and the "problematic lives" it caused.

From such brief readings, I realized I fit the definition of an "obligatory homosexual." I even wrote a paper on why homosexuality was (and should continue to be) considered a disorder. I was in my own early stages of coming out. Not wanting to be gay, I sought literature to support my denial and help me write that paper, which I still keep as a reminder of my journey.

Back then, I was starving for information about who I was and how other "homosexuals" lived. *Gay* was the affirmative term, but it didn't apply to me, because I couldn't see anything affirmative about it. Then a gay friend gave me a little paperback titled *Loving Someone Gay* by Don Clark. I read it slowly, with much skepticism. But I dog-eared pages, highlighted various parts, and re-read it again and again. Clark was writing not just for gays but for those who loved them as well. *Loving Ourselves* is a book dedicated to us, just for us.

I believe I would have spent less time in therapy coming out and not the lengthy time it took recovering from the lack of information, from neglect and internalization of negative messages about my gay identity if my therapists, school, family, and rabbis had just embraced that I was a gay little boy who loved other boys. How I wish there'd been a book like *Loving Ourselves* around when I was a gay teenager.

I like Dr. Hardin's position that we were originally gay and lesbian children who grew up that way—and didn't *become* gay or lesbian. Most people, therapists included, ignore or simply don't believe this and think of us as only adults. To identify a child as gay or lesbian brings up uncomfortable, inappropriate thoughts of adult sexual behavior. Too many equate gay with adult sexual behavior. However, as children and teenagers, gays and lesbians are no different than their straight counterparts. To me, denying them permission to explore their identities—romantically, affectionally, spiritually, psychologically, and sexually—is a form of covert cultural sexual abuse (CCSA).

CCSA is the chronic verbal and psychological (often, even sexual) assaults against an individual's expression of gender, sexual feelings, and behaviors. Like sexual harassment, it interferes with a person's ability to function. Its effects persist into adulthood, wreaking havoc in people's lives. Imagine what we children went through, hearing about the negative effects of homosexuality before we were even developmentally ready to understand what it all meant. In exchange for living out of integrity with ourselves, we are rewarded with heterosexual privileges. But in the end, we are the losers.

Loving Ourselves addresses the neglect, abuse, and trauma that we gays and lesbians grew up with and tells us how to undo the injuries and retrieve our self-esteem. It shows us how to come back into integrity with others and ourselves. Dr. Hardin promises to help readers of many different backgrounds, upbringings, and levels of professional or personal success, and makes good on his promise. Reading this, I was amazed how he manages to be inclusive in a clear, succinct way. No matter what your age, gender, race, or religion, or how you identify yourself, you are guaranteed to find yourself in these pages.

Most mental health books tell you what the problem is, how much worse it can get, and leave you with only a few pages, a chapter, if you are lucky, on what to do about it. Halfway through, however, this book gives you specific ways on how to heal yourself and build your self-esteem through cognitive restructuring, explaining what the process is and how it's helpful. Dr. Hardin leaves no gay stone or gay gem unturned, focusing on how our schools, peer groups, religions, and family of origins not only impact our developing self-esteem while growing up gay or lesbian, but also how these factors affect our later career choices, relationships, parenting, and creativity as adults.

The author gently accompanies you through each step of the path on how to help yourself. Along the way, he shares his own personal struggles and how he is able to apply the strategies to his own life.

Loving Ourselves will help you not only care more about yourself but help you find *your* own identity, what *kind* of lesbian or gay individual you want to be, and what feels good to *you*! Consider *Loving Yourself* your one-stop source for achieving this with the tools and the information you need for every aspect of your gay life.

Kimeron Hardin was one of the openly gay therapists who published books and inspired me to write my own. I had tired of reading heterocentric books and wanted to read—and write—books for us and about us. I feel honored to write the foreword for *Loving Our-*

selves and for an author who's been instrumental in restoring our sense of belonging and showing us that it is never too late to have a happy gay childhood.

Joe Kort, M. A., MSW, ACSW
author of 10 Smart Things Gay Men Can Do to Find Real Love

Introduction

I'M GOOD ENOUGH, I'M SMART ENOUGH, AND DOGGONE IT . . .
PEOPLE LIKE ME!

—*Stuart Smalley*

bout ten years ago, I was feeling that queer identity was on the brink of evolution—that moment when an organism is ripe for change and maturation. Cultural change happens sometimes slowly, like the movement of an iceberg over thousands of years, and sometimes quickly and unexpectedly, due to a novel technological advance or, sadly, a catastrophic tragedy.

My hunch at that time was that gay and lesbian people were starting to move away from focusing on being a part of a larger "community" that had to bond together to fight for basic recognition and rights, to a phase of developing individual identities that incorporated a healthy sense of sexual orientation, but with the freedom to question politically correct ideas of what a gay man or a lesbian should be like. Like other people who belong to oppressed, minority categories, initially, the fight is about creating our own identities instead of buying into the oppressor's stereotypes and to win equal status under the law to live our lives happily and fully. As we win these battles and gain more rights, however, a shift begins to occur away from lockstep community identity and towards personal intro-spection and pursuits of satisfaction. The explosion of "post gay" identities including such sub-communities as bears, lipstick lesbians, Log Cabin republicans, queer and trans youth, all suggest that we are indeed attempting to reach beyond the stereotypes, and to create spaces for ourselves that "fit better." I felt that we were particularly ripe for a book that could help us better cast off the social messages that negatively affected our self-confidence or self-esteem. Queer people were ready to start accepting themselves as full citizens, enti-tled to a place at the table with more energy to devote to enhancing their own individual quality of life.

Just as we were about to make this shift, however, after years of significant political and legal gains, something awful happened. George W. Bush was elected president and within months, one of the most horrific tragedies in recent history happened, referred to now simply as 9/11. I cite them both because who actually knows what might have been if a different person had been president dur-ing this event? Or what would have become of Bush without this shocking attack? He certainly looked like a one-termer to me, before the rush to war. His four years might have been a tiny blip on the world stage in the big scheme of things, a conservative backlash for a blowjob in the White House.

Unfortunately, however, he was elected (or *selected* as many of my friends say), with the backing of some of the most virulently anti-gay right wingers in the country, focusing on war and terror rather than on other important domestic issues like poverty and health care. We have been at war now in Iraq for over four years, with thou-sands of lost lives. Most pundits believe that the single most signifi-cant reason that Bush was re-elected to a second term was that most

Americans are hesitant to change leadership during an active conflict, no matter how badly it's going.

What that means for us, however, is that we now have been governed by a White House with strong ties to the religious right for almost seven years, with strategists who recognize the political value of stirring up anti-gay sentiment at every possible turn. If fear of terrorists doesn't get 'em, then throw in a bit of gay hysteria and the threat of "the breakdown of family values" to keep the public in lockstep.

Therefore, as of late, we've been subjected to a fairly continuous stream of public queer bashing, moralizing, and hyperbole. We've gone from eight years of a fairly gay-friendly Bill Clinton, to a stage full of Republican presidential hopefuls who take pride in stating for the record that they are opposed to gay marriage (with a few of them claiming that they don't believe in evolution either).

When I sat down to write this book, I did so because I felt the time was right to address the subtle signs that queer folks were ready to become more introspective and to take the legal and political gains that we had made and solidify them and repair some of the damage done by growing up in a homophobic society. My goal was to help the reader undo some of the deeper injuries that occurred early in life that had negative consequences in their lives today, especially in relationships, jobs, and other creative pursuits.

What makes our job of building healthy self-esteem more difficult generally, say than your average heterosexual, is the continuing daily confrontation with anti-gay rhetoric and challenges to our basic life, liberty, and pursuit of happiness. We not only have to overcome some of the leftover baggage from how and when we were raised that continues to affect our choices today, but we also have to develop strategies for dealing with the headlines that suggest that our rights are "debatable" rather than givens.

My goal is to empower you, the reader, to take control over the content of the messages that you receive and process about yourself. Some of these messages are external, from mean-spirited sources like Fox News and Rush Limbaugh, while others, perhaps the most important ones, come from inside you, internalized from your youth and affecting your identity even today. My goal is to provide you with proven ways of inoculating yourself from distorted societal messages and healthier ways of recognizing and changing old self-talk that may be forming obstacles to your happiness.

I hope you enjoy the experience and I hope that it helps you feel more confident, more proud, and more fulfilled as you read and work through this material.

WHY AND HOW

Stuart Smalley's words at the beginning of this chapter from Al Franken's hilarious *Saturday Night Live* sketch are a clever parody of someone in "recovery" from childhood abuse, alcoholism, and overeating. Stuart, having found a method of boosting his very low self-esteem, faces a mirror, looks lovingly into his own eyes, and repeats his catch phrase, with results apparently so successful that he now has his own TV show.

If you've struggled to overcome problems with self-doubt or a difficult childhood or chemical dependency, you probably also get an extra chuckle because you've met people in real life like Stuart who believe they have found simple answers to life's difficult problems. In reality, you know that life is not so simple.

Recent studies have shown that growing up gay or lesbian, or even living as an "out" adult, is often both difficult and dangerous in this society. Gays and lesbians are at greater risk for attempting or committing suicide and are more likely to abuse alcohol or other drugs than their heterosexual counterparts. Queer youth are also at significantly higher risk than heterosexuals for suicide attempts, substance abuse, school problems, running away from home, and prostitution. A study by the US Department of Health and Human Services in 1989 found that gay and lesbian youths are two to three times more likely than heterosexuals to kill themselves. The evidence suggests that being lesbian or gay doesn't lead to these behaviors, but that self-destructiveness is more likely the result of verbal and physical harassment or social rejection. Other risk factors include social isolation, depression, negative family interactions and social attitudes, and low self-esteem.

Society is full of mixed messages for gays and lesbians. Stigmatizing and hostile messages exist in the form of anti-gay rights initiatives, brutal hate crimes committed against lesbians and gays, and right-wing political strategists promising "cures for homosexuality" through religion or behavior modification. On a less hostile level, but equally as damaging, gay and lesbian couples are currently not afforded the rights of marriage on a federal level, thereby eliminating many social reinforcers of marriage such as tax breaks, wedding showers, and automatic joint custody of children. At the same time, we are often condemned for "living in sin," or having sex outside of marriage, putting us between a rock and a hard place.

DOES LOW SELF-WORTH LEAD TO SELF-DESTRUCTIVENESS?

I've often wondered whether there was a link between being oppressed and personal risk-taking. Could having healthy self-esteem mitigate high-risk behaviors in oppressed minority groups?

One study that looked at the self-esteem of adolescent girls in a suburban high school found that those with the lowest self-esteem were more likely to have eating disorders, higher anxiety, to smoke, to use drugs and alcohol, and to be sexually active with more partners than girls with higher self-esteem. Another study of homeless or drug-abusing women found that those with higher self-esteem and a stronger sense of coherence, were less likely to be emotionally distressed or to engage in high risk behaviors. A recent study of gay men who reported frequent and compulsive sex, found that they also engaged in more frequent unprotected sexual acts with more partners, reported greater use of cocaine in conjunction with sexual activity, rated high-risk sexual acts as more pleasurable, and reported lower self-esteem.

Recent studies have raised some other interesting questions

about the link between self-esteem and high-risk behavior. Apparently, high self-esteem alone is no guarantee of choosing safety or in boosting performance, success, or happiness. These studies suggest that children raised to think *too highly* of themselves, without concern for others and based on no real achievements, may behave like *narcissists*, placing their own needs above others at all times and lashing out when their pride is wounded. Sometimes, narcissists feel invincible to risk and make choices that aren't too healthy based on inaccurate beliefs that they aren't subject to the same rules as others. The researchers also point out that how we define and measure self-esteem has been a problem and that there are different qualities of self-esteem, some more likely than others to lead to greater satisfaction and success. Good self-esteem incorporates both self-confidence (based on actual accomplishments) and self-efficacy (the belief that you can handle problems effectively), as well as social awareness and responsibility.

I agree that high self-esteem, without basis in reality, is like a self-deception that will likely lead to no long-term benefit. Valuing yourself above all else may indeed make you insensitive to making good choices. People who believe that self-indulgence is the same thing as self-esteem are likely to make unhealthy choices, to go with short-term pleasure over long term happiness. My goals for you are to help you find a balance, to help you recognize and stop the self-sabotage. I'd also like to have you learn to see yourself in a more realistic, loving, but firm and responsible way, much like a good parent loves, but provides healthy guidelines for, the child they value.

I've written *Loving Ourselves: The Gay and Lesbian Guide to Self-Esteem* to help lgbt's of many different backgrounds, upbringings, and levels of professional or personal success with the ongoing process of healing from the past, coping with the present, and planning for the future. Regardless of where you are in your life, or how you came to read this book, you will find something here that relates to your own personal journey.

Why a Book Just for Gays and Lesbians?

Self-esteem is something that anyone, regardless of sexual orientation, might need to improve. Why then a special book for gays and lesbians?

First and foremost, I've always despised reading a book about self-healing or growth and having to translate the exercises or examples from a heterocentrist viewpoint. Books that say things to male readers like "Think of your first special relationship with a woman," or articles assuming that all women want to be with men make it harder for me to relate. It's challenging enough to try to understand the principles of change without having to take the extra step of mentally shifting the examples toward something that fits your own situation. In some cases, trying to play the translation game may leave you feeling even more confused and frustrated than before you started reading.

The other reason for writing this book specifically for gays and lesbians is that there are clear differences between heterosexuals and homosexuals. Understanding the factors affecting a committed relationship between two women or two men is vastly different than understanding the various forces in a relationship between a woman and a man. This book will address many of the unique issues faced by queer people. I will discuss the messages about homosexuality that you likely received as a child, but even more importantly, the messages that you continue to face every day. Racism and sexism continue to exist in our country, but I would argue that often the strongest public language is still reserved for lesbians and gays. Although mainstream society has started to shun the word "fag" in polite circles, many kids today freely use the term "That's so gay" to describe someone or something as stupid. Hate crimes against us are being tracked, but it's a double-edged sword because it increases our awareness of how much fear and disgust there still is for us.

Although queer people have made tremendous political gains in recent years, I believe our next frontier is within ourselves. We can finally organize, demonstrate, and flex our political muscle; the next step, however, is to move beyond self-hating ("I am disgusting"), beyond the community identification only ("I am a lesbian"), to a place of true self-respect, self-nurturing, and internal peace ("I am worthwhile").

How to Get the Most out of This Book

The process of loving yourself means not only learning to accept who you are, but also to change self-destructive behaviors and habits that are the opposite of self-respect. I don't want you to stare blindly into a mirror like Stuart Smalley and repeat silly phrases until you somehow start to believe them. My hope is that this book will help you undo old habits of self-doubt and internalized negative messages.

This book was not designed like a good novel to be read as quickly as possible, but as a paced, self-help guide. Learning to recognize the old distorted messages and the current negative messages society feeds you is covered in Parts I and II while Part III teaches you to stop the influence of these messages.

Yet blocking the negative is only a part of building self-esteem. To begin your healing process, you must learn how to explore the real you, your true self—the perfect and the not-so-perfect, the excellent, and the average parts—from a more objective viewpoint. The last chapter of Part III will teach you ways to expand the way you view yourself, both alone and with help from others you trust. Each chapter will provide you with many questions to ask yourself so that you can explore emotionally. In some chapters, I will even give you specific exercises to do to help you understand the concepts and apply them to your own experience. It's important for you to take your time when doing the exercises to get the most from this book. If you prefer, you can read through the book from beginning to end initially and then come back for a second, more in-depth read that includes doing the exercises. The key is to be patient with yourself since, after all, it took many years to come to the place you are at now. You may need to re-read some chapters, even after attempting all the exercises, as you reach deeper layers of self-awareness. Part IV includes the special chapters that address how self-esteem affects getting older, deciding to raise a child, gender identity, and people who have secret same sex relationships.

My goal is not only to help you stop the constant battering (from outside and inside), but also to help you see the wonderful parts of you that have existed all along. All babies are born innocent. It takes many years of distorted and harmful information to make a baby believe that she or he is imperfect, less than, or bad. As an adult, you have the opportunity that you didn't have as a child to make more rational judgments about the information that bombards you. You can decide what is objective, realistic information and what are negative and warped messages that should be discarded. You now have the opportunity to provide the nurturing, loving environment for yourself that you may not have had as a child.

If you are currently in psychotherapy, you may find this book to be a helpful adjunct to your therapy. You may even decide to work through the exercises with help from your therapist. If you are working through this book alone and find that it brings up intense feelings for you that make you uncomfortable or uneasy, consider seeing a psychotherapist to help you work through the feelings. This book is not a substitute for therapy, especially if you find that problems exist or arise that are causing you immediate harm or distress, such as depression that interferes with your everyday functioning, feelings of hopelessness, suicidal thoughts, or significant alcohol or other drug use.

I hope that when you've finished this book, you will have found a sense of peace, better self-esteem, and a greater appreciation for the person that you are. As you now embark on this process, let me congratulate you for taking the first steps toward learning to love yourself.

PART I

Origins:

Influences on Your

Self-Esteem

ONE

....

What Is Self-Esteem and Can You Really Change It?

ALL THAT WE ARE IS THE RESULT OF WHAT WE HAVE THOUGHT.
THE MIND IS EVERYTHING. WHAT WE THINK WE BECOME.
—*Maharishi Mahesh Yogi*

Most people have some idea about what the term self-esteem refers to, and most usually have a sense of whether their self-esteem is generally positive or negative, but what does the term really mean?

The National Association for Self-Esteem defines it as "the experience of being capable of meeting life's challenges and being worthy of happiness." Another way to describe self-esteem is in terms of the quality of the relationship that you have with the deepest and most authentic parts of yourself. While we all make mistakes in judgment from time to time, a person with lower self-esteem tends to be more self-critical, unforgiving, and less compassionate in the way that she views herself and therefore is more likely to choose an ultimately self-punishing or self-depriving behavior in response. People with better self-esteem tend to hold themselves to higher standards of behavior, choosing to feel honest disappointment or shame when they make mistakes, and accepting responsibility for them, but without resorting to harsh or even at times abusive, internal critique.

Many of you have never stopped to objectively examine your basic view of yourself, or your abilities, and therefore may have no idea about how such a deeply held belief is affecting your daily choices—in your career, your health, and your love life. One of the major goals of this book is to help you begin to take a better look at the inner relationship that you have with yourself, your sense of your personal capabilities, and your deep-seated sense of self-worth. My second major goal is to then help you begin to build the kind of self-esteem that allows you to feel more satisfaction, more freedom, and more happiness in your life.

How Does Self-esteem Develop?

We've just talked about esteem, but what exactly is the *self*, that we keep talking about? Humans are different from animals because only we are aware of an abstract concept we call the self. This self, also known as your *identity*, is really a way of thinking about who you are that is shaped by all of your life experiences, both positive and negative. For example, if the majority of your life experiences have been positive, and the only kind of feedback that you've ever received about yourself from others has been favorable or encouraging, then you will generally think highly of yourself and exhibit good self-esteem. On the contrary, if your life experiences have been primarily negative, then your identity is likely to be based on feeling worthless, incapable, or in some cases, even evil.

Early Life Experiences and Self-Esteem

When you were born, you had no concept of "self." Imagine how in the womb you must have floated in the nice, warm amniotic bath, with only muted sounds in darkness—and then were suddenly thrust into bright lights, strange and loud sounds, and an intense sensation of cool air on your skin. Your biggest concern was probably finding warmth again, getting away from the lights and noises, and snuggling into any comfortable spot. You had no sense of who, or even what, you were, and your only needs were for food, warmth, comfort.

If your parents were very responsive, and provided these basic necessities, you didn't have to scream quite as much for attention and therefore had the freedom to explore your world and yourself, both physically and emotionally. You probably learned first about your physical self by discovering your hands and feet, maybe by sucking your thumb or toes. After a while, you figured out what those tiny hands could do and then what sounds you could make with your mouth. Soon, you became a child who learned to communicate, first through crying, then babbling, and finally talking. Your brain grew rapidly and expanded during this time, enabling you to put together the meanings of events that happened to and around you.

Once you began to understand and use language, you learned not only the meanings of words, but most likely, you also learned the meanings of specific facial expressions (like frowns and smiles) and tones of voice (silly, happy baby talk versus stern, angry, serious voices). You probably knew what "No!" meant even before you knew how to talk. You learned to comprehend both verbal and nonverbal forms of communication. The information that you used to develop your understanding of the world came from your immediate surroundings and, as an infant, most of your time was spent with parents or other primary caregivers. When you imagine that time of your life (or reconstruct it from family stories), were your basic needs taken care of quickly? Or did you have to wait to have your hunger satisfied or your skin dry and warm?

How you answer questions like these most likely provides some insight into how you view yourself and your value today. The way your parents treated you, and the messages they intentionally or unintentionally gave you, helped form your identity, both then and now.

Messages and Cues

As you got older, and you ventured out into the world, you received messages about life, living, and your value from other sources besides your parents—from your teachers, your neighbors and friends, your place of worship, and even from the shows you watched on TV or at the movies. Millions of little girls have dreamed of being like Annette Funicello or Hilary Duff while boys long to play ball like Mickey Mantle or LeBron James. They watch for cues and imitate those they feel will bring them acceptance and recognition from the people whose opinions matter the most. A child's mind is hungry for new information and experiences that will help it be able to interpret the sights and sounds and meanings of the world and gain this recognition.

Child psychologists believe that your earliest years are important in shaping your later view of the world and yourself because a young child is not born with the ability to screen out inaccurate or negatively distorted information from dysfunctional sources. Therefore, if the messages you received about yourself when you were very young were mostly positive, loving, or nurturing, you are likely to have a more positive, compassionate view of yourself today. If, unfortunately, the majority of those messages about you were negative, you were just as likely to have believed these pieces of data no matter how inaccurate or dysfunctional and then you set about incorporating them into your overall view of yourself. Unfortunately, as an infant you didn't choose the *source* of the information (i.e. parents) that you received about who you are and about your worth, nor did you have the ability to step back from the situation, evaluate the messages about your value objectively, and reject the pieces that were harmful.

Self-Perpetuation

Not only was your identity shaped by early messages, but you also tend to repeat these messages about yourself, often leading to feelings of insecurity, fear, despair, or inadequacy.

Your level of esteem or regard for yourself depends a lot on how you formed your identity during your childhood and later growing-up experiences. In this book, however, we won't be rehashing too much old material that you'd just as soon forget, but helping you improve the quality of your life right now.

SELF-ESTEEM AND SELF-CONFIDENCE

Your self-esteem impacts every aspect of your current life—romantically, professionally, spiritually, and recreationally. It affects how you see your face or body in the mirror, your ability to socialize at a party, your dating options, and your job promotions. Your self-confidence will either be undermined or enhanced by the overall view you have of yourself. In short, *how effective you feel you'll be in any situation is highly influenced by whether you view yourself as powerful or weak, attractive or plain, intelligent or average.*

If you are satisfied with who you are, you will be able to navigate through life fairly effectively—taking challenges as they come and feeling self-confident in your ability to handle them. You may take some reasonable risks because you know that even if your plans fail, you have the resources to rebound and move on. You like yourself enough to forgive mistakes that you might make and move on without needing to punish yourself with negative thoughts like, "That was stupid!" or "You are such a loser!" Without a pervasive sense that you are basically good enough, self-doubt lingers and affects your ability to take the kinds of risks that could propel you toward satisfying relationships and careers. Good self-esteem leads to higher self-confidence, which then allows you to take chances and make choices without fear of the inevitable mistakes. Everyone makes mistakes sometimes, but people with good self-esteem rebound faster, shake off the disappointment, and get back into the saddle!

Changing Your Self-Esteem with Cognitive Behavioral Therapy

Over the last 30 years or so, a powerful new form of therapy has emerged that focuses on changing negative styles of thinking. This treatment, referred to as Cognitive Behavioral Therapy (CBT), has been successful at changing many problem behaviors. It involves learning how to recognize and replace negative messages you say to yourself with healthier, more adaptive alternatives.

One of the founders of this type of treatment, Dr. Aaron Beck, for example, found that depressed clients tended to focus more on the *negative* than positive aspects of a troubling situation they were discussing, much like a natural pessimist sees the glass half-empty. And not only did these clients tend to focus more on the negative in bad situations, but when they were depressed, they also tended to actually distort the meanings of events that were relatively benign or neutral. This means that they took an event that had no real negative effect on them and interpreted it negatively or in a personally relevant way. An example of this type of personal distortion would be if you jumped to the conclusion that someone who didn't call when they said they were going to did so because their feelings had changed about you, with no other information upon which to base this idea. Your tendency to interpret that behavior negatively could be based on prior experiences, your mood at that moment, or at a deeper level, your sense of self-esteem.

Albert Ellis, MD, another founder of CBT, found that his clients tended to hold beliefs about themselves that were long-standing and were completely unreasonable or illogical, like believing that because you were picked last for dodgeball in the third grade, you must be clumsy or non-athletic today.

Both men then applied their observations to their clinical work with patients by focusing on helping them to recognize overly negative, irrationality, or distorted cognitions (belief, thoughts, and attitudes) as they occurred and changing to something more reasonable.

They noticed almost immediate improvements in patients' moods, suggesting that changing thinking was a key to emotional health.

Over the years, CBT has gained in popularity and has gone through many refinements. It continues to be one of the fastest growing forms of psychotherapy in the world, and its effectiveness has been demonstrated with many different types of problems, from depression and anxiety to obsessive-compulsive disorders (think Jack Nicholson's character in *As Good As It Gets*), and even schizophrenia. Because CBT is so straightforward and simple, many self-help books have been published about using the strategies for many problem issues, including self-esteem.

As I mentioned in the introduction, however, none of these books has been written specifically for gay and lesbian people struggling with self-esteem. In my opinion, building self-esteem in people who identify as a sexual minority (lesbians, gay men, bisexuals, or transgender people), includes a challenge unique to us that heterosexuals do not face. In most cases, heterosexuals who suffer from lower self-esteem based on distorted information from their childhoods can grow up and leave the environment that provided those bad messages. They can get married, move to the suburbs, and stay as far away as they need to from the parents, family, or neighborhood that sent them negative messages about themselves. They then can begin to rebuild their self-concept by challenging those negative or distorted internal messages left over from when they were young. Their experiences as adults help them to disconfirm old childhood messages more easily.

Queer folks must not only identify cognitions fueled by old negative messages, but they must also learn to resist the homophobic messages that continue in our everyday culture. Despite the enormous political gains we have made in recent years, we still wake up to morning headlines debating our civil rights, our impact on society, and even our humanity. I woke up recently to hear that the Governor of California, Arnold Schwarzenegger, had vetoed gay marriage legislation for cowardly reasons. Now, more than ever, we need powerful strategies to inoculate us against these ignorant, political, and distorted messages.

The Cognitive Behavioral Model

This part of the chapter will teach you the basic concepts of CBT and how to apply them. Once my clients understand these concepts, and learn to apply them to themselves, the benefits generalize across many areas of their lives. They find that old negative images or messages, that previously went unchallenged, are much easier to recognize, challenge, and change.

The basic premise of CBT is simple. *Negative thoughts* lead to *uncomfortable emotions* that lead to *ineffective or self-destructive behaviors.*

THOUGHTS ➤ FEELINGS ➤ BEHAVIORS

In order to improve your effectiveness in the world or to reduce feelings of insecurity, fear, worry, or helplessness, you must learn to *identify* a negative thought, *evaluate* its validity, and–if necessary–*replace it* with a more realistic or healthy thought.

IDENTIFY
↓
EVALUATE
↓
REPLACE

According to the model, there are three layers of cognitions: automatic thoughts, conditional beliefs, and core beliefs.

Automatic Thoughts

When you perceive that you have been rejected or you have failed at something, you tend to have a very quick, automatic thought about the situation. Automatic thinking is triggered by a situation that carries some kind of emotional significance or importance to you. Such situations are often either *personally* relevant (meaning that they remind you of a specific traumatic or negative experience in your past) or they may be *culturally* relevant (like when someone tells a gay-bashing joke not knowing that you are gay).

Sometimes, you may be fully aware of the thoughts that pop up in these situations (e.g., "I hope this doesn't turn out like that last coffee date!"), but sometimes, they can be just below the surface of your usual awareness (meaning that you aren't fully aware that you are making an interpretation, but it still has an impact on you). If you have low self-esteem, chances are that most of your automatic thoughts are negative and self-deprecating, so you may then immediately blame yourself when bad things happen (even if you had nothing to do with it) or you may interpret even ambiguous events (like no phone call when you expected it) personally and negatively. Because these negative messages, also known as negative self-talk, are automatic, replacing them with healthier, less negative messages takes some commitment, but doing so is an essential part of improving your self-esteem.

Here's another example of a situation that provoked automatic negative thoughts.

Christina has started dating someone new, Ellen, and after a few weeks of romantic bliss, her love interest promises to call her after work at 5:30 P.M. She excitedly prepares for the call, lingering close to the kitchen so that she makes sure to be there when it rings. Then 5:30 comes and goes...and no call. So Christina waits and waits, going through the various possibilities, innocent ones at first...flat tire? An accident?

Another thirty minutes pass and her thoughts turn more ominous. Christina feels glimpses of shame, rejection, and anger and eventually finds herself saying, "I knew this could never work out" and "She's already tired of me." Christina's evening is ruined as she turns to the TV and the refrigerator for comfort.

Obviously, Ellen was not able to keep her promise, perhaps for any number of valid reasons—a dead cell phone on the freeway, an unexpected illness, a delayed flight...issues that of course are important to Christina's peace of mind and trust in Ellen. Christina's main problem in this particular example, however, was her tendency to interpret the unknown negatively. In this example, an ambiguous event (Ellen not calling) is seen through a cognitive "lens" that distorts the meaning into negative self-doubts leading to hurt feelings and, potentially, an angry confrontation. A more rational, healthy approach in this case might have been for Christina to recognize that Ellen "not calling" was of concern, but then quickly remind herself that there are many reasons that someone may not call, such as a personal emergency or no access to a phone, neither of which had much to do with Christina's value to Ellen.

Making an emotional judgment about the friend who didn't call, and her intentions, before she had adequate information is emotionally inefficient and potentially inhibiting for Christina. By stepping back from her automatic thoughts and examining them more objectively, Christina would have probably found that the feelings of rejection and abandonment she felt began to change, to become less intense and less pessimistic.

Conditional Beliefs (or The Rules You Live By)

Conditional beliefs are the spoken (and sometimes unspoken) rules by which you live your life. These beliefs function to help you survive and, like most other types of deeply held beliefs, are formed early in childhood. The rules you learned and followed as a child were sometimes discussed directly in the family, like, "My goodness Sarah Lee, you must *neva'* wear white pumps after Labor Day," but many rules that you incorporated were never spoken directly. You most likely developed your own personal rules that were unique to surviving in your family household.

In your family of origin, there may have been clear rules about when and where sexuality was discussed, if ever. For example, in my own experience growing up in a fundamentalist household, it was *not ok* to even say the word "S-E-X," much less have a conversation of any depth about the subject. There were also rules about what sexual behavior was acceptable and when it was acceptable to have it, such as having missionary position (man on top) intercourse *only* after heterosexual marriage. That means, of course, even if no one ever said it, same-sex attraction or activity was off limits.

As a gay or lesbian child, you most likely learned to avoid discussing your budding sexuality, particularly the parts that were considered "deviant" or "abnormal" at the time. A *conditional belief* that became established for you, therefore, may have been something like, *"Never share your true intimate feelings with anyone or they'll reject you."* You can see how such a rule might inhibit your ability to form close relationships. You'll read more about the development of conditional beliefs in Chapter 2, entitled Hand-Me-Down Messages.

Core Beliefs (Getting to the Bottom of Things)

After a while of paying attention to the rules you live by, and the automatic thoughts that pop up in emotionally relevant situations, you can begin to see consistent themes or patterns emerging that reflect the kind relationship you have with yourself at your deepest levels. These patterns, also known as *core beliefs*, can usually be grouped into one of three main beliefs:

1. Your ability to trust others (e.g. "Other people will hurt you if given the chance")
2. Your beliefs about the safety of being in the world (e.g., "Pain and illness is everywhere")
3. Your beliefs about your value and self-worth (e.g., "I am unworthy of love, acceptance, or compassion.")

These beliefs may be held so deeply that you've never acknowledged them, even to yourself; yet they are often experienced as absolute truths and affect every choice you make. Some theorists believe that negative core beliefs are particularly activated when a person is suffering from depression. The depressed person then tends to focus almost exclusively on information that *confirms* the negative core belief and then filters out any positive evidence that might disconfirm the core belief. An example would be someone

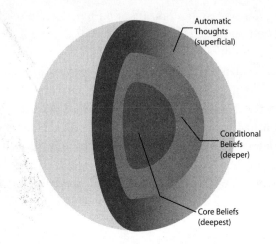

Figure 1. Structure of Cognitions and Depth of Awareness

who can't take a compliment, but is overly sensitive to even constructive criticism.

Other psychologists feel that core beliefs are active all the time and affect every decision you make, either by making choices that support the belief or choices that are a reaction against them. The beliefs act as a lens through which you see the world—if the core beliefs are distorted (e.g., "I have nothing to offer anyone"), the lens will provide a distorted picture of each person or situation that you come into contact with (e.g., "He couldn't possibly find me attractive"). The old phrase, "He's seeing the world through rose-colored glasses," is based on this concept; a person who does this tends to see everything from a positive frame of reference. According to the cognitive model, your lens (or beliefs) can range from very positive and optimistic to very negative and pessimistic.

The concept of an "information lens" helps explain why you continue to buy into the old distorted beliefs even though intellectually, you understand them to be untrue. Core beliefs tend to be rigid and influence the conditional beliefs or rules that you set for yourself to live by, which in turn then influences your automatic thoughts. For example, if your *core belief* is, "*Being gay means you're not good* enough," one of your *conditional beliefs* might be, "*I must work twice as hard as straight people to prove I'm just as competent.*" If you don't live up to your expectations in a given situation, your *automatic thoughts* will reflect the thought that you're not good enough (e.g. "*I knew that I'd never be able to succeed at this*"). You can see how this might be both emotionally and physically exhausting for you over the years as you struggle to prove yourself. Figure 1 is a graphic representation of these constructs and their relationships to each other.

Later in this book, you will read about exploring the kinds of messages you received as a child, and how they affect your life today, in more detail. In fact, I will not only invite you to explore your early family life in order to uncover and challenge the foundations for your negative self-talk, but I will also encourage you to examine other important influences on your self-esteem such as your local community, cultural heritage, religion, and the politics of the day. Once you learn to identify the origins of your self-esteem, you can then begin to retrain yourself to challenge old, negative beliefs.

RECOGNIZING NEGATIVE PATTERNS

Before you can begin challenging and changing those long-standing, negative ways of thinking, you must first train yourself to recognize patterns in the way you think and catch yourself when they occur. Reading about such patterns on the page is one thing; identifying your own patterns is another. Here's an example that may help you recognize some ways you think negatively and then talk negatively to yourself:

Let's say that you have an assignment at work with a deadline that according to your supervisor must be met or you and the organization will suffer. Also imagine that you have a limited amount of time to complete the task and while it's difficult to get started, you work very hard on it and complete it just before the deadline. The local copy center closes at 5 p.m. and it's 4:30 p.m. now. You jump into your car, and on the way, you hear on the radio that there's a huge traffic jam just ahead. You start feeling a little irritated and anxious to get there. The jam finally breaks at 4:50 p.m. and you continue to make your way there, perhaps at an unsafe speed. You finally arrive at the parking lot at 5:02 p.m., just in time to see the shades being lowered and the "Closed" sign illuminated. Your first reaction is one of numbness and horror, but then you slowly become aware of a heavy feeling in your gut and you take a little gasp for air. Then the self-talk begins. Imagine what you might be saying to yourself in this situation. What are the feelings you might be having...the sensations in your body?

For some people, the voice in their heads that follows such an event will be harsh and punitive with phrases such as, "You can't do anything right!" or "You are incompetent" or "You failed again." You may be particularly hard on yourself if you were raised to have unrealistic expectations of yourself, or if making mistakes or having an accident when you were a child was followed by humiliation or other punishments. The emotions you might expect to feel following such harsh self-talk would likely include intense panic, fear, despair, or maybe a desire to run and hide. You might feel like dropping the whole project out of frustration and self-disappointment.

For others, the voice may be less harsh, but it still serves to promote a self-image of incompetence or an inability to succeed. This voice may sound something like, "I did my best, but it's just not good enough . . . I'm not as smart as most people." While you may not be overtly punishing yourself at this level, you experience a de-motivating effect.

There are also those types who might blame the traffic jam or the copy place for closing on time and become incredibly angry and agitated. The voice is harsh, but it is directed at someone (or something) else. You may be so agitated that your sleep that night is disrupted or you are short with family and friends. If you explored a little deeper, you would likely find that the anger is directly proportional to the amount of underlying anxiety you have about how your boss will react the next day or about how horrible you expect to feel when you have to admit that the work is not ready. Regardless of your reaction, the net effect is disruptive emotional upset.

Another healthier way to respond to this unfortunate event

would be to take a more balanced and accurate appraisal of the situation that focused less on punishing yourself for missing a deadline and more on encouraging yourself to deal with the situation effectively. Recognizing your inner voice, evaluating it for accuracy and utility, and then actively making changes if necessary is the cognitive-behavioral basis for enhancing your self-esteem. Learning some basic techniques to help you recognize and evaluate your self-talk will help you confront situations throughout the day that may threaten your confidence and initiate feelings of anger, depression, or sadness.

You may have found that in the preceding example, you did not respond with negative self-talk, but managed to focus on solutions to the problems immediately. There are two reasons that this may be the case. First, we all develop areas in our lives that we feel better or more confident about than other areas. Professional competence may be that area for you, so your *professional* self-esteem is relatively healthy. However, you may find that events related to situations outside of work trigger the negative self-talk and uncomfortable feelings.

The second is that you may not recognize your own negative self-talk because of the relative depth of your negative beliefs. You may be so used to burying the negative self-talk that it takes time for you to learn to hear the messages more directly. It may take a little extra work on your part to recognize your negative self-talk, but having better self-esteem will be well worth the effort.

Where to Start?

Automatic thoughts are typically the easiest to recognize and begin to address. In fact, most cognitive behavioral therapists begin treatment by having the client keep track of automatic thoughts as they happen and then teaching the client to analyze the thoughts carefully and objectively. Examining the patterns of your automatic thoughts will help you determine the rules you live by, which can be assessed for effectiveness. Then the core beliefs that underlie all beliefs and rules will begin to emerge and can be assessed for accuracy and usefulness.

As a child, you didn't have the power to assess the accuracy of these beliefs as they were forming. One of the nice things about being an adult is you now have the ability to make more objective and healthy choices about how you view yourself. You have the power to change a self-image that is not healthy. So make a decision to begin the process today. For the next week, keep a record of your daily thoughts and how they affect your mood. Use the blank Daily Thought Record to help you keep track.

After you have kept track of your automatic thoughts for a while, take some time to go back through them and look for patterns. These regularly recurring thoughts can begin to give you insight into the core beliefs you hold about yourself. Once you recognize some of these themes or patterns, and the emotional costs they have for you, you can then begin the process of challenging negative or dysfunctional thoughts, replacing them with more healthy, accurate, or effective self-statements, and feeling the positive changes in your self-esteem.

Recognizing your negative self-talk is an effective beginning; but it's often not enough to lead to significant change. The next step, an important one, is to engage in a rational debate with these old messages, evaluating their effectiveness, usefulness, and distortion.

It can be difficult to effectively recognize and challenge old ways of thinking. This battle is made more challenging when you continue to hear distorted and negative messages on a regular basis. Every time you hear a story about gay-bashing, listen to a homophobic joke, or watch a heterocentrist advertisement, you receive direct and indirect messages that suggest you are inferior, damaged, evil, or worthless. Your special challenge is to overcome the negative distortions from your childhood as well as to actively challenge current negative messages in the media and community around you. You must become especially skilled at recognizing distortions or biases that are held as universal truths.

Before you begin your self-exploration, make sure that you understand the following central concepts of CBT:

1. Like all human beings, you are constantly talking to yourself; you may or may not be fully aware of the things that you say to yourself.
2. You are constantly interpreting events that occur in your life by using old information about yourself and your ability to handle a situation.
3. Most events trigger automatic thoughts, or self-talk, that help you interpret the situation. These automatic thoughts are habitual and can be negative and can also trigger unpleasant emotions such as anxiety, sadness, anger, or a sense of failure. Automatic thoughts are usually situation-specific.
4. Your typical pattern of thinking is maintained by deeper beliefs called conditional beliefs, which are the rules you developed to live by. These rules are usually established early in life and may have been directly taught by your parents or other caregivers. The rules may work well in childhood, but often, they don't apply as well to adulthood.
5. At the deepest level of your personality are your core beliefs-including the absolute value you place upon your worth.

Although your family is one of the main influences on your early self-concept and your self-esteem, there are multiple other factors that shape the way you view yourself and the world. In the next few chapters, I will help you examine the origins of the core and conditional beliefs that underlie your automatic thinking. You will begin by examining family factors that shape your self-view and will go on to explore other important influences such as your religious background, your school experiences, and memorable media images. By understanding these influences more thoroughly, it will be easier for you to evaluate your self-talk more accurately and dispute it more effectively.

DAILY THOUGHT RECORD

For the next week, when you find yourself feeling down, anxious, or angry, keep track of what was going through your mind at the time. Write the time, day, and date in the first column, the particular event or situation that triggered the reaction in the second column, the automatic thought or thoughts that went through your head in column three, and the feeling you experienced in the last column.

DAILY THOUGHT RECORD

TIME/DAY/DATE	EVENT	AUTOMATIC THOUGHTS	FEELINGS
5:02 p.m., Monday, 7/15	Copy store closed	"What if I get fired?" "I'm so incompetent."	Fear, anxiety despair, sadness

RESOURCES

Association for Behavioral and Cognitive Therapies

http://www.aabt.org

National Association for Self-Esteem

http://www.self-esteem-nase.org

Two

Hand-Me-Down Messages: What You Learned from Your Family of Origin

WE ARE BORN INNOCENT, BELIEVE ME ADIA, WE ARE STILL INNOCENT

—*Sarah McLachlan and Pierre Marchand, "Adia"*

The adults, who took care of you when you were a newborn and toddler, were also responsible for teaching you about the world around you and also about your place in that world. The image that your family had of you then, and in some cases may still have of you, shaped the core beliefs you now have about your value, your effectiveness in the world, and your lovability. Your core beliefs are like the original software that comes with your new computer—your parents' early reactions to you were recorded onto your mind's "hard drive," and these files continue to function the way they were originally written, until you learn to alter or re-program the software.

The deepest beliefs that you have about yourself usually come from very early childhood and are typically repeated many times over, by you and your parents. Some of you reached a stage of adolescence where you actively rebelled against these "identity" messages (e.g., "You must always be well-behaved") and outwardly rejected some or all of your family's values and preconceived ideas about who you are. You may have even gone to the extreme while attempting to assert your own identity by running away, hanging out with the "wrong crowd," or dressing against the norm. Unfortunately, even though you may have changed the outside behavior and look, those deeper messages about yourself and your worth often remain and continue to affect your choices to conform or rebel.

In some particularly rigid or hostile families, you may never reach a safe place to reject family values for fear of physical or mental harm; either the rebellion doesn't take place at all or it happens after you've been able to leave this family environment. Several aspects of your family of origin affect your self-esteem, namely parenting styles, their expectations, your role in the family, and ways that they communicate (or don't communicate).

PARENTING STYLES AND WHY THEY MATTER

The way you were raised has a major impact on the development of your core beliefs and your self-esteem. Social psychologists have identified three basic styles of parenting referred to as *authoritarian*, *permissive*, and *authoritative*. Each style sets the tone for the family communications, rules, and expectations.

You may find that your core beliefs were shaped by a parenting style that is similar to one of these three. It's possible, however, that your parents may not fit neatly into one of these categories. They may have qualities of one, two, or all three types of parenting styles. They may also have changed their style over time or following a major family crisis like death, divorce, or separation. Parenting style may also change after the birth of a new brother or sister. Just as your family might not fit one style of parenting, your own automatic thoughts can at times be fairly reasonable, and at other times, they can be harsh and self-punishing. How often you are hard on yourself depends on the specific situation and your previous success or failure experiences. Listen for familiar voices from your upbringing in your own internal self-talk.

Authoritarian Families: The Power of Threat

In authoritarian families, who's in charge defines the family organization. Control is exerted through a show of power and sometimes force. This style is most often associated with the lowest self-esteem in later adulthood. The central figures in this type of family include a dictator (or dictators) at the top of the hierarchy, with children clearly in subservient, submissive roles. Dictators often have little regard for the needs of the children, physically, or emotionally. The children are taught directly and indirectly (by not allowing the children to grapple with tough decisions for themselves) that they are incompetent and that their opinions do not matter.

The emotional needs of the dictator, usually the parent or parents, are the primary driving force of the family, and children may never be allowed to express feelings directly, especially when those feelings are in conflict with the dictator's needs. Dictators often will attempt to invalidate the children's feelings to avoid any challenge to their own rigid, but amazingly fragile and easily threatened, belief systems. They often rely on harsh and forceful physical disciplinary techniques such as spanking and slapping, as well as verbal abuse (such as name calling, insults, and public humiliation), to force compliance with their view of the world. Respect for authority and work, order and tradition, and conformity are highly valued.

This type of rigidity, when mixed with excessive physical punishment, often leads to extreme dependence, submissiveness, and a strong desire to conform. It also makes children less confident in their own abilities, less self-reliant, emotionally immature (which means they have difficulty developing mature emotional attachments to others), and occasionally overly aggressive.

It has been hypothesized that authoritarians are generally anxious about their own self-worth and feel they must rely on harsh disciplinary methods to force their children to give them respect and be obedient. They cannot tolerate open defiance or hostility from their children and therefore make it unacceptable for the children to express such feelings, or even healthy questioning, openly.

Some psychologists believe that the roots of prejudice toward other races or socioeconomic classes lie in the quashing of these early angry feelings. In order to justify a hierarchical organization of a family, its members must believe that there are people who hold more correct views than others. A typical paternalistic, authoritarian family, for example, would believe that men are the head of the household, women are lesser than men, and children are lesser still (although male children would rank higher than female children). This is not to say that women cannot be authoritarian, and in some cases they may become the dictatorial force in the home, even if the actual discipline is carried out by the father figure.

Typically in an authoritarian household, the dictator must see him or herself as more powerful than those outside the family in order to feel important. The more unlike the authoritarian figure a person is, the more negatively that person will be viewed because he or she represents a challenge or threat to the dictator's way of thinking. People of a different race/ethnicity, a lower socioeconomic status, people with more education, different religious beliefs or social values, and different sexualities may all pose threats to the authoritarian personality. Dictators tend to be overtly judgmental about differing opinions, often not only devaluing the opinions or traditions of those who are different, but belittling, actively shunning, discriminating against, or perhaps even being aggressive toward people who are different and threaten their authority.

Children of authoritarians often learn to continue this devaluing process, toward themselves as well as others. They learn that they have a certain place in the world and that there is no room for questioning the authoritarian parent or making decisions about even their most intimate likes and dislikes on their own. The official word from the dictator is "You are whatever I say you are." By not allowing freedom of thought, the parent is saying, "You are incapable of making these decisions," leading to difficulty making decisions later in life. These dictums are based on the fragile personality of the parent, *not* typically on any objective evidence about the child.

Not all control in an authoritarian household is exerted directly. Aggressiveness, or threats, may be implied or expressed passively. *Passive-aggression* can be particularly difficult for a child to see clearly, since the parent's displeasure may not be as obvious as a slap or immediate verbal put-down would be, but comes more indirectly, for example, through the silent treatment or becoming emotionally detached or rejecting. Passive-aggressive parental behaviors may not immediately follow the "transgression" of the child but may come later when the child least expects it, say as an embarrassing comment by the parent at a party or in front of the child's friends. It's difficult to link these angry behaviors to the event that prompted them because the passive-aggressive person cannot handle his or her own anger effectively and directly, thereby thwarting healthy communication.

Passive-aggressive parents use shaming and guilt rather than direct aggression as methods of control. They know exactly when and how to emotionally "blackmail" a child into conforming to their wishes. Implicit threats of rejection, literally or emotionally, may be all it takes to extinguish the child's initiative, questioning, or exploration. Whether the control is direct or indirect, the same message underlies it: "You must live according to my rules or risk the consequences." We will discuss styles of family communication and their effect on self-esteem again later in this chapter.

An authoritarian does not believe in accidents and punishes the child for her or his mistakes. Spilling the milk is attributed to stupidity or irresponsibility rather than simply to normal human imperfection. This leads children to develop self-talk like, "I must be perfect" or "When I make mistakes, I am a failure."

Permissive: Too Much Freedom?

On the other side of the spectrum are permissive parents. These parents may offer emotional support or caring but few limits or boundaries. They allow children to do as they please, make all decisions for themselves, and have everything they want. These parents may make this choice intentionally, believing that children learn to be independent by making their own decisions early in life and facing the natural consequences. They assume that if a child makes a decision that results in discomfort, the child will learn not to make this choice again. Parents might be considered permissive for other reasons as well, such as the need to work long hours with little support, or self-absorption in their own lives and problems. It's also possible that they had inadequate models of good parenting from their own parents when they were young.

Children of permissive parents can, like children from authoritarian families, have problems with self-esteem. Some studies have suggested that these children behave selfishly when interacting with others and may be insecure and emotionally immature. Most importantly, however, they often interpret their parents' lack of control or discipline as emotional neglect, even if the parents feel great love and caring toward them. The messages children hear from feeling unacknowledged may include such statements as "You are unimportant," "You do not exist for me," or "Nothing you do matters," and they then may start to incorporate these messages into their inner identities in the form of, "I am not important," or "Nothing I do matters, so I can do anything I want or I can do nothing."

At times, children of permissive parents may consciously or unconsciously seek to test their parents' limits, looking for any response that signals an emotional connection. Sometimes when children "act out," or break a rule, what they really may be looking for is acknowledgment by the parents that they exist in their parents' world. All children have a need as part of the natural development process to be recognized as independent and powerful. Having parents acknowledge children by attending to their wishes, thoughts, and feelings allows the children to gauge their effectiveness in the world by observing the parents' reaction. For example, sometimes behaving badly may be the behavioral equivalent of saying "Look at me, look at me!"

Narcissism, a deep-seated form of insecurity, often manifests in adulthood as selfishness, self-centeredness, and self-aggrandizement (building up one's sense of self-importance). It may be that children who are unattended to emotionally and physically go on to become narcissistically oriented adults, constantly looking for the attention and recognition they did not receive at home, but simultaneously being unable to let down the barriers enough to become vulnerable and intimate. This core, yet unfulfilled, need may have an impact on one's ability to develop mutually gratifying, adult relationships.

David, raised in the 1960's by parents who were young and caught up in the social and political changes happening in the world, felt happy at times that he had more freedom than his peers in school and among his friends. While his buddies often had to be home by 8 or 9 p.m., he could basically set his own schedule and would often stay out past 10— even on school nights—for much of his childhood. He loved feeling "mature" and responsible and even taunted his friends about being "babies" and needing to be "tucked in" before bed.

At times though, David felt lonely and like a bystander in his household's flurry of protest marches and poetry readings. When he began to notice that he wasn't developing the same interest in dating that his closest male friends seemed to be excited about, he felt confused and even a bit frightened at his lack of passion. When he tried to sit down with his dad to talk about things, he found that his dad was distracted, uncomfortable, and generally of no help at all. He felt particularly embarrassed to talk to his mother about something so intimate and started to feel that he was keeping a secret that probably shouldn't be discussed at all.

It wasn't until his junior year in high school that he started to put two and two together, when he found himself thinking about his best friend Roger in a sexual way—something that both shocked and excited him.

As an adult, David finds himself a comfortably "out" gay man in his forties who has trouble maintaining intimacy in relationships and therefore has never been in a relationship that lasted more than two to three months. His typical pattern is to feel huge excitement initially with a new beau, but then things begin to deteriorate after he finds that he cannot share his innermost feelings with his partner. The boyfriend feels frustrated, believing David either doesn't really care or doesn't feel that it's necessary to talk about how he feels. David, realizing that he does care, but believing that he will somehow be hurt by sharing his feelings, is trapped between what he wants and how to get it. Sometimes, he wonders if his early experience of feeling unimportant has contributed to his problems today.

Authoritative: Fair and Balanced

The authoritative parenting style appears to be associated with higher levels of self-esteem later in life. Although still the ultimate source of authority in the family, like authoritarians, a major difference is that authoritative parents are *more democratic and allow children to have a role in family decision making*. Children are allowed to question the authority figure, and reasons for rules are explained at a level they can understand. When the parents and children reach an impasse, and the parents exert their ultimate authority, they allow the children to have feelings about the decision without condemnation. Children are taught that their feelings are valid, but that some behaviors are socially unacceptable. The children learn invaluable methods of dealing with adult situations by being allowed to question and reason.

Authoritative parents attempt to establish an atmosphere of respect, trust, and open communication within the family. They establish clear and firm rules and usually spell out the consequences for breaking them. The consequences are applied uniformly across the household and in a non-hostile and non-abusive way. The goals are to allow children to learn mastery of their environment by providing clear guidelines for living, which ultimately increases children's sense of personal power and positive self-image.

Beyond the effective limit-setting, authoritative parents provide consistent emotional support and love during stressful events. Children learn that they don't have to feel alone, but can reach out for comfort when they feel frightened or needy. Reason is valued and encouraged, as well as the need to respect yourself and others. The messages you may learn and incorporate into your self-talk from authoritative parents may sound like, "Your feelings are valid, but we all have to live together" or "You exist and have value in this family."

RELEARNING TO SELF-PARENT

It's important for you to learn to recognize when you may be internally perpetuating the negative parenting you may have received as a child. It's also essential for you to become more balanced in your cognitive dealings with yourself, more like an authoritative parent who controls with love and respect than an authoritarian who controls with fear, or an emotionally neglectful, overly permissive parent. You can learn to tend to yourself, to respect and nurture yourself when you have feelings, to validate rather than invalidate, and to allow yourself to make mistakes. I will ask you to explore more about your family's primary methods of parenting at the end of this chapter to help you examine your own inner parenting style.

Rules and Boundaries

Boundaries are limits that you attempt to place between yourself and others, and rules are made to enforce boundaries. Knocking before entering someone's room is an example of a healthy boundary that indicates respect for privacy. When someone does not respect your rights, physically or emotionally, that person has violated that boundary. Good boundaries are absolutely necessary for healthy development of the self.

As children grow from completely dependent infants to healthy independent adults, they must learn to construct barriers between themselves and the world around them in order to protect themselves from harm. They must learn to say "no" when something does not feel safe. They must develop private thoughts, ways of coping with the world, and decision-making skills. The parents' role in this process is to model and teach effective and healthy ways of being in the world.

Boundaries can be healthy or unhealthy in a family. Too many boundaries might be considered rigid and lead to feelings of isolation and alienation. You may be able to protect yourself with the walls you construct, but then you cannot open doors to intimacy or affection. Too few boundaries, or weak boundaries, allow others to take advantage of you through disrespect or abuse. Parents with unhealthy boundaries themselves will often raise their children with few or no boundaries. These children may not have the tools to protect themselves as adults and allow others to push them around. Their self-talk sounds like, "I deserved that" or "I'm useless anyway," which leads them to be passive when treated unfairly.

Babies cannot initially establish healthy boundaries when they are born. Only through exploration of their bodies and their environment do they learn that they are separate from the world. They also learn about their ability to affect change, protect themselves, and reach out for what they need through their experiences as they grow. The adult caregivers shape a child's experiences, thereby shaping the child's beliefs about their effectiveness in making change, also called *self-efficacy*. When parents provide everything or nothing, children learn distorted messages about their own ability to cope with the world. Parents who continually violate the boundaries of growing children teach the children that they cannot or do not have the right to say "no" or to fend for themselves. Children also learn by watching their parents interact with others.

A family that has unclear or too few boundaries is referred to as *enmeshed*. At some point in a child's development, she must be given opportunities to make decisions for and about herself so that she will be able to apply this skill later in life. Parents who will not allow children to think independently because of their own insecurities are effectively crossing the children's healthy boundaries. Other, more overt, forms of boundary violations in families include incest and emotional abuse.

When attempts to establish effective and clear boundaries in the family are met with resistance, sometimes the child, adolescent, or young adult may try to establish an ultimate barrier by leaving the family system altogether. Running away from home may be a form of separating from dysfunctional family systems and can be viewed at times as healthy individuation (development of a healthy and independent identity). The pressures in some family systems may be so intense that children see only two options—escape or conform.

Gay and lesbian children are much more likely to run away from home and attempt suicide than their heterosexual peers, as a form of escape from a dysfunctional family system that resists the notion of a child with a nonconforming identity. Sometimes, a family chooses to send the child, who does not conform, away to boarding school or military school with the goal of re-establishing family rules and with the wish that the child be "transformed" into a conformist. Often healthy lesbian or gay children or adolescents learn to compartmentalize their lives, placing the secret parts of themselves (namely their sexuality) deep inside. They develop a conformist "exterior self" that follows the rules of the family system and allows them to function in relative safety until they are able to arrange to move to an environment that is more healthy or accepting.

Family Roles

You may have learned about your value by the role you were asked to play in your family. Often, each member of a family is assigned a task or role to play in the family. In most cases, this is an unspoken act, with family members taking on certain roles because of the behavior of other family members. Common family roles include the scapegoat (the one who always gets the blame), the caretaker or rescuer (of siblings, mother, father), the black sheep (similar to the scapegoat but more overtly rejected), and the hero (the one who must succeed).

John Bradshaw, author of several books dealing with the effects of families on development, including *Healing the Shame That Binds You*, is an ardent supporter of the notion that the family role you were expected to play as a child has an influence on your adult self-esteem.

As an adult, you may find that you continue to play the role that was assigned to you as a child. You may have chosen your career because it fits the early role you assumed. For example, people attracted to helping professions, such as psychotherapy and nursing, may have grown up tending to the needs of their parents and siblings, continuing to place their own needs lower on the personal list of priorities. Gay and lesbian children often take on the caretaker role in the family, both to focus attention away from their own unmet needs and to gain recognition and attention for their care-giving behaviors. They may learn from this that their value to the family comes from attending to the *others'* needs, rather than feeling they have intrinsic value in and of themselves. Common messages that result from rigid role playing include, "I must take care of others even at my own expense," "Taking care of my own needs or listening to my own feelings is selfish," or "I won't fit in if I act the way I truly feel."

WAYS THAT WE TALK TO EACH OTHER

Much of the language in the messages you give yourself comes from the forms of communication in your early family life. You may hear those messages in the voice of the person who said them the most when you were young. You may, for example, always hear your mother's voice when you have a failure experience sternly commenting "You see, I told you we Thompsons weren't meant to win!" Maybe you see the look of disappointment on your father's face instead of hearing the words he used. It's important to recognize the various forms of communication your family used to help you see how you may be continuing to communicate in an unhealthy way with yourself and others even today.

Nonverbal Messages

While some messages are conveyed with words, many of the messages you receive and observe are unspoken. In fact, it's been suggested that up to 90% of all communication is nonverbal, including behaviors like smiles or frowns.

Many families develop their own system of nonverbal codes that they can use at home and in public; these codes are so unique to that family that others may not recognize their meanings or importance. Other nonverbal forms of communication include body language (such as whether someone hugs you or stiffens as you approach), giving or avoiding direct eye contact, or even stretches of silence at the dinner table.

Sometimes, your negative internal messages are in fact visual images, rather than auditory, drawn from the stern looks or negative events that occurred in response to your behaviors as a child. For example, you may have always received looks of disgust or disapproval whenever you tried to discuss issues of sexuality or intense emotion, sending you the message that there is something wrong about discussing that particular issue or something wrong with you for wanting to discuss the issue.

Tone of voice can also suggest that you or something you wish to express is unacceptable, even if the words the other person uses suggest that he or she is willing to listen. This is called double-bind communication, since a parent may say one thing, but tone or body language says something else. This type of communication is confusing and teaches children to mistrust what they are told. Body language can also contradict words, sending confused messages. For example, a parent may say, "I need a hug," but will stiffen when the child approaches to do so. Sometimes what people say they want and what they really want are two different things. You may in fact have developed this indirect style of communicating with others without realizing it until this moment. Pay attention to your own tone and body language for the next few days to see if your body and words are in sync.

Expressing Anger: Taming the Tiger

You may treat yourself in a passive-aggressive way if your family was not comfortable with the direct expression of anger. Rather than saying harsh things to yourself such as, "You are foolish and unworthy" (a directly aggressive self-statement), you may unconsciously (and indirectly) sabotage your own success at times. It may be difficult for you to recognize the messages your family's passive-aggressiveness taught you if the messages were never spoken out loud, but always inferred. It may be easier for an experienced psychotherapist to help you sort out these kinds of messages when nonverbal communication and passive-aggressiveness were the primary forms of communication in your family.

Dawn's mother, Doris, would always give Dawn a look of shock whenever Dawn tried to speak up for herself. Although Doris never verbally chastised Dawn, from her facial expressions, Dawn felt her mother was saying, "You are disappointing to me. I may withdraw my love from you if you continue on this path." If Dawn persisted in her argument, her mother would become cold and distant, sometimes for days on end. Without words, Dawn learned from those experiences that, according to her mother, there are correct and incorrect ways of expressing herself. Although Dawn had always maintained that her parents had never been abusive and were always willing to talk about issues with her, it was not until she was an adult with difficulties in her own relationship that Dawn realized how much of her mother's communication style she had brought to her own relationship with her partner. Dawn found that she was passive-aggressive with herself at times. Instead of allowing herself to feel disappointed when things didn't work out the way she wanted, she realized that she was more likely to turn down invitations to socialize with friends or to reject support from her partner because she felt she didn't deserve it.

Rewarding and Acceptance

Families tend to recognize and reward standards of behavior that they value, like compliance, conformity, academic achievement, and beauty. You may or may not be able to live up to these standards. When you are able to meet the family's expectations, they will likely reward you with praise or acceptance, and you will likely continue to try to meet those standards again in the future. Academic achievement is a common area where many children learn that if they excel, they are then rewarded for their success at home. I'll discuss the impact of school on self-esteem in greater detail later in the book.

THE SECRET SELF

Many queer adults remember feeling a disdain for same-sex attraction in the family. Even while your family may not have discussed the issue of your homosexuality, you probably knew the family's attitudes toward these issues and learned to hide those feelings.

Your early recognition of same-sex attraction in a homophobic family or culture may have led you to develop a split self—one that is *public* and one that is *private*, or secret. When you are the "public self," you behave in ways that are most likely to please parents, friends, and society. This part of the self follows all the rules and behaves in ways that are expected, even when your real, deeper feelings or experiences don't match those of friends or family.

Heterosexuals may have "secret selves" as well. For example, girls may prefer activities that are viewed as more traditionally masculine, like playing aggressive sports or working on cars, but they learn early on that they might be ridiculed for pursuing these interests openly so they pretend to accept more traditionally feminine activities. This can eventually lead to feelings of chronic boredom or even depression. Lesbian or gay children often are invalidated not only in their budding sexuality, but also in their other inclinations that may fall outside of sex role expectations. Some gay men can identify with the story of being forced into participating in wood shop rather than learning about music or art, to avoid Dad's humiliation or scorn. Many lesbians share similar war stories of being told to wear a dress or makeup or being scolded for "unladylike" behavior until they complied.

Not all gay men or lesbians feel this type of gender discomfort. There are lesbians with more traditionally feminine interests and gay men who enjoy traditionally masculine pursuits. What most gay or lesbian people have in common, however, is the constant invalidation of their sexual interests. The overwhelming messages a child learns from living a split life are, "I must live to please others rather than listen to my own feelings or needs," "My true feelings are invalid or unacceptable and I must always hide them," or the more deeply held belief, "My secret self is shameful, unworthy, or evil." I will address this issue of the "secret self" later again in the "Down Low" in chapter 16.

Abuse and Neglect: The Painful Part of the Continuum

No one would dispute the fact that abuse is harmful in many ways— physically, emotionally, and spiritually. Abuse can be divided into different types, such as physical abuse, sexual abuse, and emotional abuse. These types of abuse are also most commonly associated with the authoritarian style of parenting.

Common types of *physical abuse* include beating, slapping, restraining, or otherwise causing physical discomfort or pain. This abuse may or may not be a punishment in response to a child's behavior. Sometimes physical abuse stems from the parent's mood or their self-centered need to release anger or anxiety. In this case, the message conveyed is a confusing one, since the child will often try to correlate his or her own behavior with the parental outburst ("What did I do to cause this?"). If there is no logical correlation between the child's behavior and the parental outburst, occasionally arbitrary associations can be made between innocuous behaviors like wearing the color blue with the parents' abusive behavior in the mind of the child. The pressure of attempting to predict the parent's outbursts and avoid provoking them can lead to chronic feelings of anxiety and stress. Even limited physical punishment in the past has the power to shape your self-esteem for many years.

You may have been a convenient target for a psychologically immature parent with poor emotional coping skills because you were powerless to resist and could be intimidated into silence. The messages are loud and clear: "You do not have the power to defend yourself," and "Great harm will befall you if you make the wrong step."

Sexual abuse includes such behaviors as outright rape (forcing a child to accept sexual behavior) to seduction (convincing the child that inappropriate sexual behavior is acceptable and consensual). Specific behaviors include all forms of intercourse, fellatio, cunnilingus, and other touching of private parts, as well as less obvious but also sexualized forms of behavior like voyeurism, exhibitionism, flirtations, and making embarrassing sexual comments. Sexual abuse can occur inside the family (incest) as well as outside the family by someone of the same or opposite sex. Victims of sexual abuse can often have unresolved or mixed feelings about the abuse itself, particularly if they experienced any pleasure from the act sexually or emotionally. They may feel guilty and responsible for the abuse, especially if the abuser framed the abuse as consensual or mutually pleasurable. When sexually abused children grow up, they also often feel guilty and ashamed of not speaking out about the abuse earlier.

Sometimes, gay or lesbian people have been convinced that sexual abuse when they were young was responsible for their later-emerging sexual identity. This argument is often made as an explanation for the origin of homosexuality, suggesting that something abnormal has occurred in order for a gay or lesbian identity to develop. Republican Representative Mark Foley, outed as a gay man after being exposed for dalliances with male congressional pages, claimed, as an excuse for his behavior, that he was sexually molested by a Catholic priest as a youth. While the molestation may have indeed happened, it does not fully explain the other factors that also contributed to his violation of appropriate social boundaries in a position of authority.

Another problem with this type of reasoning is that it's self-invalidating. One could argue that a woman became a lesbian both because she was sexually abused by a woman (and liked it) or because she was sexually abused by a man (and didn't like it). Conducting research to validate these types of theories is both ethically and practically difficult to carry out since it would involve measuring sexual orientation before childhood sexual abuse and then again after the abuse. Although more and more evidence is surfacing suggesting that sexual orientation begins to take shape very early in life, we still are relatively ineffective at determining which children might grow up to be gay or lesbian. The most current data suggests that sexual orientation is shaped by many factors, including non-environmental factors like genetics or biology.

Emotional abuse may be overt or covert and therefore not everyone agrees on what exactly constitutes emotional abuse. It doesn't necessarily involve physical or sexual abuse, but each of these most certainly includes emotional abuse. Clear examples of overt emotional abuse include subjecting a child to frequent yelling, insulting or degrading comments, and both verbal and nonverbal threats of physical, sexual, or emotional harm. Less clear examples include implied threats, rejection, avoidant behaviors, smirks, passive-aggressive behaviors, and sarcasm. Emotional abusers share many of the same general characteristics of physical and sexual abusers, if not the specific behaviors. For example, they often respond to children in an abusive way because of their own needs or inability to control impulses, rather than in direct response to the behaviors of the child. The sting of emotional abuse carries the same effect on a child's self-esteem as physical or sexual abuse. Emotional abuse may be particularly damaging because the parent may be able to abuse in this way more often with less challenge from other family members or outsiders. Emotional abuse may not be exhibited in discrete episodes, as is often the case with physical or sexual abuse, but may exist constantly in the form of insults, intimidation, and verbal or nonverbal threats. A child who grows up in an environment with a constant barrage of negative evaluation (e.g., "You will never amount to anything!") will most likely have low self-esteem. The more negative the messages, the lower the self-esteem.

Often, if parents indulge in one form of abuse, they may also indulge in others. A common thread for all forms of abuse is boundary violation. Boundaries are healthy in many ways and are particularly relevant to people who were raised in abusive families. Parents who do not encourage the formation of healthy boundaries in their children or do not respect these boundaries when they are formed are in effect teaching their children to be victims. They teach their children that their thoughts, feelings, and desires are invalid and that the needs of others are more important. They also teach their childen that even if these desires are valid, the children are not powerful enough to reach for these desires or wishes. Repeated violation of physical, sexual, or emotional boundaries teaches the child that they are unworthy of respect, love, or happiness. The cognitive messages that abused children develop sound like this: "You are not worth respect from others," "You don't deserve to be loved," and "You are meant to be abused by others."

There are many reasons that parents abuse their children beyond a conscious intent to inflict short-term and long-term damage. Many of the parents grew up in homes that were violent and abusive themselves and learned their parenting styles from their own parents. Many of these parents also have problems that are overwhelming, such as poverty, loss of a job, or marital difficulties, and they have few effective means for coping with these pressures. They may also have psychological problems or conditions, including alcohol or other substance abuse or dependency. It's important to keep in mind that the abuser may not realize that their choices are inappropriate and harmful. In many cases, they may be intending to do the right thing, but their own backgrounds prevent them from making the right decisions in parenting.

Another potentially harmful type of parental behavior, neglect, is less likely to raise the public ire, except in extreme cases. Such extremes include leaving a child alone for long periods of time or not attending to life-threatening health or safety needs of a child. Less extreme forms may simply be the emotional or physical unavailability of a parent, lack of attention to longer term health issues like proper nutrition or exercise, or ignoring signs of potential problems for a child in school or in relationships. Parents can be both loving and neglectful, selecting issues that are appropriate in their minds for discussion and ignoring the child's other needs. These children learn to believe that they are unimportant, not good enough to be attended to, or incapable of making a difference.

Children who grow up with parents who have significant psychological illness or drug or alcohol abuse/dependency often take a backseat to the needs of the parents or other family members exhibiting the most serious problems. The children may learn from this that in order to be attended to, they must be sick or otherwise disruptive. These families tend to form an unhealthy system around the individual's (or individuals') sickness and disruptive behavior and emotional health or striving for independence is discouraged. Parents who have an untreated mental illness or substance abuse/dependency problem may exhibit physically, sexually, or emotionally abusive behaviors toward their children due to difficulty with impulse control or intense self-absorption. Children who grow up in this type of environment learn that the world is an unpredictable and frightening place and they must attend to the needs of others rather than their own needs. Inconsistent messages of support or nurturing may, indeed, make it more difficult for the children to form clear expectations of the world and themselves.

CRITICALLY EVALUATE THE AUTOMATIC MESSAGES

The goal of this chapter is to help you understand the origins of your personal internal messages—both direct and indirect. By learning to recognize these messages or beliefs that are sometimes just under the surface of your awareness, as an adult, you have a distinct advantage over when you were a child: You can evaluate the messages more objectively and choose to reject the ones that are not accurate.

How We Replay the Old Stories

Many times, my lesbian or gay clients have not been aware of how they perpetuate feelings of inadequacy, doubt, anxiety, or depression by continuing to play the old family messages etched into their "hard drive" through their ongoing and sometimes unconscious self-talk. It's important for you to begin to recognize the beliefs and hidden messages that you carry with you from your childhood.

Answering the following questions will help you clarify family beliefs, values, and messages that you received when you were growing and forming your self-concept. It will then be important for you to consider the validity of these beliefs and their usefulness to you now as an adult. Remember that just because your family believed something about you does not make it true. Just because they taught you what they knew does not mean what they taught you is helpful for you. In fact in many cases, what they learned as heterosexuals about gays or lesbians, or about sexuality in general, may be quite unhealthy and unhelpful for you.

QUESTIONS FOR REFLECTION

Take some time to ask yourself the following questions derived from this chapter's concepts. You do not have to write down your answers, but you may choose to begin keeping a journal of memories, thoughts, and feelings for later review.

- Which style of parenting—authoritarian, permissive, or authoritative—was most evident in your family when you were growing up?
- *If you were raised in an authoritarian family:* Who was the "dictator" (or "dictators")? How did this person use discipline? Was he or she physical with you or did that person use psychological or emotional strategies to control you? How was punishment, or the threat of punishment, used when you thought or felt something that the dictator did not value? Were you scolded or punished for accidents or mistakes? How do you feel today when you make mistakes? In what other ways do you recognize your upbringing affecting your life today?
- *If you were raised in a permissive family:* How often did you feel totally accepted? Were there times as a child when you

felt alone, neglected, or unattended to? Were there times you secretly wished for an argument in order to feel some emotional connection with a family member? Could you "get away" with things you did wrong? What happened when you brought home a good grade or received some other recognition for good work? As an adult, do you ever feel the need to have an argument with a friend or significant other just to break the silence? Do you sometimes feel like you have to be the life of the party at social gatherings? In what other ways do you recognize your upbringing affecting your life today?

- *If you were raised in an authoritative family*: How often did you feel totally accepted? Was there a time when your parents changed their parenting style? Was there an event that had a significant impact on your family, such as a divorce, death, or change in financial status? How often were you included in major family decisions? In what other ways do you recognize your upbringing affecting your life today? Did your family exhibit characteristics of two or all three family styles? In what ways? How do you perpetuate the same kind of parenting you were raised with? Can you identify which style you use with yourself now? To motivate yourself? To deal with mistakes? Do you say things to yourself or others that are aggressive or do things that are passive-aggressive?

- What were the family rules about privacy? Were you allowed to have time and space alone? Were your thoughts, feelings, and possessions respected? Did your parents have healthy boundaries with you? Were you aware of a secret self that you felt you had to hide? Were you physically, sexually, or emotionally abused?

- Did you have a parent (or parents) with mental illness, substance abuse problems, and so on? How did you compensate for their problems?

- What unresolved emotional issues do you have from your childhood? What patterns do you perpetuate with yourself now?

THREE

*Inescapable Messages:
The Media, Culture,
and Politics*

HOW DO YOU DOCUMENT REAL LIFE WHEN REAL LIFE'S GETTING
MORE LIKE FICTION EACH DAY?

—*Jonathan Larson, Rent*

We are all a product of our society and the times; we may conform to it, rebel against it, or both. The family system that you explored in Chapter 2 is a part of the larger society that contains it. If your family members conform to the neighbors' expectations and attitudes, then they will likely expect you to conform. People conform both to feel *accepted* and to *avoid the pain of rejection and isolation.*

Lesbians and gays often are blamed or scapegoated by members of our culture for certain social problems. For example, some right-wing religious groups suggest that gays and lesbians are responsible for the breakdown of what they call "traditional family values." If you tend to feel guilt or shame when you hear such messages, you may be a *high internalizer*. People with low self-esteem tend to accept responsibility for problems, rather than look for someone else to blame. If you are a high internalizer, part of your strategy to raise your self-esteem will be to begin evaluating external reasons for problematic behavior, rather than always accepting full responsibility and blaming yourself. In the example, then, nuclear family "breakdown" might be viewed as a result of economic factors rather than moral ones.

PREJUDICE, STEREOTYPES, AND DISCRIMINATION IN THE CULTURE AT LARGE

People's attitudes and attributions affect how they evaluate and treat other people. Positive attitudes/attributions will lead them to treat those people favorably. Negative attitudes can quickly lead to prejudicial behavior toward, and stereotyping of, the person or people toward whom they hold those negative beliefs. A *prejudice* is defined as a negative attitude toward a person solely due to her or his membership in a group. A *stereotype* is a set of beliefs about the characteristics of people in a specific group that is then expanded to all members of that group. *Discrimination*, in simple terms, is the behavioral expression of prejudice and involves actions that harm members of the targeted group. Although most gay or lesbian people can quickly name instances of discrimination they have encountered, both directly and indirectly, many do not recognize the ways that they may internally stereotype, hold self-prejudicial attitudes, or even discriminate against themselves.

As products of a generally gay-intolerant culture, you cannot help but internalize the negative attitudes that may be held by your family, friends, or larger culture. This can create an ongoing internal battle between your desires and your behaviors. This tension, sometimes referred to as *internalized homophobia*, may result in self-punitive thinking, self-censorship, decreased assertiveness, and destructive self-fulfilling prophecies.

Miriam was worried that being a lesbian would cause her to lose out on a high level job she really wanted. Before she even went in for her interview, she had convinced herself that being a lesbian was going to be a liability. In her home life, she was "out" to everyone she knew and she believed that her company was much too conservative to tolerate someone at upper management levels who was openly lesbian. Her thoughts, just before the interview, ran the gamut from, "My sexual orientation will be a handicap to me in this job," to "I should just be happy with what I already have," increasing her anxiety about the interview to the point of having sweaty palms and a racing heart. Although she knew that questions about her sexual orientation would likely not come up during the interview, she didn't perform nearly as well as she knew she could have. As she had predicted, she did not get the job, which she took as a confirmation that being an out lesbian was not compatible with this level of management. Unfortunately, Miriam could not see that being a lesbian in itself likely had less to do with not getting the job than did her anxiety. Her lowered self-expectations actually interfered with her ability to present herself as the competent and capable employee that she was.

SOCIETY'S DEEP-SEATED ANTI-GAY MESSAGES

Although society's rules for conforming often are made explicit through laws and ethics codes of formal organizations (such as the government and religious institutions), many of society's rules are communicated more subtly and informally. Just as parents can communicate messages overtly by yelling, name-calling, or beating—or subtly through facial expressions, silence, and other covert forms of rejection—society's messages about homosexuality can also be obvious or hidden. Society's overt homophobia can be found in anti-gay employment policies, anti-gay marriage amendments, sodomy laws (finally on their last legs), and hate crimes. The indirect negativity toward homosexuals is more difficult to see, just as the nonverbal cues within a family may be more difficult to recognize as inappropriate. Examples of covert homophobia include such societal behaviors as the stereotyping of homosexuals in the media and public conversations, voting against pro-gay issues or HIV funding initiatives (which may be easier for some homophobes with a conscience because they feel uncomfortable with voting directly for an anti-gay initiative), and teaching children distorted information about lesbian and gay sexual behavior.

Some segments of society often have a need to stereotype groups of people in order to exert control over them. Stereotyping allows for the marginalization of minorities or subgroups and thereby allows the majority to disseminate inaccurate information that keeps the oppressive attitudes alive. Depicting the "lesbian" character in a TV show or movie as the murderer or crazy, condoning or not speaking out against the telling of "fag" jokes by heterosexuals, or making assumptions about gay families or friends based on general expectations for "those people" are forms of covert homophobia—no direct intent to harm may be obvious in these examples, but may indirectly lead to harm nonetheless.

Historical and Cultural Contexts of Society's Messages

In order to evaluate the negative messages you might hear in your world today, let's take a look at their origins. It's clear from the history books that various world cultures have had different attitudes regarding sexual relations between people of the same sex. And while cultures themselves may have held varying attitudes, positive or negative, toward same-sex attractions during the same period of time, each culture may have changed its views of this behavior across different time periods. In other words, many of societies' attitudes toward same-sex attraction are dynamic, constantly changing as the society evolves and changes. Nowhere is this more obvious than in one well-known historical record we know as the Bible. Part of the value of this book is its documentation of the attitudes, laws, and customs of Judeo-Christian peoples thousands of years ago.

Most people observe the change in customs and values that have occurred since the original writings due to cultural advances in areas such as science, medicine, and technology.

We also know from this record that, at times, even standards of behavior within the Bible changed over time. For example, polygamy was a common practice during the time of Abraham, but went out of fashion when Paul suggested the concept of "Christian" monogamy. Other major religious historical texts outside the Judeo-Christian perspective, including Eastern, Native-American, and African perspectives, also document changing cultural practices across hundreds or thousands of years.

Neil Miller's book *Out of the Past: Gay and Lesbian History from 1869 to the Present* includes a treasure trove of information about American (and other cultural) views of gays and lesbians. Miller points out an inherent difficulty in the study of lesbian and gay history: The term *homosexual* did not even exist prior to the nineteenth century. Most likely, even the concept of homosexual identity was not understood the way we understand it today. He effectively argues that same-sex attraction or behavior has occurred throughout history, but that the behaviors themselves were either tolerated or prohibited without identifying people who exhibited the behaviors as having a separate "homosexual" identity. He goes on to argue that only as industrialization allowed for more economic independence from extended families did people develop unique lifestyles identified around their sexualities.

It's only over the past 150 or so years that gay and lesbian people have been identified as separate sub-populations within the dominant culture and therefore have been subject to the development of the larger society's prejudicial and discriminatory attitudes. Even today, there are widely varying opinions about homosexuality both within this country and in other countries. For a deeper perspective on society's attitudes toward homosexuality, I recommend two other excellent books by Neil Miller, entitled *Out in the World: Gay and Lesbian Life from Buenos Aires to Bangkok* and his significant *In Search of Gay America*, an American Library Association prizewinner and Lambda Literary Award winner.

All of this ultimately suggests that there are no cultural absolutes. Just because the regional/geographical or chronological attitudes are gay and lesbian intolerant, it does not mean that these attitudes are correct and should be readily accepted by you without careful reflection and assessment. Luckily, you are not a sponge that soaks up the liquid around it without a filter. You have the ability to evaluate the values that the culture around you puts forth as absolutes and certainties and you can apply the same objective reasoning process to dispel these ideas that you are learning from this book.

You can assess whether specific cultural prohibitions or negative attitudes are healthy, helpful, or beneficial and rationally make your own decision about their value to you.

This is not to say that cultural norms are never helpful. There are standards of behavior that are rational, healthy, and beneficial for the greater good, including sanctions against murder, rape, and other behaviors that directly or indirectly harm others. But it takes some extensive twisting of logic and history by people in positions of authority to justify the persecution of two consenting adults who wish to enter into an affectionate, mutually satisfying, integrity-filled relationship! Such arguments often include vague warnings of "the decay of the moral fiber of America" if homosexual relationships are accepted and honored, usually based on fear and ignorance rather than on facts.

History and Homosexuality

Let's look at a few examples of the types of attitudes and beliefs that Americans have held about homosexuals and homosexual behavior in recent times and the messages they convey. Since the concept of homosexual identity did not begin to form until the mid-nineteenth century, specific sexual behaviors were more likely to be judged as wrong rather than the people themselves being deemed entirely evil. Before that time, an individual's sexual behavior did not define them as a person. Societal standards for what was considered appropriate and inappropriate changed with the times.

With greater industrialization, and subsequent economic independence, people were freer to move away from the traditional extended family setting and into urban areas with larger populations and greater anonymity. People with attractions to the same sex eventually found each other and established their own social networks and customs. But with the self-identification of men and women as "homosexual" came the greater society's reaction to a fledgling and minority community.

By rejecting traditional roles of husband and wife, several problems were created. First, the society as a whole may have felt frightened by people who would not conform, and therefore attempted to pathologize or demonize this behavior. Then, once lesbians and gay men rejected the norms for behavior, with no prior role models, they had to determine what their own social norms would be. Early attempts to explain why people were homosexual included the concept that the "correct" way to relate sexually for males was to females and females to males. People who related sexually to other people of the same sex must be a separate, or third, sex.

Heterosexism and Heterocentrism

Society communicates negative messages to you about your worth through heterosexism or heterocentrism. These two terms are similar but have subtle distinctions. *Heterosexism* refers to the economic exploitation and social domination of homosexuals by heterosexuals. For example, there are groups of people who assume that gay or lesbian employees do not deserve domestic partner benefits because in their view we cannot marry, do not maintain long-term relationships, or are simply not deserving of what they feel are special privileges. Certainly heterosexists can and often do base their voting decisions and beliefs on their "heterosexual is superior" attitude.

The term *heterocentrism* is based on the term egocentrism, which refers to the worldview that everything in a person's life should and does revolve around that person. Egocentrists tend to focus on their own needs before they focus on the needs of others. At times, they may not even acknowledge the needs of others or understand that by focusing only on themselves, they deprive or harm others. Heterocentrism, therefore, refers to the view that heterosexuality is all that exists. People who think from a heterocentrist perspective assume that single men they meet must be looking for a woman to date or that two middle-aged women who live together must be "very good friends" or "old maids" just waiting for the right man. Heterocentrists may not intend to be harmful; they just cannot see beyond their own values and experiences. Heterocentrists may be equally as discriminatory as heterosexists in the lack of recognition of the needs of the lesbian or gay community, but it's out of self-absorption rather than an overt need to dominate.

Javier's family had always voiced support for him as he was coming out and assured him that his sexual orientation had no effect on their love for him. He felt accepted at family gatherings and was always included in important family discussions. When he compared himself to his gay friends who had not been so lucky and had been rejected or abused by their families because of their sexuality, he felt he should consider himself lucky.

It came as a surprise to Javier when his partner of six years, Rusty, expressed to him that he felt as though he was an outsider at Javier's family gatherings, never becoming more to them than "Javi's friend." Javier began to realize that, although they were always nice to Rusty, his family had often extended invitations to family events to him that did not include Rusty. He remembered that his sister's husband was instantly considered a part of the family after they married four years ago and that most family discussions always included his brother-in-law.

As he paid more attention to the differences in how his family responded to him as a part of a couple and how they responded to his sister and her husband, he could clearly see the subtle signs of heterocentrism, without an obvious intent to harm.

Double and Triple Negatives

The messages of these attitudes, both formal and informal, are clear: "Homosexuals are inferior to heterosexuals and thereby deserve less privilege." Sometimes the message is stronger: "Homosexuals deserve to be jailed, abused, or killed." Many people receive complicated messages like, "If you act like a heterosexual and never speak of your true nature, then you can have some of the privileges of society." Lesbians may receive these messages about homosexuality in addition to negative societal messages toward women such as, "Women are inferior to men," or "Powerful women are freaks." People of color have a whole other contingent of negative societal messages. Lesbians of color have been referred to as having "a triple strike" against them in this culture for their sex, their race, and their sexuality.

Sexual Stereotypes: Male and Female Characteristics

One of the most pervasive stereotypes about gay men and lesbians is that gay men are effeminate and lesbians are masculine. Some theories have suggested similarities in brain tissues, hormones, or other brain chemistry between gay men and straight women and lesbians and straight men. Early reasoning assumed that males who were attracted to males must actually have female characteristics. Since physically they still looked like "regular" males, then they must be internally (or psychologically) more like females. The argument is reversed for lesbians (i.e., they must be internally more like men). In fact, an early term for lesbians and gay men was *inverts*, a shortened form of the term, inversion. This early logic has continued in some form even until today, despite scientific advances in the study of homosexuality and sex role development.

It would not be unexpected for gay people themselves to buy into old explanations and understandings of themselves and having done so, begin to adopt other features of the sex role to which they have now been assigned. If you accept, for example, that you, as a biological male, are in fact internally like a female, then you may readily accept (and even cultivate) other traditionally feminine characteristics. You might adopt stereotypical behaviors of the opposite sex for many reasons, but it may simply be to reduce conflicting self-expectations that produce anxiety. For a woman who loves women, the only largely available role models for loving women are men. The woman might therefore feel as though she must act like a man if she loves women.

Another theory is that if people who are attracted to the same sex reject the larger society's view of what constitutes normal sexuality, then they may also feel freer to reject other social roles that do not fit. This leaves them freer to express characteristics that fall outside of the acceptable norm. For example, women may choose to be more athletic, assertive, or independent, all of which continue to be stereotypically masculine characteristics. Men, thus, may choose to express characteristics such as nurturance and emotional expression, which are stereotypically seen as feminine.

The stereotype that gay men are effeminate and lesbians are masculine is so commonplace that this view of homosexuals is often the first information that children get about same-sex attraction. Whether or not your parents held this view, many adult gay and lesbian people were exposed to this idea as they were growing up through the larger culture (movies, TV, books, and so on).

One of the earliest gay male icons, Oscar Wilde, became a household name following a long and scandalous trial during which his private life was held up for public scrutiny in the 1890s. Many of Wilde's personal attributes—wit, flamboyance, and hedonism— were quickly assumed to be characteristic of all men with homosexual inclinations, leading to further embellishment of the stereotype. It was commonplace after this trial for men suspected of being gay to be referred to as "the Oscar Wilde sort," as in the E.M. Forster novel, *Maurice*. A similar figure for lesbians in twentieth-century history is Radclyffe Hall, author of the influential lesbian novel, *The Well of Loneliness*, who faced a similar courtroom scandal in 1920 with major media coverage. Hall's novel became widely distributed (sometimes through the lesbian underground) and her conceptualization of the lesbian characters as "femme" and "butch" likely influenced later social views of lesbian roles.

The messages that a large segment of our society continues to send to children include "gay men are effeminate sissies" and "lesbians are masculine." Not only does straight society send this message, but gays and lesbians often perpetuate these myths unknowingly.

We now realize that gay men and lesbians manifest the same range of masculine and feminine characteristics as the heterosexual community. Some theories suggest that the dichotomy between heterosexuality and homosexuality is an artificial one, with human sexual variations falling on a continuum between the two extremes and that most people are in fact bisexual (or capable of attraction to both sexes), with very few people attracted exclusively to the opposite or same sex. Exclusive heterosexuality might, for example, suggest that an exclusively heterosexual woman could not judge the attractiveness of another woman because she did not feel a desire to have sexual relations with her. Many heterosexual males claim to be unable to determine whether another male is handsome, yet through social science research, we find that most males and females rate an attractive male higher than an unattractive male on scales of personal attributes such as strength, intelligence, and friendliness. Human sexuality is complex, involving both behavior and attraction, the former of which can be altered and the latter of which cannot.

In reality, all minority groups defy the general stereotypes associated with them. While some members of the group may indeed seem like the view held by the larger culture, there are many who do not fit the stereotype. There are indeed effeminate gay men and butch lesbians, but I also know gay men and lesbians who would not fit those descriptions.

Other prominent stereotypes for gay men include being unathletic, weaker than straight men, passive, dependent, sensitive, into the arts, "bitchy," and fastidious. For lesbians, often-repeated stereotypes include being "butch," loud, aggressive, insensitive, nonmaternal, athletic, clumsy, and co-dependent. Many other stereotypes exist both outside and within the gay community. Many comedians use community-based stereotypes as a basis for humor. Of course, even the humor itself can be harmful if it clearly perpetuates attitudes that may lead to harmful behavior. Gay and lesbian comedians may be able to get away with this type of humor because, ultimately, the humor mocks the stereotyping, rather than using the humor to mock the individuals themselves.

SOCIOECONOMIC MESSAGES:
YOU ARE WHAT YOU MAKE

Your socioeconomic status while growing up (and as an adult) can have a significant effect on your self-esteem. While it is beyond the scope of this book to discuss the many ways that low socioeconomic status can affect a child's development, it is a powerful influence on physical, emotional, and cognitive growth. Clearly, our culture maintains many negative stereotypes about the poor, stigmatizing this group as "lazy," "stupid," or of "low character." Unfortunately, it often seems in the current political climate that the poor in the United States are used as pawns in the political struggle between political groups. Describing with contempt the "welfare mother" and the "liberal agenda" to devise ways of enriching the already wealthy are subtle and not-so-subtle themes discussed by middle-class and wealthy voters. Contempt for the poor is encouraged by arguments that maintain that most poor people are intentionally "bilking the system." The messages that filter through are meant to shame and vilify: "You are poor because you are lazy" and "You cannot escape because you are worthless." If you are gay and poor, you are doubly stigmatized.

VEHICLES FOR SOCIETY'S MESSAGES

We learn about societal messages from many sources including the media (TV, movies, print, and internet) and the government. Two other obvious and primary sources include religious institutions and schools, both of which teach you directly about appropriate ways to worship, think, and act from their own perspectives. These last two sources are important since they often serve to reinforce the attitudes of parents and family, toward you and your self-concept.

The Media Around Us

How gay or lesbian characters are portrayed in literature and film may have the effect of establishing, perpetuating, or contradicting social stereotypes. We also know that while the media is—to a degree— reflective of our larger culture, the content of the images is subject to the control of publishers, studios, the large corporations who own the studios, government regulators, and pressure from special interest groups of all types. The portrayal of homosexual characters in the movies in a negative way is largely ignored by anti-gay religious groups, which suggests that it is okay in their opinion for the gay character to fit unflattering stereotypes or to be portrayed as the bad guy or to ultimately suffer and die. However, when a gay or lesbian character is portrayed in a healthy, positive light, these same forces mobilize to protest, boycott, and condemn the movie's makers and sponsors. It is not the portrayal of a homosexual character that is condemned; it only becomes a problem when the characters are portrayed in ways that are contradictory to that group's purposes or values.

Vito Russo provides a wonderful and detailed history of homosexuality in films in his book *The Celluloid Closet* (as well as in the DVD version inspired by the book).

Think about the portrayal of lesbian or gay characters in the literature or media of your childhood and adolescence. Do you remember any positive portrayals of gays or lesbians? If the character was not "evil," was she or he stereotypically flamboyant or butch in an exaggerated way for humor? Did the character ultimately change his or her sexual orientation (that is, "choose" to be heterosexual), go to prison, or die? Obviously, there were and are subtle messages about being gay or lesbian that you learned from these portrayals. Even the absence of positive portrayals of gay characters subtly communicates that healthy gay people don't exist in our culture.

Steps have been taken in recent years in an attempt to remedy the terrible and distorted messages in literature and the media. Movies are beginning to allow gay and lesbian characters to live, to be "normal," and even to reflect higher values of integrity, loyalty, and honor. Television took a big step in 1997 by allowing lesbian comedian Ellen DeGeneres to continue with her hit sitcom, even after she publicly acknowledged her sexual orientation. For the first time in history, the main character of a TV series was an out lesbian. DeGeneres has taken her place in history as she attempted to move public opinion by portraying the "real life" experiences, feelings, and dreams of hundreds of thousands, if not millions, of gay and lesbian people in this country. I was especially impressed with her attempts to avoid using old gay male and lesbian stereotypes for humor. She continues to win fans and change opinions with her daytime talk show and her predictable good nature and modesty.

A special organization that has been monitoring the portrayal of lesbians and gays in the media is known as GLAAD, Gay and Lesbian Alliance Against Defamation. One of this group's main goals is to attempt to exert some pressure on writers and the show business industry to portray our community more accurately and sensitively, rather than resorting to inaccurate stereotypes.

Stories about gays in the evening news can perpetuate or disconfirm gay stereotypes. Ethical journalists attempt to present a story in a balanced manner. This means that if reasonable conflict exists about an issue, both sides should be allowed to represent their opinion so that viewers can make their own decisions. Some people, however, suggest that ethics in journalism is waning, with the rise of entertainment-owned networks focused on ratings and advertising dollars. This translates into the "trash talk show" version of news stories where people representing the most extreme points of view regarding an issue are invited to participate in a "debate" with the intentional desire to create conflict and thereby attract viewers. Many times, I've watched what appeared to be a serious, issue-oriented news story about gay legal rights take a dive when the journalist interviews a radical right-winger espousing a distorted and irrational perspective that is shared by only a tiny fundamentalist organization. To say that this is a balanced perspective is to seriously underestimate the intelligence of the viewer and it moves the debate from the rational, fact-based arena to sideshow status. By granting "moral" extremists the opposing perspective in an issue-oriented debate, the media in fact lends an air of legitimacy to the extremist, non-mainstream, and often irrational, propaganda. For a more in-depth discussion of the influence of dualism in the American culture, see Deborah Tannen's 1998 book, *The Argument Culture*.

Politicians and the Government

Our country's government is largely shaped by our culture's moral values, which are in turn shaped by predominant religious institutions in the country. The government can be a cause of discrimination and distress in the way that it encourages or discourages intolerance or acceptance of its people. The government at all levels—local, state, and federal—shapes public attitudes through the laws that it makes and enforces. As the keeper of legal authority, the government has the power to define as criminals those the church defines as immoral. Although sexual activity between consenting adults would not technically constitute a crime, most states in the early part of this century made certain specific sexual acts—homosexual and heterosexual—a crime. Yet even people who are known to have "broken the law," but are not arrested or convicted, are stigmatized by the culture at large. The threat of being arrested in itself has been used throughout the years to control gay men and lesbians through intimidation.

Fortunately, a major shift occurred in this country when the US Supreme Court ruled that sodomy laws were unconstitutional. Although it's probably hard to notice an immediate impact by this ruling (after all, it's not every day that police are staking out our homes just to break in on oral sex between adults), the effect in reducing stigma and fear for sexual minorities has been staggering. Breaking down this barrier has led to unprecedented progress in establishing civil rights even in the face of a very gay-intolerant controlling party in the government.

Sometimes, the laws don't threaten to punish us directly, but simply do not allow us to fully participate in the cultural traditions that the heterosexual majority enjoys. We were not allowed to marry anywhere in the world for many years, and were then condemned for "promiscuous" sex or sex outside of marriage, a double-standard. Again, since this book was first released in 1999 there have been major shifts in this country despite serious opposition. Massachusetts became the first US state to allow lesbians and gays to marry. Other states like Vermont and California have taken steps just up to the brink of allowing marriage as well.

Unfortunately, even those couples legally married in Massachu-setts or Canada are not recognized by the U.S. federal government. We cannot file our IRS taxes jointly with our partners and enjoy the tax benefits afforded to a married couple. When our sexuality is made known at our jobs, we can be fired, and the employer suffers little penalty. When we want to join the country club, move into an exclusive apartment building, or join the Boy Scouts or military, we can be turned away. When we want to visit our partners in the hospi-tal or adopt a child, we must rely on the kindness of strangers rather than the protection of our constitution.

Children reason that if the government does not protect them from ignorance and intolerance, then surely they are worth nothing. As an adult who is continually bombarded with these messages in your own life and in the news, you may find it hard to maintain the sense of well-being you are entitled to and the motivation to keep working for change. The messages from the government sound like this: "You are second class," "You are not worthy of the rights granted all other Americans," and "You are part of a dispensable voting block that would be better used as a political wedge issue than treated as a human being with rights." You may find yourself frustrated or hot under the collar with each anti-gay pronouncement by party or reli-gious leaders.

Theoretically, our government is meant to serve the needs of all the citizens of this country. However, the welfare of the people often seems to take a backseat to the needs of the political process and the politicians themselves. Lesbians and gays are often a convenient sub-group within this country for attacking, scapegoating, and fund-rais-ing. It's not unusual for politicians to blame minority groups for economic problems and/or "moral decay" whether or not they personally feel this way. Over the years these scapegoat groups have included people of color, non-Christians, the poor, the disabled, and immigrants.

A few years back, George W. Bush involved himself in the case of Terry Schiavo, a woman in Florida living in a persistent vegetative state after loss of oxygen to her brain years ago from bulimia. This issue of course is extremely complex, with many emotional dynamics for both sides of the struggling family. Despite the polls that suggested that an overwhelming majority of Americans, both Republican and Democrat, supported keeping the government out of this very personal issue, members of the US Congress and Mr. Bush decided that it was important to take steps to intervene in an issue that had been reviewed by over 19 different judges at the local, state, and federal level. Although I try to understand the legitimate reasons it might have been important to intervene in this specific case, the skeptical part of me had to wonder if this issue was seen as an opportunity to shore up support with the political "base" rather for true moral/ethical reasons. I wonder sometimes also if using gay marriage as a wedge issue has less to do with Republican morality and everything to do with "stirring up the base" as well.

Recently, it has become unacceptable to directly attack many minority groups for the sake of getting votes, especially on the basis of race or religion. Much of this may be due to the rising political clout these groups have enjoyed as they have organized politically themselves. Gays and lesbians, however, remain a convenient target for doom-crying politicians (and some religious leaders) since we are still in the process of organizing our political muscle.

DISSECTING THE MESSAGES

This chapter has been about recognizing the anti-gay messages embedded in our culture in addition to the ones specific to your family of origin. Although at one level, our society seems to be slowly moving away from condemnation of lesbians and gays, negative messages still exist and have actually become much more prominent during the first part of the 21st century. In order to effectively protect yourself from these direct and hidden messages about your worth, you must take steps to evaluate them and dispute, challenge, and change them. Keep in mind that society's values are not absolutes but have changed over time and will change again. When the culture at large sends signals that you are "second class," or not worthy of rights, remember that it is those values that are wrong and those beliefs that are misguided. The problem is with *them*, not *you*!

QUESTIONS FOR REFLECTION

- What were the social values concerning homosexuality where you were raised? Was it accepted and tolerated? Were lesbians or gay men mocked, repudiated, or condemned?
- What was the first book, TV show, or movie you remember that mentioned lesbians or gay men? What was the tone of the book, show, or movie? Was the gay or lesbian character portrayed as a positive figure or role model? Did the character suffer or die? Were the characters stereotypical? What were those stereotypes for lesbians? For gay men?
- What have been your personal experiences with discrimination or harassment for being gay or lesbian? A woman? A person of color? Do you know anyone personally who has been the victim of discrimination, heterocentrism, or heterosexism? How did these experiences affect your self-concept and behaviors?
- In what ways have you internalized the homophobia of the culture in which you live? How do you perpetuate society's negative stereotypes within yourself? Toward others?
- How does it make you feel to hear an anti-gay politician use lesbian and gay rights as a way to mobilize voters? Refer to basic civil rights as "special rights?" Do you hold onto these feelings or can you let go of them quickly and easily?
- When something goes wrong, to whom or what do you tend

to attribute the blame? Are you an internalizer (blame yourself) or externalizer (blame others)? How does this affect your self-esteem?

Resources

Gay & Lesbian Alliance Against Defamation

www.glaad.org

Four

Messages of Faith:
Religious Authorities

In my family, religion was a part of our everyday life. My parents were devout, tea-totaling, fundamentalist Christians who followed the rules of both their church and their local preacher. We attended services every Sunday morning, Sunday evening, and Wednesday night, and my brother and I also were raised going to Sunday School, designed specifically for teaching children about church doctrine with local twists. In my tiny Southern hometown, there was little distinction between church standards and community standards. Everyone understood the importance of an affiliation with a church, since one of the first questions you could be guaranteed to be asked was "Where do you go to church?" after you met someone new. There was a bit of disagreement here or there between the Southern Baptists and the United Methodists, over whether smoking was a sin or opposite sexes could swim in the same pool, but for the most part, a good Christian was a churchgoer.

In my own family, sometimes it was even hard to tell whether the "rights" and "wrongs" we were taught actually came directly from the Bible, the interpretation of the local pastor, or purely from the minds of my own parents. It all seemed to run together. The important thing though was never to question adults or the teachings of our church. Questioning was a sin in and of itself.

THE LAW

Religion plays an important role in the moral development of both the individual and the larger culture. Even if you were not raised by a religious family, you still were affected by those around you who adhered to religious values and teachings. While the framers of the Constitution were explicit in the separation of church and state, the United States' legal system nonetheless is highly influenced by larger cultural and religious attitudes. In fact, most US society is heavily influenced by the Judeo-Christian values of its founders.

Our country, in fact, was born out of reaction to religious intolerance in Europe and the desire for freedom from religious and governmental oppression. In some current world cultures, theocratic forms of government are headed by clerics. Even today in the United States, religious organizations and leaders continue to have direct influence on our government's policies and laws and often attract candidates from all parties during campaigns who are anxious to appease this segment of America.

While many religious organizations help to maintain social control, governmental laws are also made to control behavior in the larger society. Sometimes religion and the government have overlapping goals—to reduce killing, rape, and theft. Often, society seeks to redefine the phrase "life, liberty, and the pursuit of happiness" and challenge basic American principles regarding "freedom for all."

Who exactly is entitled to life? Should we extend liberty to everyone or just a few and if so, what behaviors should we use to decide when to limit one's liberty? What *kind* of happiness are we talking about pursuing? Religion is all too eager sometimes to provide simple and clear (albeit biased) answers to these questions, even in a complex, multicultural society like the United States.

The larger and more diverse our society becomes, the more we need laws (and clarifications of the law) and each step is usually hotly debated. Some people believe that while certain behaviors do not directly harm another individual, they have the potential to cause harm through gradual social decay. ("If you give them an inch, they'll take a mile" or "We'll be going down the slippery slope . . .") These types would prohibit behaviors that appear to them to lead to greater problems with social control later on. Unfortunately, many of their fears are irrational and unprovable.

Morality

Although religion heavily influences our culture's moral debate, morality itself is subject to interpretation. According to psychologist Betty Berzon, in our culture there are two interpretations of what morality is. One is based on intrinsic, personal experience and the other based on religious dogma. The ability to know right from wrong and to behave in a way that is consistent with what you know to be right (particularly with regards to how you treat others) is the first type of morality. Conforming to what a particular religion says is the right way to act and live without question is often mistaken for morality. People who believe in this interpretation are considered immoral if they do not conform and moral if they do conform to the religious teachings.

Many people believe that morality can be definitively decided and should be the same for everyone. Today laws exist that attempt to legislate moral issues which ultimately may not have a clear "right" or "wrong" position. Unfortunately, determining an absolute has not been easy. Abortion laws, for example, attempt to determine at which specific moment life occurs, an issue that stimulates many differing opinions.

Moral values can be relatively dynamic or changing. Even the mainstream religions, in existence for thousands of years, have made changes in policies and teachings. Prior to the fourth century, the Roman Catholic Church did not insist upon celibacy for priests and the Church has continued to make slow, but constant change in many dimensions of faith. For example, in 2000, Pope John Paul II issued a broad apology for the Church's wrongdoings in the past that led to harm during the Inquisition and then later forced conversion of Jews. Yet fundamentalist segments of almost every religion persist in believing that absolute morality exists and is unchanging despite changes in society and the discovery of new ideas and science.

Christian fundamentalists propose that we take the Bible, or "word of God," literally for our legal and moral guidelines. There are many ways, however, that this view creates conflict. For example, not every situation that needs guidance is discussed directly in the Bible, leaving modern "interpreters" (that is, ministers) to extrapolate God's intent from the words. At that point, we not only have introduced a fallible, human element to the Biblical "absolutes," but we also have questions about how the ancient languages of the original written materials were translated and how and why some early writings were included and others excluded from the current version of the Bible.

There are also contradictions within the Bible itself that cannot be explained if you take a literal approach to the interpretation. Even literalists are making interpretations based on their own personal history and biases, since language itself is often imprecise and single words can have multiple meanings.

What seems clear is that while there appear to be a few universally accepted values (about not killing, stealing from, or harming others), there are many issues upon which religious people do not agree and, in fact, may have completely opposite teachings. It appears that many of these "lesser" values, such as those dealings with appropriate styles of dress or ways to prepare food, are incorporated for culture-specific reasons at the time of the founding of the religion. This makes them appropriate at that time and place, but less appropriate in a modern world. Many experts feel that even if you take a literalist's interpretation of the Biblical passages typically used to justify anti-gay rhetoric (e.g., Leviticus 18:22: "You shall not lie with a man as one lies with a woman"), these passages had specific cultural relevance for the times in which the passages were written and have little to no relevancy now. Others argue that since the concept of homosexuality as we know it did not exist then, those same passages are best interpreted as metaphors for deeper messages and values, such as respecting the rights and dignity of others, honoring a commitment to a spouse, and being truthful or faithful.

RELIGIOUS SYSTEMS

Religious organizations function very much like other systems. Just like families, they can exhibit varying degrees of dysfunction. Communication within the system can be direct or indirect. Religious organizations usually have a structure and are organized hierarchically, with one ultimate human authority figure (such as the Pope for Catholics) or governing body, with successively lower levels of authority, down to the local congregation leader. Each level of organization has its own designated leader or leadership committee. Even the local level of organization (e.g., a church, synagogue, mosque, etc.) functions as a system.

Just like city governments must cooperate with county, state, and federal levels of authority, so do most local religious institutions. Also, just like family systems, these successive systems may be organized in authoritarian, authoritative, or permissive ways. Ultimate decisions in questions of morality are often decided by holy texts (as interpreted by the local leaders). Sometimes, the final judgment about moral questions rests with the titular head of the religious organization or sometimes with the local leader. As with parenting styles, some religious organizational styles are more associated with promoting individual feelings of autonomy and self-worth than others. These styles promote messages like, "You are born good and loved by God (or the Universe, etc.) no matter what."

An authoritarian organization, however, may diminish the value of a person in this "earthly form" so as to promote the focus on the next life (the "otherworldly" form). These teachings encourage the acceptance of suffering and the basic premise that all human beings are born evil with "original sin," and only through practicing specific religious tenets can they hope to find peace. Redemption from evil is always precarious and may be lost at any particular time should thoughts, feelings, or behaviors become less than holy. This type of religious organization promotes thoughts like, "I am unworthy of respect or love without penance or suffering," or "If I can only reach perfection, then I may become worthy of peace and forgiveness." Authoritarian religions often use psychological, if not overtly physical, threats to keep followers under control; much in the way authoritarian parents try to control their children. Interestingly, it appears that people who tend to be more rigid or authoritarian personally, choose religious organizations that reflect these personality attributes.

Mark's family belonged to a fundamentalist church that taught that all thoughts, feelings, and behaviors were reflective of one's degree of moral purity. Having thoughts deemed impure was the same as acting on it and must therefore be confessed and punished. Mark's feelings of attraction to other males began at a very early age, but he knew, without ever having had a conversation with anyone about these feelings, that they were unacceptable to his church and his family. He tried to deal with these feelings the best way that he could by developing a secret self that he was ashamed of, that he could try to either eliminate or control. His attempts to eliminate his secret self included prayers to God to "take it away" and to make him "normal," sometimes viciously condemning himself whenever he had feelings of attraction to another male. Eventually, Mark realized he could not control his feelings and after much mental preparation, spoke to his minister. Almost immediately, Mark's fears were confirmed. His minister told him that these feelings were evil and that Mark could only be saved from hell through intense spiritual cleansing. Mark's family was immediately notified about Mark's conversation, and Mark spent many months being watched and prayed over. He was sent to a counselor within the religious system, who tried even more intense and painful forms of conditioning and behavior modification.

For a while, Mark believed that he had successfully eliminated these attractions to men, and was convinced that he could establish a successful relationship with a woman. Eventually, though, the old feelings returned despite his earnest religious practices and sincere desire to change. This time, he chose to seek help outside of his religious institution. He read a number of books and articles and after a thorough search, he found a psychotherapist who helped him learn to accept himself as he was and realize that he could live a happy and satisfied life as a gay man. Mark continues to work on reducing and eliminating the strong negative messages he received from his church and his family and feels much more hopeful about himself and his life.

Some religious organizations are less hostile to lesbians and gays, and less rigid overall, than Mark's religion. Some are more like the authoritative forms of parenting, with firm rules but an overall respect for the follower's dignity and inherent worth. A few may be more like the permissive parents, focused on validating the individual's belief system or understanding of how the world is organized, rather than supporting the overall organization's doctrine.

Many lesbians and gays have felt that they needed to leave the religious organization of their upbringing for many of the same reasons they have left their families—to find complete acceptance as individuals and to diminish the constant barrage of negative messages. Some choose to avoid religion altogether and have many unpleasant memories about the rejection or degradation they felt at the hands of religious organizations in their early lives. Others find more contentment with religions that are either more accepting of gays and lesbians in general or are at least less overtly condemning. A few continue to try to find ways to work within the religion of their upbringing because they have positive memories of their religious experiences. They find specific local congregations that are more tolerant, continue living with a secret self, or work within the organization for change.

Faith and Acceptance

Both the beauty and the irony of a religious belief system is that you accept central constructs based on faith, not logic or proof. When believers encounter a part of the dogma that doesn't intuitively or logically make sense and begin to ask questions, they are often told to "have faith" and comply with the teaching anyway. Not only might there be no attempt made to answer the question itself, but even the process of questioning is discouraged. Depending on how threatening the questions are, the response from religious leaders can vary from loving words meant to encourage the development of an "unquestioning faith," to threats of expulsion from the organization or threats of spiritual condemnation. I got the message very early on in my childhood that some questions were simply not to be asked and that if I kept on asking those types of questions (like "If Mary became pregnant by God, did that mean that God had semen?"), I risked being ostracized or even punished for the thought! Now when I look back, I recognize that those were the early stages of training to accept absolute definitions of morality and to "just stop thinking so much!"

Religious Indoctrination

Many religious institutions have ways of educating children about the larger values of the organization. In many Christian churches, education begins in Sunday School, where children learn about the beliefs and values of the larger organization. Church educators often use stories based on Bible passages that have been interpreted through the lens of the organizational authorities. The stories can range from happy, cartoon-like representations of a loving, accepting God to a raging and judgmental God who sends "bad" children to eternal torment.

If you were raised to be religious, your view of God may be shaped by these early lessons, with reinforcement from parents, and sometimes school (particularly if you attended a private, religious school). If all of these sources of information were strongly anti-gay, then you likely continue to perpetuate strong anti-gay messages with a heavy "moral" tone within yourself.

Kathy was raised by religious parents who attended services regularly, at least several times per week. She also was sent to a private school associated with her family church. Because Kathy's worldview did not extend much beyond those of her parents and her church, she developed core beliefs about herself that reflected what she had been taught about lesbians and gays. Because she had only heard strongly anti-gay information all of her life, Kathy felt a deep sense of shame and guilt about her attraction toward other women. The anti-gay rhetoric all around her led her to develop strong negative messages about her own self-worth and value. Because she had never been exposed to other ideas and ways of thinking about things, it was initially much more difficult for Kathy to change the harmful self-talk about her sexuality. With much practice and support, eventually she was able to find new, more positive ways of viewing herself and her sexuality.

Religious Harm

There are many ways that a religion can be harmful to gays and lesbians, both as growing children and active adults. The public positions that religious organizations hold about our sexuality can themselves be harmful. While Pope Benedict XVI may consider himself a good and moral man, his proclamation that gays and lesbians have a "tendency toward an intrinsic moral evil, and thus the inclination itself must be seen as an objective disorder," he is promoting harm towards lesbians and gays. When he teaches that homosexuality is a moral "choice" that is wrong, he gives license to people who look for justification to act out their own frustrations by harming lesbians and gays all over the world, both directly and indirectly. Whether or not religious figureheads like Benedict, Pat Robertson, and James

Dobson accept responsibility for the effects of harmful statements they make about gays, their behaviors foster an atmosphere of hate, distrust, family division, and even death—acts regarded as immoral within their very own traditions.

Homosexuality is not a choice, but self-acceptance is.

SUBTLE AND NOT-SO-SUBTLE RELIGIOUS MESSAGES

Some institutions teach that sexuality in general is bad, except as a means for procreation. Thus, according to these institutions, sex using birth control, sex only to express emotional intimacy or affection, or sexual practices that could never lead to pregnancy, such as masturbation and oral or anal sex, are all wrong and should *never* be practiced. It logically follows from this stance that since homosexual sex cannot lead to pregnancy, it must also be wrong. You didn't have to actually hear the words "gay and lesbian sex is wrong" to glean from this message that you would be a sinner if you engaged in sex for reasons other than having a baby.

In some churches, the messages children hear are more direct about the prohibition of homosexual sex, thought, or feelings. Some queer adults can recall the specific language that was used to chastise them and incorporate this language into the messages they replay to themselves. Extreme forms of condemnation such as "You are unworthy of social acceptance," easily become part of the core belief system in a child with a developing self-identity. Challenging these specific messages will become a part of your strategy to increase your self-esteem as you work through this book.

SPIRITUALITY OR RELIGION?

The terms *religion* and *spiritual* are often used interchangeably, but in practice are quite different. Religion usually has some central organization and is generally more formal than spirituality, with rules, doctrine, and guidelines that function to maintain social control. Spirituality, on the other hand, is much more personal and incorporates the emotional, perceptual, and mystical aspects of religious experience. It is the idiosyncratic way that you answer the larger questions of life—for example, "Why am I here?" "What is the meaning of life?" "What is my purpose?" "Where is my place in the universe?"

Typically, people are chronically unhappy, anxious, or unfulfilled when they cannot understand the answers to these types of existential questions and organized religions attempt to provide these answers. For example, reincarnation is a concept that helps explain why we may have tragedy or success in our lives today. It suggests that these events are linked to a larger purposeful progression through many lives that increase our experience and understanding of the world and lead to our ultimate enlightenment.

Often, however, a gay person's experience is different from what he or she is told by a religious institution. For example, while some anti-gay religions clearly condemn same-sex relationships as choices that are sinful, many lesbians and gays do not remember *choosing* to make themselves attracted to certain same-sex individuals (as if this was possible for either homosexuals or heterosexuals). This difference between an individual's experience and what the doctrine of the religion says you *should* feel can blunt or confuse the experience of spirituality.

The underlying philosophical systems within a particular religion may vary from a more positively focused, nurturing, or soothing emphasis to a more negative, fear-based emphasis. Some institutions attempt to limit themselves to a creation-centered spirituality, focusing on the life-affirming side of religion (the basic idea that all humans are valued unconditionally by the universe or a God-figure), while others focus on the fear-of-God theme (the idea that if you don't follow the rules, you will suffer). In addition to the basic philosophical differences, most fear-based religions attempt to answer life questions in a polarized way, that is, that there are only two ways of thinking about the world— "good and evil" or "right or wrong." This type of thinking can be effective by reducing anxiety when questions appear to have simple answers. Yet when complex questions, with no obvious right or wrong answers, need equally complex answers, dichotomous thinking can actually increase anxiety.

Religions that tend to be all black or white also preach that the love of God is conditional, meaning that if you slip up, then you will be rejected and condemned. Some religions attempt to label morally acceptable behaviors without condemning the individual, although it is inherently impossible to say that you love a person unconditionally, if you don't accept certain thoughts, feelings, or behaviors. People who subscribe to this "love the sinner and hate the sin" idea may be attempting to resolve conflicts between their personal experiences and their rigid belief system. They may also be looking to justify personal self-righteousness ("I am better than this other pitiful person") or convince themselves that they are making a "good Christian" effort to accept someone that they secretly despise. Because people are attracted to a specific religion with a particular style of thinking that makes them feel comfortable, any threat to that system represents a personal threat to that individual—a proverbial house of cards.

While some religions may not directly promote anti-gay beliefs, some homophobic followers may irrationally "twist" the teachings of their faith to justify or suit their own bigotry. Often they feel more empowered in their hostility and judgments if they believe that there is a holy precedent or justification for their personal feelings of fear, disgust, or self-righteousness. The Bible has been used in this way for many evil purposes from the persecution of Jews, discrimination against people of color, and today, to barring gays from achieving full civil rights. It's difficult to feel compassion for people who use their religion in this way, as a tool for lashing out at others. However, in many cases, these angry people may be completely unaware that they are perpetuating intolerance, because they are following the models that were available to them as they grew up or are using religion to cover deeper emotional or psychological problems.

What's Good about Religion

There are many advantages to formal worship. Weekly meetings serve to strengthen social connections and support within a community, reinforce positive values for the common good, and provide opportunities to perform good works for the community at large. Not all religions, or local congregations within a larger religion, perpetuate negative views of lesbians and gays. Even within larger organizations that have explicitly expressed anti-gay views, you can find individuals and leaders who do not support these views.

One way to stay involved with a mainstream religion is by challenging the interpretation of anti-gay Biblical or other sacred writings, based on *cultural relevancy theory* or on inaccurate linguistic interpretation. In these cases, you may want to look for institutions that either reject anti-gay teachings on the basis of flawed translation, on the principle that these passages are not applicable to modern times or argue that the original writer was personally homophobic. Another option is called the "smorgasbord approach"—meaning that you accept most tenets of your religion but ignore those that are condemning or rejecting.

Many mainstream religions now have subgroups just for gays and lesbians and their supporters, although these groups may not be officially recognized or sanctioned by the larger organization. For example, the Catholic Church has a group called "Dignity," the Episcopal Church has "Integrity," and the Church of Jesus Christ of Latter Day Saints has groups called "Mormons Concerned." In San Francisco and other progressive urban areas with large gay communities, many other types of religious institutions, such as the synagogue Sha'ar Zahav and the Gay Buddhist's Group, include the needs of gays and lesbians in their meetings and services. Each of these groups attempt to resolve the conflict for gays and lesbians within the larger organization by allowing them to participate in their chosen faith in a more directly relevant and consistent way.

Lesbians and gays now have other alternatives as well. In 1967, Rev. Troy Perry founded the Metropolitan Community Church, a Christianity-based church specifically for lesbians and gays. Other smaller religious organizations, like the Unitarian-Universalists and Quakers (Friends), have accepted homosexuals on equal footing with heterosexuals for years. Other major denominations appear to be making significant positive strides as well, such as the election of an openly gay bishop in the Episcopal Church, the Reverend Canon Gene Robinson from New Hampshire.

For a more well-rounded discussion of other world religions, I recommend that you read Arlene Swindler's book, *Homosexuality and World Religions*.

WHEN RELIGION IS NOT AN OPTION

Sometimes by opting out of formal religions, people ignore the spiritual sides of themselves, believing that the two are necessarily intertwined. Anything that remotely resembles religion has associated painful memories for some. If you have been damaged, harmed, or rejected by the people and beliefs of your religious background, the hurt and anger may prevent you from finding inner spiritual peace and self-acceptance until you find ways of working through and healing these old wounds.

Many people who have rejected religious teaching incorrectly assume that you must be involved with a formal religious institution in order to develop your spiritual side. Religious institutions do represent a formalized attempt to help the masses cultivate spirituality in most cases. For me, spirituality includes my personal search for answers to questions about my purpose, the existence of a Higher Power, and the rules of the universe. How you answer these questions can help you resolve long-standing inaccurate core beliefs. Even if you find no specific answers to the larger questions, attending to the process of asking after years of neglect can be emotionally healing.

EVALUATING THE MESSAGES

If you received messages as a child that being lesbian or gay was unacceptable, or lessened your sense of value as a human being, then you must begin to find other alternative messages that contradict these teachings.

People who have not learned how to think dichotomously can see other alternatives, specifically that some tenets of each religion may be true, and that for certain people, each may work well as a path to spirituality. However, if a particular religion does not fit you, then you owe it to yourself to search for a path to healthy human spirituality that does fit you. Find something that is healing rather than harmful. Chapter 12 will help you explore and develop a healthy spirituality.

QUESTIONS FOR REFLECTION

- If you were raised in a family that practiced a particular religion, what was that religion's view on homosexuality? Do you remember specific religious teachings that were anti-gay/lesbian? What was the religion's perspective on sex in general?
- How was guilt used as a form of control over you?
- How were you threatened with negative spiritual consequences (e.g., going to hell) for ways of behaving? Thinking? Feeling?
- How were your questions about the religious teachings handled? Was the general process of questioning encouraged or discouraged?
- What was the intensity or firmness of your family's religious belief system?
- What were the role expectations for women, men, and children within the religious teachings?
- Were you taught that certain people or acts were evil and others good or righteous?

- How did your family tolerate the beliefs of others within other religious systems?
- Was your religious upbringing from a creation-centered perspective or a fear-based (i.e., "hell and damnation") perspective?
- How might the religious views of your parents serve them psychologically? Did they experience reduced anxiety by having clear answers to difficult or complex questions? Was it easier for them to ignore the "gray areas" of life?
- What are the messages from your childhood about religion that surface in your self-talk today?
- How do you practice spirituality today?

RESOURCES

Affirmation (Gay and Lesbian Latter Day Saints), www.affirmation.org

Association of Welcoming and Affirming Baptist Churchesk www.wabaptists.org

Born Again and Gayk www.geocities.com/bornagainandgay

Brethren/Mennonite Council for Lesbian and Gay Concerns, www.bmclgbt.org

Cathedral of Hope, www.cathedralofhope.com

Christ Chapel of the Valley, www.christchapel.com

Emergence International (Gay Christian Scientists), www.emergence-international.org

Dharma Dykes, dharma.fourwhitefeet.com

Dignity/USA (Catholic), www.dignityusa.org

Evangelicals Concerned, www.ecwr.org

Freedom in Christ Church (Gay-affirmative Evangelical), www.freedom-inchrist-sf.org

Friends for Lesbian and Gay Concerns (Quaker), www.quaker.org/flgbtqc

Gay Buddhist Fellowship, www.gaybuddhist.org

Gay and Lesbian Arabs, www.well.com/user/queerjhd

Gay Muslims, www.angelfire.com/ca2/queermuslims

Integrity (Episcopal), www.integrityusa.org

The Interfaith Working Group, www.iwgonline.org

Lutherans Concerned, www.lcna.org

Orthodox Gay Jews, members.aol.com/gayjews

Presbyterian Lesbian and Gay Concerns, www.mlp.org

GLBT Pagans, www.soulrebels.com/beth/glbt.html

Seventh Day Adventist Kinship International, www.sdakinship.org

Soka Gakkai International, www.sgi-usa.org

Something Jewish, www.somethingjewish.co.uk/community_corner/jew-
ish_lesbian_and_gay_group/index

Soulforce (Rev. Mel White), www.soulforce.org

Universal Fellowship of the Metropolitan Community Churches (MCC),
www.ufmcc.com/

Unitarian Universalist Office of Bi, Gay, Lesbian & Trans Concerns,
www.uua.org/visitors/justicdiversity/6252.shtml

United Church of Christ, www.ucc.org

FIVE

Schools, Peers, and Other Influences

Like families, our culture, and our religious institutions, schools are subject to the same systemic forces. If home life was abusive and degrading, your school life may have provided a haven, with contradictory and positive information about yourself and your worth. On the other hand, home life may have been wonderful and supportive, and your school experiences could have been negative. A learning disability requiring special services, for example, may have made it difficult to feel successful in school and left you with internal messages such as "I'm not smart enough," or "I'm not like everyone else." Negative messages from a teacher ("You're a troublemaker") or rejection by peers ("You're a sissy") can add to the core beliefs you have about yourself just as powerfully as the messages you hear at home.

My goal for this chapter is to explore some of the sources of your internal messaging that came from outside of your immediate family.

Charlotte came from a quiet, middle-class home that was almost always serene and pleasant. She was the youngest of three children. Her parents were gentle people, but were always somewhat distant and generally avoided displays of affection. They were never abusive or even discouraging to her and, in fact, they often praised her for her athletic and academic accomplishments. Charlotte, however, often felt a subtle sense of loneliness and was never truly able to discuss with her family her innermost feelings about herself and her budding sexuality. She felt as if other members of her family didn't experience the depth of feelings she had and couldn't understand her desire to talk about these feelings.

At school, Charlotte excelled at all levels—in grades, sports, and social situations. She won many awards and received a lot of school recognition for her gifts and was often allowed special privileges by teachers who encouraged her to strive for her eventual goal of law school. Charlotte felt very comfortable in this academic environment and achieved most of her ultimate professional goal by the time she was thirty years old—a professorship at a prestigious university law school.

Once her life as a student was over, Charlotte started noticing that the old feelings of emptiness and loneliness were resurfacing. She was becoming exhausted from the time she devoted to her career and had nothing in her personal life that was satisfying. She began to realize that perhaps her attention to her academic success, which gave her wonderful feelings of accomplishment throughout the years, had been at the expense of exploring the emotional side of her life. Although she had quite high regard for herself professionally, personally she felt unfulfilled and undeveloped. She had never connected on an intimate level with anyone; she'd only had a few, almost superficial, friendships over the years.

While she had recognized an attraction to women, she never acted on these feelings in any way. So at the age of thirty, Charlotte began searching for ways to correct the imbalance, to explore ways to "find herself" emotionally.

Charlotte never had models of how to deal with emotional or sexual feelings in a healthy way. She would not consider her parents abusive, but they were emotionally distant and were uncomfortable with intimacy. Because she was rewarded for achievement both at home and at school, she took this path all the way to its logical conclusion for her, which included law school and a professorship. This was the only way she could feel accepted and capable. This left her, unfortunately, with mixed feelings of self-esteem. She knew she was intelligent and professionally competent, but she felt emotionally immature.

Most schools are set up to reward academic achievement. Occasionally, through interaction with a warm and positive teacher, principal, or counselor, you may have learned that you had value as a person in addition to your value as an academic achiever. School has the potential to be a powerful agent for building positive self-esteem for queer and questioning youth by providing accurate portrayals of gays and lesbians in the classroom and encouraging respect for alternative ways of thinking, feeling, and believing. While several progressive school systems in this country are beginning to actively encourage programs that foster gay-positive curricula and positive self-esteem skills, most schools don't have such programs.

Many schools, teachers, and counselors remain ignorant or are homophobic, and encourage the same negative and stereotypical views of homosexuality held by the larger society. A school often reflects the values of the larger community, and in many cases parents have chosen where they live based on values in the community similar to their own. In other words, authoritarian, conservative parents often either choose conservative communities to live in with similarly focused public schools or they send their children to private or religious schools that will teach values similar to their own. In recent years, many religious fundamentalist groups have targeted school board elections as a focus of their activities in an attempt to assure that their perspective becomes more pervasive in school systems across the United States—a frightening prospect for queer youth.

Peer Groups

People often identify with a group of peers in order to feel that they fit in. When I was in high school, I belonged to a rather bohemian group of "strays" that represented the blue collar families of our rural community, but were smart and fun to hang out with; one was an aspiring actress, one a prototypical IT guy, and the other a future Steven Spielberg. I was encouraged to participate in student government by the faculty sponsor, a beautiful African-American woman, who taught me US and World History. It seemed a risky move for me as someone outside the "popular" group but she was persistent and encouraging, and as an awkward teenager, I secretly enjoyed her support.

The groups people choose to identify with can be based on a lot of factors such as race, gender, socioeconomic status, acceptance or rejection of social norms, mutual need for protection in a hostile environment, religious upbringing, age, or education. To some degree, your behaviors are shaped by whether you felt accepted or rejected by your peer group. Adolescents and young children act in ways that would not necessarily feel satisfying except when they are receiving some type of recognition, praise, or acceptance from their peers. At times, peers can take the place of the family in supplying safety needs and a sense of belonging when family members are overtly or covertly rejecting.

Some lesbian and gay youth grow up experiencing the benefits of membership in peer groups such as sports teams, school clubs, neighborhood cliques, and religious youth groups. Most, however, feel only a limited acceptance and never discuss their sexual identity for fear of rejection by the group. They hide their secret self and only show sides that they believe are acceptable. The message you may have learned is, "You may belong to this group only if you act, or pretend you are, heterosexual." So, while belonging to a group may have some important positive qualities such as allowing for emotional support, social skill development, and increased independence from family values, it also can be a source of negative self-statements and other distorted beliefs.

Some groups are exclusive by nature and tend to view outsiders as inferior or encourage the development of stereotypes, racist or homophobic stances, and other separatist attitudes. In order to avoid rejection from a peer group, you may have behaved in ways the group deemed acceptable, but may have been harmful in the long run. Many urban youths, who join gangs for protection and the positive sense of belonging, also feel they have no choice but to follow the leaders' direction to fight, use or sell drugs, or otherwise prove their worthiness of the group membership.

David and his mother moved from a small town in Ohio to Cleveland when he was ten. It had been difficult for David to leave his friends and cousins, and he had a hard time making new friends in the city. His mother worked such long hours that he ended up spending a lot of time alone.

When David entered high school, it was clear that many of the other boys belonged to "clubs," which he soon realized were actually gangs. His mother had warned him about these groups and he generally avoided them, but after he was threatened a few times, he decided that he needed to join one for his own protection. At first, he found it somewhat satisfying to finally feel like he belonged and he did his best to stay out of trouble. It became clear, however, that he was expected to conform to the wishes of the leaders of his group. Although he considered leaving, he was repeatedly told that he could not protect himself if he didn't remain in the gang, and he understood that if he left, his own group would turn against him. Not only was he afraid to leave, but the leaders also controlled virtually every detail of his behavior, from the types and colors of clothes he wore to the way he wore his hair. They even told him whom he could and could not date.

Although David liked women, he found himself having feelings for other guys, which disturbed him. He was well aware that he couldn't discuss these feelings with anyone in the gang. In fact, "fags" were occasional targets of gang violence "just for fun." What started out as a means of self-protection and belonging had ended up as a trap for David. He found himself doing and saying things that he found unacceptable because of the incredible pressure he felt to conform.

When he turned eighteen, David moved to New York and started a new life for himself. He was able to see a counselor, who helped him deal with his past and learn to be true to himself.

Peer groups may be highly organized and hierarchical, with clear rules for membership, or rules that may be unspoken but clearly understood by all who belong. Within such a structure, there is always the threat of rejection. Being accepted by, and remaining a member of the group, may be extremely important to someone who has not developed a strong sense of self with positive self-esteem. It may be that people with higher self-esteem, especially those who value their own unique ways of thinking and feeling, can more easily withstand peer pressure to conform. That's why encouraging a child to feel good about himself for standing up to peer pressure is a frequently used theme in anti-drug and anti-smoking campaigns. Having the courage to stand on your own requires both self-confidence and self-esteem, qualities that may be lacking in queer children and adolescents.

Lesbian and Gay Peer Groups

Sometimes even gay and lesbian peer groups perpetuate the larger society's stereotypes as well. During the early years of moviemaking in Hollywood, African-Americans were limited to playing small parts in films—often the role of slave, servant, or other stereotypes. The actors who were fortunate enough to get parts in this white-dominated industry had their own acting organizations that supported and encouraged African-Americans in the film industry. However, when Lena Horne began demanding larger roles outside of the traditionally accepted "Negro" domain of roles, she was not only rejected by the white establishment (or relegated to walk-on singing roles), but she was astonished to find herself rejected by her African-American actor peers, whose own stereotyped self-images may have been threatened by her success.

You may have felt a wonderful sense of belonging and acceptance for who you really are, perhaps for the first time in your life when you came out and made your first gay friends. Because historically there has been a lack of visible role models in our culture (until recently), often the first lesbian or gay group you socialize with becomes an important source of information about what is "socially acceptable" within the community. You may have wanted to fit in with this group almost immediately, or you may have found yourself slowly becoming more like the people with whom you associate. Gay peer groups often become the source for your tastes in clothes, hair, attitudes, and behaviors.

As with other types of peer groups, you may also feel some pressure to conform to the styles and attitudes of the "fashionable" and visible lesbian and gay leaders. This may lead you back to self-disparaging messages when you find that you don't fit the socially acceptable norms. For example, aging for some gay men becomes a source of distress when the group they most closely associate with places a high value on youth and beauty. Because the peers with whom they have associated most frequently sometimes seem as if they are the whole of the community rather than a small segment of it, many men do not realize that there are other aging gay men for whom youth is not an important value. I will address this issue in more detail in Chapter 15 on Queer Aging.

You may fall victim to your own internalized stereotypes at times. You are a part of the larger American society and thereby are influenced by its general stereotypes of gay people. Some lesbian and gay writers, such as Andrew Sullivan, have discussed the role of the gay community in perpetuating its own stereotypes. Many personal ads written by gay males have been criticized for listing such desired qualities for future mates as "straight-acting" or "no fats or fems," suggesting that men who act "gay" or are not "gym-fit" are not desirable. A similar phenomenon was observed in the African-American community by director Spike Lee in his film *School Daze* in which he explores the cultural divide between light and dark-skinned African-Americans.

Hanging with other queers provides lots of benefits, such as support, education, and acceptance. But, like families and religious institutions, which also have many good features, the gay community with which you interact can also contribute to the reservoir of negative messages you may send to yourself. As with the other influences on self-statements, you do not have to reject your peer group in order to dispute the negative and inaccurate messages; you can accept the components that are healthy and supportive and reject the ones that are harmful.

Other Influences

Special Authority Figures

When you think back to your childhood and adolescence, there may be specific authority figures, usually adults, who had a significant impact on how you felt about yourself. I've mentioned some of the obvious figures that likely have had an influence on you— including one or both parents or other family members such as a grandparent, aunt, or uncle. There may have been other important figures outside your family who served both as a role model for you and as a source of information about yourself as you were developing.

These important figures include your teachers, religious leader, nannies, physicians, coaches, tutors, or neighbors. The information that they reflected back to you may have closely resembled that which your family provided. Their messages to you may have been as positive or as negative as those supplied to you by your family.

Because these people were outside of the family, it's possible that they provided you with a different perspective about yourself, your value to the world and to them, and your special talents or gifts. Their insights may have provided a safe haven for you, allowing you a respite from the negativity of other sources. The positive images these figures provided for you may have helped you survive your early years with some sense of self-satisfaction. The positive feedback you received from a coach that you admired may have helped you feel good about your athletic abilities and gain feelings of self-acceptance in this area of your life.

If you were fortunate, you had a positive role model whose influence extended beyond one limited area of your life and they provided a place where you could be unconditionally accepted and nurtured. This figure might have been able to help you recognize that some of the negativity you were exposed to in other aspects of your life was inappropriate. My history teacher was a truly kind and encouraging force in my life. I called her recently to say "Thank you for her presence in my life back then. If you were very lucky, you had a figure who taught you that being gay or lesbian was not something awful, sinful, or sick, but a natural part of who you are. Think about some of the positive influences you may have enjoyed as you grew up who may have helped salvage your self-esteem from devastation and distortion.

Sports and Other Extra-Curricular Activities

Our culture values competition. Our school systems often incorporate athletics into the curriculum at a high level.

There are a number of ways that sports can be beneficial. Aside from reaping the general health effects, if you were a particularly gifted athlete, you may have received much recognition and praise for your accomplishments. This may have been one of the most important factors in how your self-perception was formed. You may have found a great deal of value in your athletic ability and you possibly learned to value and enjoy competition as a way of demonstrating your self-worth. This positive association of competition with self-worth may later have generalized to your professional and personal life and your typical style of thinking may sound like this: "If I don't win, then I'm a failure," or "I am worthless if I don't finish first."

If you were not gifted in sports, this may also have affected how you defined yourself. Being rejected for a team or chosen last is a lasting memory for many children. Imagine the messages you may have developed about yourself if you were consistently not chosen or if you faced the wrath of the rest of the team for mistakes or clumsiness. You may still carry messages about yourself from these experiences such as "I am awkward and a nerd," or "I cannot become a team player because I may let the team down."

Being especially talented in sports may have had its own challenges as well. Teams are a powerful form of peer groups. While being a contributing member of a sports team can be a powerful positive influence in many ways, you may have felt that you could not risk expressing your sexuality openly with these very close peers for fear of rejection. You likely chose to develop a secret self in order to remain on the team. The sometimes difficult, but recently improving life stories of lesbian and gay professional athletes have been well-described in the books *Jocks: True Stories of America's Gay Male Athletes* by Dan Woog and *Lesbians and Gays and Sports* by Perry Young and Martin Duberman. Recent role models in professional sports include Martina Navratilova and Amelie Mauresmo (tennis), John Amaechi (basketball), Esera Tuaolo (football), and Billy Bean (baseball).

DISABILITY

Having a healthy self-esteem is important for everyone, but it's even more important to feel good about your strengths if you have a disabling condition. Disability exists in many forms, for example, paraplegia, deformity, or a congenital or chronic disease that may impair mobility or the ability to perform basic activities of daily living. It also may exist in the form of a mental illness such as schizophrenia, bipolar disorder, or depression. For some, the disability is in the form of difficulty with learning in academic activities, for example, difficulty with reading, writing, and arithmetic or requiring special tutoring or alternative forms of education.

When children are viewed as different by peers, because of a disability, they may become the object of ridicule or may be rejected from participation in peer group activities. Sometimes, if children with disabilities are placed in special schools or classrooms for children with similar problems, rejection can be less likely. Some disability specialists however have advocated for *mainstreaming*, or integrating children with disabilities into regular classrooms with non-disabled students. The supporters of this approach believe that it is important for disabled children to learn to get along in the larger society and that it helps non-disabled children better understand those who are disabled. Unfortunately, in both situations, children with disabilities must cope with the stigmatizing messages our larger culture has about disability. These messages can be harsh and belittling such as, "You are not normal, therefore you are inferior," or "You are to be pitied and are in need of help." Lesbians or gay men who also have a disability need to pay particular attention to building solid self-esteem and positive self-talk. They must work extra hard at refuting old, distorted messages about their value and worth in this society.

Attitudes about AIDS

The impact of AIDS on the gay community has been immense. The full impact of AIDS on our society, the world, and the individual cannot be fully discussed here. It is, however, worth mentioning as an important influence on self-talk and self-esteem.

When AIDS first appeared in the press of the early 1980's, it created a good deal of hysteria within the gay male community, who seemed to be its only victims, and later in those outside of the gay community. Because it appeared to specifically target gay males, many people were quick to draw conclusions about the connection between gay male behavior and the development of this disease. The hysteria around AIDS became a prime medium for judgmental propagandizing from the media, society, and the pulpit. Fundamentalist religious leaders drew embarrassingly naive conclusions about AIDS as some sort of retribution from God against gay men for so-called immoral behavior. The now-deceased Moral Majority founder, Jerry Falwell, owes at least a portion of his notoriety and media coverage to his outrageous and misinformed declarations about HIV and immorality.

Jeff, who came from a fundamentalist religious background, struggled with the negative and inflammatory rhetoric made by the pompous TV evangelists of the day who took the opportunity of the appearance of AIDS to gain national press and donations. He had always doubted at some level his own legitimacy, living life as a gay man. Deep down, he even wondered if there was some credence to the fundamentalists' claims. His family had never been supportive of him, so he'd always experienced a certain level of shame. Every time he heard Mr. Falwell or Pat Robertson rail against the "sinners," likening AIDS to the plagues visited by God on the pharaoh in Egypt, he felt a pang of guilt and deep sadness. His depression increased to the point that he rarely socialized, finding it hard to reach out for help or connection with others. Only through talking about these claims with his persuasive friends, and later with a therapist, was Jeff able to begin to understand that his internal conflicts ran deep. By learning to recognize and refute his negative self-talk, he was able to feel more peaceful and to live a life ultimately more satisfying.

People not only suffered from the distorted and ignorant messages that were rampant about AIDS and the stigma it now brought to homosexuality, but the actual threat of the disease and death was a significant source of distress for many gay men at the time. How could you explore your sexual identity if it possibly meant that you would die? Many felt that they must either choose sex and risk death or choose abstinence and lead an incomplete life.

Fortunately, many gay men and lesbians kept their cool and insisted on rational debate and scientific study regarding AIDS rather than allowing fear and immoral opportunism to reign supreme. Some lesbian and gay historians, in fact, feel that AIDS brought the larger gay community together in a way that it had never been before. They had common enemies to fight against: ignorance, disease, and bigotry. At some level, this was, and is, a lesbian and gay issue, rather than just a gay male one.

Gay men and lesbians who were growing up during this time were affected by the cultural hysteria. In some ways, our community was just beginning to enjoy more societal visibility and was beginning to flex some political muscle that had been gained with the symbolic "victory" at the Stonewall riot in 1969 and continued through the liberating 1970s. Initially, AIDS seemed to threaten the gains made during the prior years, setting back the gay rights movement and having a negative effect on the newly positive self-images within the gay and lesbian community. Because many gays and lesbians began organizing and educating themselves, we have seen the facts emerge above the hysteria and health education take priority over irrational beliefs. AIDS is still a concern for us all, but we now understand it for what it is—a disease, not a verdict.

Evaluate the Messages

In this and the previous chapters, I have briefly begun to explore some of the factors that have shaped the messages you give yourself about how to view yourself, the world, and others. If you have taken the time to answer the questions posed to you at the end of each chapter, you may be starting to recognize the specific influences that shaped your life and the messages you continue to give yourself, both positive and negative.

Yet, the sources of messages do not stop with these influences. There may be other people, places, or experiences you can remember that added to your self-perception that I did not discuss here—for example, living through a once-in-a-lifetime trauma like 9/11, a flood or war, moving frequently as a child, or living through divorce. Only you can begin to hear the residual voices from your past and learn to take control of them.

QUESTIONS FOR REFLECTION

What kinds of positive experiences did you encounter in school as you were growing up? What kinds of negative experiences?

- What kinds of messages did you receive about yourself from teachers? Peers?
- What messages about homosexuality in general do you remember from your school experiences? From your teachers and peers?
- How did your general experiences with school affect your current professional identity or the development of your self-confidence?
- How were your achievements (or lack there of) in school received at home? How were your negative experiences in school handled at home?
- Were there any people you thought were lesbian or gay in your school, including teachers, staff, or peers? What images of gays or lesbians do you continue to carry based on these people? Were they stereotypical? Overt? Closeted?
- What memories do you have about interacting with peers as a child? Were you accepted? Rejected? Social? A loner or outsider?
- What attitudes did your peer group hold about homosexuals?
- Do you remember pretending to be heterosexual to fit in or avoid rejection?
- Were there specific authority figures in your life that provided a source of unconditional acceptance?
- How did participation or nonparticipation in sports shape your self-identity?
- How has AIDS changed your behaviors and self-concepts?
- What kinds of pressure to conform do you experience from your current peers?

PART II

*Choices: How
Self-Esteem
Impacts Your
Daily Life*

Six

*Your Career
and Going for It*

N ow that you've explored the origins of your self-talk, you're ready to look at some ways this self-talk may be affecting your life today. Who you are in your professional life is affected by your general self-concept. If you feel unworthy of praise or attention in your personal life, you also likely feel this way in your professional life. Feeling uncomfortable with praise, or like you don't deserve it, may inhibit your job performance and prevent you from receiving special recognition.

In this chapter we'll examine how self-esteem can affect career choices, job performance, and on-the-job relationships. You can also use this information to explore whether your career may be having a negative impact on your self-esteem.

FITTING IN AT WORK

Some people find themselves in quite a double bind at work since they want the raises and promotions, but at the same time, they resist doing anything that would cause them to feel uncomfortable or put them in the spotlight.

If you believed as a child that calling attention to yourself invited public speculation about your sexuality, you may have unintentionally opted for mediocrity. By avoiding the extra look from your employer, you may be telling yourself that you are protecting yourself from being "discovered." Discrimination on the job is a fact of life in this country and people have been fired for reasons that are not related to the job performance. Unfortunately, because lesbians and gays are at this writing not offered protection against discrimination in many settings, the fear of harassment and job loss is also a reality. Thus, your career can have consequences for your self-esteem and your level of self-esteem can affect your performance on the job. Finding a comfortable balance between personal and job needs will be important to your overall life satisfaction.

How Self-Esteem Affects Career Choice

People choose a particular career for many reasons and there are many ways that self-esteem may have affected the career you chose as well. Think back to the time in your life when you were first considering all of your career options. Someone in your life may have strongly encouraged you to follow a specific path, or invalidated some of your choices as "unrealistic, or "beyond your abilities, or encouraged you to follow only careers that were approved by the family. You may have also been pushed to pursue things that you were good at, even if you would have preferred to pursue a path you were more passionate about.

Given the negative stereotypes our society has about homosexuality, many gay men and lesbians choose careers based on the appearance or level of social acceptability of the career. Some gay men, for example, avoid taking creative/artistic career paths because of the feared response from homophobic people in their community, even though they may have felt drawn to this type of work. Others choose a specific career *because of* their sexual orientation, gender identity, race, or other oppressed minority status, feeling as if they would not be accepted in other careers.

In the absence of personal validation by society, many queer people choose career paths that provide levels of prestige and validation that they otherwise may not have received. For example, if you found success through academic achievement, it is likely that you chose a profession which values or rewards similar forms of achievement. Brad, a forty-five-year-old physician, came to my office complaining of job burnout and with many signs of what most people would call a "midlife crisis." In many ways his career had been stellar—early academic success in high school led him to a remarkable undergraduate effort at a major university where he majored in biochemistry and pharmacology. His hard work paid off when he was admitted to medical school and later obtained a prestigious residency and fellowship. When he completed the fellowship, he was offered a plum position at one of the top medical schools in the country where he quickly made a name for himself as a talented clinician, administrator, and colleague.

Six years later, however, Brad found himself dissatisfied with both his work and his personal life. He readily admitted that his personal growth and difficulties with maintaining relationships were likely related to the disproportionate amount of time that he spent on his career versus the rest of his life. While he still enjoyed many parts of his job, such as the respect afforded him by the medical community, his patients' recovery and gratitude, and the comfortable salary, he found himself longing to get off of the "achievement treadmill" and find more balance in his lifestyle. Although he was good at what he did for a living, and it provided him with many positive advantages, Brad was not completely satisfied with the day-to-day aspects of his job. He had grown tired of his position of authority but felt trapped because he had little confidence that he could do anything besides medicine. He also worried about family repercussions if he were to leave medicine altogether since his parents and friends were so proud of his accomplishments as a doctor. Self-doubt and fear kept him from exploring other career options.

Brad and I began to explore how he came to choose his career path and discovered that his sexuality was one of several important factors that influenced his choices. He remembered that he chose to become a physician at some level to prove to himself and his family that he was worthy of the respect that he feared they would not give him because of his sexual orientation. Physicians were highly respected by Brad's parents and family and were held in quite high esteem at the time he was making his early career decisions.

While he had developed a healthy and positive professional self-concept (he saw himself as good at what he did and had external indicators of success), this high professional self-esteem didn't seem to extend to relationships and other endeavors. He still felt unworthy of being loved by others, especially if they really knew who he was or understood the parts of himself that he considered "less successful."

Brad's experience is not uncommon in people whose self-esteem is based on their career successes. Building core self-esteem that is not dependent upon external rewards is one way to begin to ease the feelings of being trapped or feeling like an impostor. For Brad, this meant changing careers altogether and choosing something that he felt would make him more satisfied regardless of the impressions of others. For others, it may mean learning to change how they behave on the job by standing up for themselves, making choices that may lead to success and recognition, and living more openly and authentically without fear.

While self-esteem may have had an impact on your job choice, the work you do can also have an impact on your self-esteem. Your job may, in fact, be a source of self-esteem (and positive self-messages) that feels rewarding and satisfying. There may be aspects of your job that are not as fulfilling. You may not be moving toward your career goals as quickly as you want, or maybe certain work-related situations keep your job from being as satisfying as it could be. You may, for example, feel uncomfortable talking about your personal life at work for fear of homophobic reactions of others, or you may have felt uncomfortable with jokes or remarks from co-workers. You may also feel frustrated, as you watch others get promotions and recognition that you feel you deserve but don't get, because you are afraid to confront the company. Sometimes those promotions may be based on how open or comfortable you are with others and keeping your personal life private may have worked against you.

The Secret Self on the Job

Many lesbians and gay men feel as if they must keep their personal lives exceptionally private in order to succeed in the workplace. Yet most heterosexuals don't compartmentalize in this way, often sharing many details of their home life, including how it affects their daily moods and productivity. Many of my co-workers over the years have taken for granted the ability to have pictures of their spouse on their desk or to bring them to the company party. Keeping your home life a secret can diminish your creativity and leave you feeling alienated from people at the office. Feeling limited also leads to feelings of frustration and job burnout, and may reinforce lower self-esteem as you justify living a secret: "I must keep this secret self hidden and I should be grateful for the opportunity to hold this position."

Some people who have taken the risk to be more open about themselves on the job have suffered from discrimination while others have found the environment accepting and have noticed positive effects from no longer expending energy to "hide." If you feel that you cannot make the choice to come out at your present job, you may want to consider searching for a position where you would feel comfortable about living more openly. Regardless of the choices you make, it's important for you to understand the messages you're sending yourself about the work place and change the negative self-talk that may be interfering in your day-to-day functioning.

People Who Supervise You: Who's the Boss?

Dealing with a boss can be tricky because she has the power to alter the course of your career. It can also be difficult to stand up for yourself when your boss is a homophobe unless you have a strong sense of self-esteem and confidence.

How you relate to people in authority is affected by your past experiences. Were your parents patient and nurturing, or were they demanding and rigid? If you had an authoritarian family that didn't allow you to make independent decisions, you may be indecisive as an adult. Your experiences may have made you anxious about making decisions today. You may also have difficulty working with authoritarian-type leaders now and have negative expectations of your current supervisor simply because he or she reminds you of an abusive adult from your past. Even if past experiences with authority figures have been primarily positive, it is possible that your overall expectations for your boss and yourself are lower than necessary because of your impulse to protect yourself from homophobia.

If you've internalized the idea that gay people aren't entitled to the rights and privileges of heterosexuals, then you may expect less for yourself on the job—less recognition, less value to the company, and less entitled to the perks, such as health benefits for your partner. If this is true for you, then you likely behave in ways with your boss that suggests that you don't deserve better. Behaviors that get you nowhere include saying, "I don't deserve a raise" out of modesty and missing opportunities by not speaking up when your boss tries to ask you about your needs.

Losing It: Anger in the Workplace

Expecting that you will not be offered equal status at your job can lead not only to negative self-talk, but also to intense frustration. Inappropriate ways of dealing with frustration might include passive-aggressive behaviors such as showing up late for meetings, "forgetting" deadlines, and ignoring potential problems that are not part of your responsibilities so that the workplace will suffer consequences. More direct and inappropriate expressions of anger include forms of aggression like losing your temper and raising your voice, making threats, and sabotaging a project or other employee.

An appropriate way of managing anger involves behaving assertively when you have unmet needs or when your rights have been violated. If your self-esteem is low, you may have difficulty standing up for yourself and behaving assertively at work. This may lead you to say things to yourself like, "Don't say anything about that nasty comment...just be grateful that you have a job," or "I really wanted that promotion, but they wouldn't have taken me seriously if I had said something about it." Learning to change the way you see yourself, interpreting the meaning of a supervisor's behaviors, and standing up for yourself when necessary are appropriate ways of managing anger in your job.

Keeping Boundaries

Generally, the better your self-esteem, the less likely you are to tolerate boundary violations (e.g., being exploited, devalued, or ignored) on the job. Working on maintaining healthy boundaries in your career life means giving yourself permission to ask your boss for what you want or need to perform your job well, expressing your opinions about a project or decision, saying "no" when you feel overloaded, and setting limits on personal intrusiveness by co-workers or other company personnel.

Healthy boundaries, however, are not so rigid that they require excessive energy to maintain them. For example, most heterosexual employees do not worry about keeping their private lives a complete secret, even while they may not feel that this information is particularly relevant to share at work. If you find that you spend a significant amount of time managing your personal image ("I don't want anyone to know I'm a lesbian or I will lose the respect of my peers"), then you may be depleting your creative energy by maintaining this personal/professional separation. It's like the old *Star Trek* episodes in which Scotty, the engineer, has to siphon energy from lower priority functions of the ship to "maintain the shields, Captain" while under attack. This doesn't mean that you necessarily should come out to your boss and co-workers, especially if sexual orientation is not a protected status in your company or city.

There are still many jobs in which self-identifying as a gay man or lesbian can lead to discrimination, as in the US military. As you build confidence, you may feel a strong need to come out in the workplace no matter what the consequences. Remember though that coming out to others is a highly personal decision and should be made only when you are ready to handle the reactions of the people around you.

Teamwork

Although your co-workers may not have the authority to fire you, they are important sources of support and cooperation in the workplace. They can make the difference for you in terms of overall job satisfaction and a day-to-day sense of security. Co-workers who see the results of your labor and observe your work style can shape the impression that your boss or company has of you.

As with your boss, you may spend significant time and energy diverting the topics of conversation with co-workers away from your personal life, or simply pretending as if you have no personal life.

You may not be aware of it, but years of living in a self-protective way may have led you to settle for less than total acceptance and feel as though this is normal (e.g., "I cannot expect the same emotional support as my heterosexual co-workers"). These types of long-standing beliefs may inhibit you from building relationships that could advance your career.

It's not unusual to make friends on the job that extend beyond the workplace and if the relationship is with a superior, it also can be empowering professionally. It's important when building self-esteem for you to examine your long-standing beliefs regarding what kinds of support you will and will not allow yourself to have at work.

The Leadership Role

While most positions of responsibility require self-confidence, it is particularly so for positions that call for leadership requiring patience, tact, poise, and a sense of fairness. Think about some of the supervisors you've worked with.

Supervisors with low self-esteem are more likely to take your performance mistakes personally and respond in a personal, rather than professional, manner. *The less self-confidence they have in their own abilities as supervisors, the more threatened they may be by your successes.*

In order to become an effective supervisor yourself, you must build professional self-confidence. In order to use and believe healthy self-statements, such as, "I am competent to supervise someone who is a talented employee," make sure that you have adequate support and training in this position.

Keys to Management Success

Managing employees requires that you have excellent communication skills, an understanding of company systems and expectations, and adequate support and modeling from your own supervisor. As with any position, make sure you have at least the minimum skills required for the job before launching into it. If you have these basic skills, then your goal is to avoid negative self-talk that may sabotage your performance or lead you to feel insecure, frustrated, or overwhelmed.

Your Sexual Orientation and Management

Occasionally, subordinates or co-workers can become threatened by your success, regardless of your sexual orientation. As a lesbian or gay man, being a supervisor may lead to special concerns. Often employees who have lower self-esteem take decisions that you may make personally and react angrily. You may feel particularly vulnerable to threats because of your sexual orientation (that is, you may fear being outed, humiliated, and so on). Because of these concerns, it's not uncommon for gay male or lesbian supervisors to feel as if they need to walk a fine line between being authentic, yet being protective, about their personal lives. Regardless of the way you decide to balance these two competing needs on the job, you can be in control of any self-talk that leads you to feel insecure and indecisive. The questions at the end of this chapter will help you to evaluate your self-talk regarding how you see yourself in a position of authority.

Is Your Self-Esteem Too Dependent on Your Job?

Because self-esteem is affected by many experiences, you're likely to have areas in your life where you feel self-confident and accomplished—and other areas where you don't. Some people base their self-esteem on a single aspect of their lives in which they perform well. For example, many people find helping others beneficial in raising their sense of self-esteem. For others, work becomes an important source of self-esteem.

While success experiences are important for developing positive self-talk, it's possible to place so much emphasis on outside indicators of success in your life that you risk neglecting the internal structure that's important to building good self-esteem overall. Basing your self-esteem solely on something that is dependent on your performance, like a job, puts you at risk for self-esteem crises if you reach a point where you can no longer perform that job. The key to building lasting and pervasive self-esteem is to work at learning to love yourself at your core. This means learning to accept yourself as you are, recognizing your inner resources, and being kind to yourself during your inner monologue.

QUESTIONS FOR REFLECTION

- How has your professional life affected your perspective of yourself? How has your view of yourself affected your job?
- Are you happy with your current job? Why or why not?
- How did you make the decision to follow the career path you have followed? What factors did you weigh in choosing a career? How much of your career choice was based on what others expected of you versus what you wanted to do?
- How did consideration of cultural stereotypes for lesbians and gay men affect your decisions?
- Does concern about negative consequences at your current job keep you from sharing your personal life or going for advancement?
- What are your current supervisor's attitudes toward gay men and lesbians? Upon what information is this based?
- How has homophobia in the workplace affected your day-to-day comfort level?
- What is your level of confidence as a supervisor?
- What messages from the past or about your sexual orientation affect your self-talk on the job?

SEVEN

Love and Self-Esteem

TO HAVE HEALTHY RELATIONSHIPS WITH OTHERS, WE MUST FIRST
BE AT HOME WITH OURSELVES.

—*Susan L. Taylor, Lessons in Living*

How you feel about yourself cannot help but impact the quality of your relationships with others. Your sense of self-worth, how safe you feel with others, how much independence you need, whether or not you feel you deserve love, and how you expect to be treated by others are all determined to some extent by your core beliefs. Low self-esteem can make you feel powerless to avoid manipulation or outright abuse by others. You may feel as though you don't measure up in relationships or as if you don't deserve to be in a relationship with someone who is self-confident and healthy.

Having low self-esteem also affects your ability to make close friends or feel connected to your family. Establishing trust—the building block of depth in relationships—means learning to be vulnerable while at the same time, protecting yourself from harm. You may have trouble knowing how independent you should be and how close to let someone get as a relationship progresses. What you learned about depending on others, trusting them with your vulnerable sides, and what type of person makes a good mate was affected by the models of relationships you had when you were growing up and by the messages you were given about your value to others.

It's also helpful to consider that self-esteem is a type of relationship with yourself. You likely have different standards for other people than you have for yourself. At the same time, you are probably harder on yourself than you would ever be on someone you cared about. The demands that you make on yourself may sometimes be so unrealistic that you can never successfully meet them, leading to harsh and condemning self-statements and feelings of inadequacy.

If you recognize an adversarial relationship with yourself, (i.e., one that relies on self-criticism for motivation), you may be creating barriers in your relationships by preventing yourself from experiencing pleasure when you're with others or by refusing to allow others to enjoy the real you. In Part III, we'll discuss the relationship you have with yourself and ways to improve this important relationship in much more detail.

Getting Close

While sometimes the word *intimacy* is used as a euphemism for sexual activity, in this chapter I will use the word in a broader context, meaning the *sharing of the most private or personal feelings and thoughts you have with another person*. If you learned as a child that certain feelings and thoughts were not to be shared, you may still have difficulty sharing your true feelings with someone with whom you would like to be close. Many of you who grew up with a secret self, have a hard time as adults sharing your true feelings out of a fear of rejection or abandonment. The messages you received as a child about being honest and open may have sounded like this: "Some feelings are bad or evil and must never be talked about," or "If you tell me something I don't want to hear, I will punish or leave you." Some of you have had experiences of coming out to someone you cared about and then they deserted you.

One advantage in remaining opaque about your inner life is that it acts as a form of protection, keeping people from using this information to hurt you or leave you. On the flip side, maintaining a barrier between you and others can become too rigid, preventing you from experiencing the joy of a mutually intimate and trusting relationship. Without good modeling for how to set strong but flexible boundaries, you may leave yourself too open and vulnerable to abuse or alternatively, you shut everyone out. By teaching yourself to change negative self-talk and by learning to value and protect yourself, you will simultaneously raise your self-esteem and change the way you relate to others.

Two Paths of Sexual Development

Heterosexuals are lucky when it comes to meaningful sex education. They have it all around them from the time they are old enough to walk until they take their first sexual steps with another person. If you are straight, then you probably received some direct conversations about sex that made sense to you around the onset of puberty and early adolescence. You learned about physical changes in your body and then you started to feel the effects of the physical and hormonal changes emotionally. You began to pay attention to your "physical attractiveness quotient" and how the opposite sex viewed you.

Most heterosexuals are fortunate enough also to have a lot of company as they pass through the awkward adolescent phases and "sexual experiments" common at that age. They learn to form relationships, sexual and romantic, with the opposite sex through a highly traditional and recognizable process. In the beginning of the heterosexual process, adolescents typically get to know members of the opposite sex in small safe groups (i.e., going to the movies, the mall, or a dance). As young heterosexuals gain confidence, they grow bolder and begin to date as couples. Expectations for how far one should go around the bases on these early dates are usually clearly spelled out by concerned parents—no touching, petting, or kissing until a specific age or status. It is perfectly normal for parents to educate their children about sexuality and sexual behavior in progressively more sophisticated ways as they grow up.

Some studies have suggested that most adolescents learn about sex from sources other than their immediate family. I vaguely recall one to two very tense and incredibly awkward discussions with my father around the time I discovered the first signs of puberty. For the life of me, I cannot recall any of the content, but I clearly remember my dad stuttering, shaking, and sweating through the conversation and my own horror and embarrassment about a topic that I had no interest in!

Heterosexuals have the benefit of having society's general approval as they find their way through this difficult developmental process. Lesbians and gays, on the other hand, often have to actively *suppress* these complex feelings and sensations as they attempt to negotiate the other non-sexual perils of adolescence ("I must not allow myself to feel these things," or "My feelings are invalid or inappropriate"). If they are aware that they find people of the same sex attractive, they may opt to actively hide them. Many lesbian and gay youths, however, may not recognize or be able to label these feelings because they are unconsciously holding (or *repressing*) this information away from their awareness. People who are actively suppressing or repressing uncomfortable feelings tend to focus on other activities as a way of diverting this energy. A positive diversion might be schoolwork, jobs, or other productive or benign hobbies and interests. Unfortunately, negative diversions include behaviors like rebelling against parents or drug abuse or dependency. I will explain the concepts of repression and suppression in more detail in Chapter 17.

You could also choose to handle these feelings by openly acknowledging them, but then risk the rejection of family and

friends. Being rejected has its own consequences: loneliness, isolation, and depression. In some extreme circumstances, open acknowledgment of same-sex attractions can lead not just to rejections, but
also open hostility and physical harm.

Developing a secret self for feelings that you hide from others
seems to be another alternative chosen by many. Maintaining the
separate public and private identities can be exhausting and confusing for an adolescent, leading to feelings of anger, depression, suicidal thinking, and emotional fatigue.

TIGHTENING THE LID ON THE PRESSURE COOKER

There are many ways that avoidance, or suppression, of normal feelings may be harmful to a developing youth. First, queer youth are
not allowed the same support and guidance throughout the process
of reaching sexual maturity that heterosexual adolescents are universally offered. We must be our own guides through the dating and
sexuality aspects of our development and create our own rules and
expectations. Having to do this alone, however, has its own bumps
and bruises, and for many, their own struggle with self-acceptance
during an important phase of development leads to delayed experimentation and self-awareness. Heterosexuals proceed through these
stages at roughly the same times in their lives, while many gay people cannot explore themselves fully until later in their adult lives.

Heterosexuals have an advantage of going through sexual development at relatively the same age, while lesbians and gay men may
have a much larger range of ages when these sexual identity
processes occur. In some ways, this wide variation makes it harder to
find a compatible partner. For example, a forty-five-year-old man
who has just come to realize that he is gay may in some ways relate
more to a twenty-five-year-old man who has also come out, than to
other forty-five-year-olds who have been out since they were teens.
Hopefully, with greater social acceptance of lesbian and gay youth,
and support for age-appropriate sexuality education, gay youths will
enter self-discovery and exploration phases more in sync.

Self-Esteem and Stages of a Relationship

Although you might meet people you find exciting and attractive easily, expect to take some time to develop trust and emotional intimacy, like the aging of a fine wine. Building a trusting bond happens in phases, and each phase can be affected by your self-talk.

Phase One: Meeting Others

Meeting someone to date can happen anywhere, from the local supermarket to networks designed to bring singles interested in dating together, like gay.com, personal ads, or gay "speed dating." Most people who feel isolated can think of places or groups where they might be able to meet someone, but they feel "blocked" because they cannot imagine themselves fitting in, or they can't otherwise find the motivation to get there. Often, these blocks are related to inhibiting self-talk like, "I'm not very experienced with hiking so I probably would look like a klutz if I went to a hiking club meeting," leading to expectations of disappointment and inhibition.

Feeling Like You Don't Fit In?

You may have felt as though your alternatives for meeting people are limited because you don't think you fit an "image" expected by the lesbian/gay community. A common complaint I hear from urban gay (mostly white) men is that they consider themselves as average, overweight, or not buffed enough to fit into the local "gay male scene." Many of my clients assume that because they don't use alcohol or they tend to have more conservative views of sexual behavior than what they believe the gay norms are, they will not be accepted in gay social circles.

Sandra, who has had only a couple of short-term relationships, is opting out of the search for a relationship altogether, dooming herself to a life alone. She has a close circle of friends but has given up on finding a potential partner. She tends to focus on what she can't offer someone in a relationship rather than what she can. Her low self-esteem is perpetuated by the messages she sends herself: "I'm too fat, boring, or poor to be of interest to anyone else." Rather than face anticipated rejection, she stays at home, feeling lonely and sad, watching reality TV.

Learning to value yourself and your positive qualities can help you overcome such negative thinking and can help you find the motivation to seek out friends and partners who share your values. Keep in mind that lesbians and gays represent a full range of physical, emotional, intellectual, and professional types, including your own. Those people that you see in the bars, the social clubs, or the political groups that seem trendy or ideal, are all subgroups of a larger, diverse queer population.

Communicating Is the Key

Queer people, who have grown accustomed to avoiding the spotlight, often feel awkward in social settings, stifled by anxiety. If you didn't develop effective ways of initiating, or carrying on a conversation, early on in your life, your feelings of anxiety now about socializing may be interfering with meeting the right person. Recognizing that you need to work on your social skills is the first step. In order to increase your range of communication strategies and tools, practice these skills on friends or family before you attempt to reach out for new relationships. Two excellent books about developing communication skills are *Messages* by McKay, Davis, and Fanning and *Couple Skills* by McKay, Fanning, and Paleg. Consulting a psychologist who specializes in building solid relationships can also be helpful by teaching you ways to feel more comfortable in new social situations using such techniques as role playing (a way of practicing your conversation ahead of time) and assertiveness training (to help you understand how to speak up more effectively).

When you are getting ready to meet new people, examine what you are saying to yourself about how you will be perceived in a new situation ("They will see me as a geek"), who you feel you are able to approach ("Someone like her would never talk to someone like me"), and your likelihood of making a positive connection ("Even if I can get up the nerve to say something, he would never be interested in going out with me"). These negative self-statements reduce your motivation to reach out to someone and can leave you feeling depressed, awkward, and intimidated. They also set you up sometimes to choose people you may feel are safe or approachable, but are not necessarily who you *want* to meet. The questions at the end of the chapter will help you analyze the self-statements that you may be making to yourself.

PHASE TWO: FOLLOWING THROUGH

Once you've met someone that you're attracted to, the next step is to *follow through* so that it's more likely that you will develop a relationship. People with low self-esteem often assume that if the initial contact went well, it was a fluke. They say things to themselves like, "If he only knew the real me, he wouldn't want to get together again." Because of a fear of being rejected, they may not take the next step of making a call to set up another meeting, or stay too quiet on subsequent dates, or even turning down invitations.

Replacing statements like, "If she really liked me, she would call me first" with "Things seemed to go well the first time we met. I'd like to see her again and I find out if the feeling is mutual. Even if she is not interested in meeting again, it doesn't mean that it's because of a shortcoming on my part." Learning to talk to yourself in a more rational and respectful way takes practice, but will be worth it when it comes to dating.

PHASE THREE: DEEPENING THE RELATIONSHIP

After beginning a new relationship, you are faced with deciding how quickly or completely to trust the new person in your life. The real work of developing an honest and sincere relationship begins here.

You may have been raised to keep your true feelings, reactions, and thoughts a secret from your family and friends. Living as though you are someone you are not, however, can lead to feeling chronically like an impostor or fraud. Developing relationships can then be both confusing and complex because you can never be sure if what they care about in the relationship is the image you portray or the real you.

You may have learned that the way to deepen a relationship is through making yourself indispensable to the other person or by doing things that please the other person even if it means sacrificing your own needs. People with low self-esteem often have learned to value the needs of others over their own needs and desires, then later can feel the frustration of not being attended to by those whom they have cared for. The thing that they most want, namely being cared about for who they really are, doesn't happen because the messages they repeat to themselves include "My needs and wants aren't important here." If you have this type of self-talk, you may find yourself in a cyclical and self-reinforcing spiral: The more you focus on your partner's needs, the less your needs are attended to, leaving you feeling ignored, betrayed, or even frustrated. Messages like this are often deeply embedded, so it's important to examine your core beliefs about relationships to be able to develop honest and mutually satisfying relationships.

Protecting Yourself

Even if you feel that you can be honest with your partner about your thoughts and feelings, it is important during this phase to maintain self-protection as you move into deeper trust in a relationship. Particularly if you have no experience in trusting, honest relationships or have been hurt in the past by someone whom you trusted, it's important to take your time as you become more honest with your friend or partner.

Healthy boundaries are important in this phase to protect you, while at the same time allowing you to open the gate to other people who have proven themselves trustworthy. This means that you share some of the vulnerable side of yourself, until you have enough evidence that your special someone respects and values you. Evidence for moving forward includes how she treats other people with whom she has relationships and how she handles the private details you shared with her in the beginning of the relationship.

These steps are primarily designed for people who recognize in themselves a difficulty with trusting others and developing deeper relationships. The idea is not to create tests for the people in your life that they must pass in order to gain your trust, but to make well-informed choices about the people in your life with whom you want to take emotional risks.

PHASE FOUR: MAINTAINING THE CONNECTION

After you have built substantial relationships in your life, just like a precious antique, you have to care for it to keep it in tip-top condition. Healthy self-esteem allows you to experience high quality intimacy in the form of feeling close to someone, allowing yourself to ask for what you need, and allowing yourself to accept affection. If you have low self-esteem, however, you can feel as though you don't deserve such experiences. Movies, literature, and popular culture are full of images of ideal love and friendships, often portrayed unrealistically. Lovers who never argue or disagree, friends who are always faithful, and people who make no mistakes are unrealistic models. Learning to have reasonable expectations for yourself and others is an important part of maintaining a connection and growing together. Examining unrealistic expectations, such as hoping your partner or friends can read your thoughts, and learning to be flexible is a part of expressing mutual respect and support.

Healthy self-esteem grows as you negotiate between your own needs and the needs of your partner, without minimizing either person's experiences, feelings, or ways of thinking. Intimacy grows as you realize that two people do not need to feel the same way about an issue to be able to accept the other's perspective. In a healthy relationship, you learn to respect yourself and your partner, each maintaining your own individuality.

Learning to accept your own responsibility during a conflict with someone you care about is equally important. While some people with low self-esteem assume all responsibility for mistakes in a relationship, it is important to stand up for yourself when you feel that your rights have been violated or your feelings not considered. This is not always easy, particularly if you tend to send distorted and negative messages to yourself.

People with low self-esteem are often afraid to admit mistakes; feeling as if making mistakes proves that they are worthless. They avoid accepting responsibility for their part in disputes, which in time can lead to further problems.

Elizabeth and Sharon began to have problems in their relationship because Elizabeth never admitted when she was wrong. Their arguments always ended with Sharon apologizing and shouldering the responsibility for their problems.

After a while, Sharon began to resent Elizabeth for this and would pick fights just to get a reaction from her.

In this case, it is likely that both partners suffer from self-esteem problems since no one always is correct or always to blame in every single conflict during a relationship. The best strategy is to have open, honest discussions about feelings, perceptions, and assumptions and to accept your part in the argument or misunderstanding. Learning to understand and forgive a partner who has made a mistake is important for both people as you grow as a couple or close friends.

Successful Relationships

Negative self-talk can hamper your ability to have a successful relationship at every level. Just as you may be talking yourself out of putting your best foot forward on the job, you may also be inhibiting or sabotaging yourself in relationships with rigid, self-negating messages that rule you out before you are even in. Once a relationship is formed, learning to accept yourself more completely and present yourself more genuinely (warts and all) to the other person can help you experience greater satisfaction in your relationships. Answering the following questions can help you examine your own negative self-talk and determine where you need to begin making changes.

Questions for Reflection

- What lessons did you learn as you were growing up about depending on others?
- What did you learn about being vulnerable in relationships?
- What kind of model did your parents provide you about adult romantic relationships?
- What kind of models did you have for adult lesbian or gay male relationships? What were the stereotypes for these relationships?
- At what age did you begin to experiment with sexual behavior? Dating? Committed relationships? Did these ages correspond to the ages that your heterosexual friends began their experimentation? At what chronological age did you go through your "adolescent" phase of development in terms of sexual exploration?
- How do your past experiences with intimacy affect your current relationships or attitudes about having a relationship?
- Does your self-talk create a barrier to developing satisfying relationships? How does it adversely affect you in meeting others? In following through? In deepening the relationship? In maintaining relationships?
- Do you question your ability to have a relationship? In what ways?
- Do you try to diminish anxiety or reduce the potential of rejection and subsequent pain by talking yourself out of a relationship? How do you do this?
- How might you keep sexual activity apart from intimacy? How does sexual activity get in the way of intimacy?

Eight

Lifestyle

WHAT AN ABSURD AMOUNT OF ENERGY I HAVE BEEN WASTING ALL
MY LIFE TRYING TO FIGURE OUT HOW THINGS "REALLY ARE,"
WHEN ALL THE TIME THEY WEREN'T.

—*Hugh Prather, Notes to Myself*

This chapter is about exploring ways that self-esteem affects your choices—in friends and whether or not you use alcohol and other drugs, interact with the bar scene, or protect yourself from AID or other diseases.

ALCOHOL AND OTHER DRUGS

Using chemicals to enhance mood, reduce pain, encourage healing, contact the spirit world, or escape from reality has been a part of our world for thousands of years. The decision to use them is often influenced by social messages such as "When you are sick, take some medicine," and "Alcohol will make you more relaxed if you are nervous." If you've learned not to trust your own experiences, thoughts, and feelings, you are more susceptible to the influence of others around you. You may drink or take drugs in an attempt to fit in, reduce uncomfortable feelings (such as anxiety, anger, or grief), or to prove your worthiness or "coolness."

Take a moment to examine the messages you give yourself about when, how, and why you use alcohol and other drugs. Many of these messages may be distorted, irrational, or not healthy. While traditional twelve-step programs, such as AA or NA are a part of a successful chemical dependency treatment program for many people, an alternative approach based on cognitive theory, was developed called SMART (Self-Management and Recovery Training). This program is based on the assertion that cognitive distortions and irrational ideas keep people using chemicals in a harmful way and includes a step-by-step guide to overcoming negative self-talk related to harmful use of alcohol and drugs.

Research supports the link between low self-esteem and substance abuse. Children and teenagers with low self-esteem tend to experiment with alcohol and other drugs more often than children and teens with higher self-esteem. Low self-esteem appears to make youths more vulnerable to peer pressure, taking more risks, and like many adults, using drugs or alcohol to escape from their own volatile self-talk.

If you use alcohol or other drugs, at some level you may be telling yourself it's okay to use chemicals to "make things better" or that substances are better than your own coping skills. If you have less confidence in your own abilities to handle pressure for example, you might believe that alcohol or drugs are acceptable to use as a performance enhancer, as long as you get the job done. If you've come to believe that you have little worth, you may feel that you can't cope with stress without alcohol or drugs. Even when you make minor mistakes, you may begin to verbally berate yourself and then drink or use drugs later to reduce the emotional pain.

Short-Term versus Long-Term Hedonism

People who seek pleasure in the short-term, through the excessive use of alcohol, other drugs, or cigarettes, often tell themselves that the long-term effects of these activities don't matter because "we all die anyway." Chemical dependency is a complex phenomenon with multiple causal factors including genetic makeup, family history, and modeling of substance use by people you looked up to. Sometimes, however, actively continuing to use substances excessively may be an indication of deeper problems with self-esteem.

Dr. Albert Ellis, a founder of CBT, suggested that leading a healthy lifestyle is a form of *long-term hedonism*. He recommended that we make our choices today with an eye on our future. He believed that if we truly valued ourselves, we would choose not to engage in behaviors that lead to short-term pleasure but that ultimately shorten or reduce the quality of our lives (like smoking, drinking excessively, binge eating, etc.). He linked the notion of taking care of ourselves (an aspect of self-esteem) with the choices that we make and the irrational beliefs that we hold today. Examples of these beliefs include "My life is so bad that it doesn't matter if I have an accident and die," "I can't take another rejection; it'll help if I take a drink," or "I really can't control myself." He was widely known for his blunt challenges to his clients' irrational beliefs and his strong emphasis on replacing irrational self-statements with more honest, intentionally healthy ones.

The Club Scene

A common problem for gay men and women is that many urban social activities are centered on gay or lesbian clubs or bars. While there is nothing inherently wrong with going to a bar or dancing for hours, they can be problematic for those who have difficulty controlling their alcohol and other drug use, or for those who don't feel like they "fit the norm" of the club crowd.

Because we can "pass" so well in the straight world, it's not always easy to identify and meet potential partners. Avenues are limited for meeting people, particularly if you are from the 'burbs or more rural areas. Even if you do have access to larger group events, it can be quite hard on the ego if you attend and then aren't approached by someone or are rejected outright. For some, the bar scene can feel like a meat market, where looks are valued over deeper qualities. You may compare yourself to others and feel inferior, particularly if your self-esteem is low. You may find that you avoid going out at all because of extreme self-messages about not fitting in, such as, "No one would want me, looking like this."

When Justin was younger, he loved going dancing at the hot clubs in the city. He had no trouble making friends or meeting people when he was in his twenties and thirties, but now that he was approaching 50, he found that men his age made up a much smaller proportion of the crowd. He also felt less attractive as his waist began to spread and his hair began to thin. Justin had always believed that he would be in a comfortable relationship by the time he was fifty, and now he felt uneasy about his chances at a long-term relationship at this age. These days, when he went out to bars, it was rare that anyone would ask him to dance or even speak to him if he didn't initiate the conversation. Because of these experiences, Justin began to feel old and unattractive. He began to avoid going out to clubs, feeling that they were too youth oriented. Since bars and dance clubs had been his primary sources of socialization, he found himself becoming more isolated, lonely, and more depressed, particularly as his old group of friends paired off into relationships or moved away. He told himself that he would probably die "alone, old, and bitter."

Fortunately, Justin heard about a social group for gay men over forty that met at a local Unitarian church. With some encouragement from his friends, he went to a few meetings and found other men like himself who were single, attractive, and energetic. He realized that gay men could age gracefully and that not all gay men were attracted to youth and external beauty. He began to change how he viewed himself and the self-talk that he used when he was alone. His depression began to lift and he felt able to make new, more comfortable choices for socializing.

SELF-ESTEEM AND HIV

AIDS has had a major impact on the queer community. The mere presence of HIV has altered innumerable lives and choices, with the relationship between AIDS and self-esteem often complex and reciprocal. In a recent study of 301 gay men between the ages of eighteen and twenty-seven, 46% of men who were found to have lower levels of self-acceptance reported having unsafe sex, while only 30% of men reporting higher levels of self-acceptance engaged in risky sex.

Researchers like Rafael Diaz at the San Francisco AIDS Foundation are also finding a significant relationship between low self-esteem and the transmission of HIV in men, particularly as they look for experiences that make them feel, even temporarily, better about themselves. Hazel Betsy of the Women's AIDS Network believes that self-esteem is also an issue for women with HIV, particularly in terms of the difficulty women have in saying "no" to people pressuring them to engage in risky behaviors.

Although the great losses caused by AIDS are overwhelming, some people feel that AIDS may have affected the community in some beneficial ways. The world's attention became focused upon gay and lesbian issues in ways that made them more difficult to ignore or deny. The more exposure the general population has to the gay and lesbian community, the more likely it is that they will begin to confront inaccurate stereotypes. AIDS has also served to bring the community together in an effort to fight the disease and the stigma. People have joined forces to create AIDS service delivery organizations across the globe, to challenge the political and economically motivated systems that ignore or abuse gay and lesbian rights, and—by virtue of AIDS education—to increase the visibility of other gay and lesbian issues. Because many employers had to deal with the issues of HIV in the workplace, for example, they had to deal with policies affecting gays and lesbians as well. There were, of course, people who took the opportunity to discriminate against and harass people with AIDS or who were lesbian or gay; a few noble businesspeople took the opportunity to do the right thing by expanding benefits and family policies to include lesbians and gays in a supportive way.

Lesbians' and gay men's initial response to the AIDS epidemic was also positive in that it helped the community organize around the common goal of survival. Many AIDS organizations developed all over the country, providing models for health education and support services that had never been accomplished before on such a scale. AIDS activism helped challenge old, antiquated drug approval systems and helped forge new policies that affected not only people with AIDS but also people with other diseases who were waiting for new drugs to enter the market.

The AIDS epidemic unfortunately gave homophobes and other ignorant people the opportunity to make inappropriate and hurtful links between sexual behavior and retribution. They claimed it justified their positions that homosexuality is wrong, evil, or sick. As author Susan Sontag suggested in her book, *AIDS as Metaphor*, AIDS became a kind of shorthand in the minds of many in the general public for sexual perversion and death. Many AIDS sufferers were led to feel guilty and ashamed of contracting the disease early on, leading some to self-destructive or suicidal behavior. Gay men who became infected in the early '80s were often terrified of this mysterious and virulent illness as they watched larger and larger numbers of their friends and family die with little medical attention.

The President of the United States at the time, Ronald Reagan, completely ignored the issue in terms of discussion, action, or funding, some say largely because the first victims were gay men. Urban areas, such as San Francisco and New York, with large lesbian and gay communities, saw rapid and devastating changes as the hospitals and health clinics filled up with patients who would die sometimes frightening and painful deaths.

The effect on gays and lesbians as a group was powerful. Many who tested positive but were asymptomatic and those who were not infected often suffered multiple losses of people they loved and cared for. The collected works of author/activist Larry Kramer including the play *The Normal Heart* and the book *Faggott*, portrays both the deep grief and intense rage experienced by many gay men and lesbians during this time. Many who have survived the early years of AIDS feel as though they are veterans back from a war, emotionally burned out with too many faces to mourn.

The effect on self-esteem in someone who has survived such loss, fear, and turbulence is significant. Facing mortality is difficult for anyone. Most Americans live in some form of denial about eventually dying in order to stay focused on the present and continuing to function. If you thought about your death every second of every day, you would likely not be able to make appropriate choices, perform your daily tasks, or keep your attention focused on your job. People who are HIV-positive, even if they are asymptomatic, often struggle to regain some sense of normality in their lives as they try to psychologically adjust to a diagnosis that remains without a cure, with seemingly infinite variations of opportunistic infections, and recently the threat of a new "supervirus" that is immune to standard treatments. It is not the inevitability of death that can be so devastating since this is true for every human being. It appears that the constant daily reminders of mortality—every benign physical symptom, every medication dose, every evening news story about AIDS—seem to prevent some people with HIV from settling back into a comfortable, moderate level of denial of death. Too much denial can lead you to avoid proper medical treatment, too little overwhelms you emotionally. Many lesbians and gay men carry messages in their daily self-talk that relate directly or indirectly to AIDS.

Even though Margaret did not have HIV, and she did not know anyone personally who had HIV or died from it, she had friends who did have these experiences and had been deeply affected by them. Although the rate of transmission of the disease in the lesbian population was low compared to other affected groups, Margaret had found her own sexual behavior altered by her awareness of AIDS. She was aware that there were women who identified themselves as bisexual and that some of them had contracted HIV by sleeping with men. She also had heard about needle-sharing by lesbians who used IV drugs. She tried to practice safe sex with her partners, but occasionally found herself wondering if she might become infected. She began to wonder whether she should even have sex at all or whether she should just be comfortable with a nonsexual companion. She found herself even wondering about whether it was possible to contract some type of new and equally horrible disease that affected lesbians in the same way that AIDS had affected gay men in the beginning of the epidemic. The messages she heard herself saying as she began to try to form new relationships were things like, "She looks nice enough but she may have a history that she hasn't told me about. I think I'll pass on that dinner invitation."

Margaret's self-talk regarding the potential of contracting a disease became more extreme over time. In fact, her fear actually dovetailed into her negative self-talk about herself with statements such as, "I won't go out with her because she wouldn't really understand my need for safety," leading her to continue to avoid relationships. For Margaret, her fear of contracting a disease, stimulated by the larger gay and lesbian population's emphasis on disease prevention, actually provided her with a comfortable way to avoid relationships altogether.

Aside from providing an excuse to avoid intimacy, AIDS has other effects on self-esteem. Sometimes, it is difficult to resist the negative messages perpetuated by the media and public figures. During an interview, former US Senate majority leader Trent Lott (R-Miss.) answered the interviewer's question, "Is homosexuality a sin?" by saying "yes" and then went on to say that homosexuals should be treated as if they were people with problems like "kleptomania . . . alcoholics . . . sex addicts." Amazingly, in just one statement, he condemned gay men and lesbians as *immoral*, but then made a comparison of homosexuality with "other *illnesses*." Most religious leaders would agree that an illness is not a sin and a sin is not an illness. The senator's rhetoric was either incredibly ignorant or blatantly political, attempting to placate voters who believe either one model or the other. Recent political leaders, like Rick Santorum, the former Republican senator from Pennsylvania and Tom DeLay, the former Republican majority leader of the House of Representatives, make equally outrageous and ignorant remarks on a regular basis. Both men have been relieved of their political responsibilities in part due to their ignorance and lack of humility.

Attaching the stigma of having AIDS with the stereotype of hypersexuality and promiscuity allows other people like Lott, Santorum, and DeLay, to also make inaccurate and distorted statements. It can be difficult to resist the constant messages in the media about who you are, particularly when the messages are sent by politically powerful figures in our country. Even if you have no problem dismissing such ignorance, the ripple effect of such talk likely encourages, and in a way even endorses, discrimination and overt harm toward gays and lesbians.

People who live with HIV must not only deal with the negative messages about being lesbian or gay, but the residual fears about AIDS left over from the time when not much was known about the epidemic. They may find that once a stranger whom they have just met finds out that they are HIV-positive, the attitude and behavior of that person changes dramatically—perhaps becoming negative and avoidant. People who are HIV-positive may feel as though they are now treated as a disease instead of as a person or as if they are dying instead of living.

If you are HIV-positive, it's important to be aware of challenges to your self-esteem. You must evaluate negative thinking about the future ("Why bother planning for the future since I won't be around for it"), self-blame about the past ("I was so stupid to have contracted this disease"), and distorted messages in the present ("It's not worth trying for a relationship because no one will want to be with a "sick person"). Maintaining a healthy self-image may be difficult with constant reminders of the HIV battle, such as reports of fluctuating viral load and T-cell counts, opportunistic infections, and medication side effects. Low self-esteem that existed prior to the contraction of HIV, or as a result of repeated losses or health scares, can decrease your motivation to take care of yourself properly. It may be more difficult when you are tired and sick to challenge the inaccurate messages from the media and from your internal critic. Getting enough emotional support is both important and effective, as is learning to view yourself with compassion and self-nurturing.

For some individuals with HIV or AIDS, there can be personal gains. Some of my patients have found that being HIV-positive forced them to examine themselves at deeper levels and to re-examine the priorities in their lives. Some have found themselves connected or reconnected to their family and friends in ways that didn't seem possible in the past. Others have explored deeper levels of spirituality and found new meaning and self-value. Facing your mortality, often a frightening experience can help you learn to listen to what's important and to make your choices more thoughtfully and with self-compassion—a worthy goal. Thankfully, with new treatments emerging regularly, the life expectancy of someone with HIV is significantly longer these days.

Everyday Choices

Every decision you make throughout the day is affected, at some level, by your self-esteem. Your brain forms a hybrid of incoming current data and messages from your past experience, in a matter of milliseconds, to affect what actions you next take. Depending on those past filters, you may pause or instantly react in any given situation, thus creating the basis for your individual personality.

Cliff, a twenty-eight-year-old, African-American gay man, was raised in a predominantly white, Midwestern, small town and was often the only person of color in his class during his elementary and high school years. His main contact with other African-Americans came when his family visited his relatives in Chicago, once or twice each year. Cliff loved his family dearly, particularly his cousins, but he had never revealed his sexual orientation to them out of a fear how they'd react. He often didn't feel as though he fit in at school because of his skin color, leaving him feeling like an outsider most of the time.

Cliff was conscious of trying to fit in as best he could. He generally tried to look and act like his friends at school, but also became quite adept at adopting the language and patterns of his family in Chicago. He became quite good at matching the style of almost any with whom he interacted, which provided him with at least some acceptance and from being rejected outright. Unfortunately, although Cliff could always make himself fit in no matter where he was, he never felt satisfied. He rarely took risks to explore his own likes and dislikes for fear of standing out or being subject to ridicule, rejection, or potential harm. He developed a *secret self*, where he hid both his sexual orientation and other personal likes and dislikes. As an adult, he often worked quietly and effectively at his job, but didn't interact much with his co-workers or do anything to draw attention to himself. His self-talk often revolved around messages like "Don't rock the boat. Just do what you have to do and leave. You don't fit in here anyway."

Never having truly explored his African roots or his sexuality, Cliff was unhappy with his life on many levels. He finally sought out a counselor to help him understand his chronic feelings of emptiness and dissatisfaction. She helped him to recognize the negative self-talk and to understand how his family and society affected his self-esteem. He began to understand that he developed his approach to life as a way of surviving as a man of color in a white community and a gay man in a heterosexual world. His counselor began to help him explore his true feelings about the choices in his life instead of always making the choice that was least obtrusive or most conservative.

Cliff learned to quiet the stifling self-talk and to listen to his true likes and dislikes, which led him to make some significant changes in his lifestyle and ultimately to feel more satisfied. He began to take more risks in the way he dressed, the music he listened to, and even in the food he ate, often finding that there were many more choices available to him than he had imagined. Occasionally, Cliff found that his friends, co-workers, and family disapproved of some of his choices, but he learned to trust his own judgments and recognize that it was not his responsibility to deal with other people's distress about conformity. As he began to trust his own choices, feelings, and opinions, Cliff found the chronic emptiness subsiding and a growing sense of well-being and self-confidence.

SOCIAL COMMUNITIES

Some social and psychological theorists have proposed that the development of a healthy lesbian or gay identity involves identification with a larger community. Although social/political organizations for lesbians and gay men existed earlier, many historians point to the riots at the Stonewall Inn, a Greenwich Village gay bar, as the single pre-AIDS event that sparked social and political activism. Tired of being humiliated and harassed by New York City police, the queer patrons turned on the police that night, yelling and throwing bottles, uprooting parking meters, and loudly protesting the years of abuse with chants of "Gay power!" Newspaper headlines the next day proclaimed to the world the beginnings of a new, historic movement in which lesbians and gays would no longer passively accept identification as second-class citizens.

For many gay and lesbian people, *coming out* involves finding and bonding with others who are similar. Many remember fondly the first time they attended a gay or lesbian social or political event. They felt frightened as they made the choice to attend, often taking weeks or months to work up the courage to venture into a gay or lesbian bar, a Metropolitan Community Church service, or a lesbian or gay AA meeting, potluck, or community center. They may have felt disoriented initially, but found that this feeling gave way to excitement and later a sense of belonging. That feeling of acceptance and understanding provided a powerful bond between the strangers with a common identity. For many, such meetings became a safe haven and place to share the secret self before returning to the heterocentric worlds in which they lived.

As more and more people became aware of their sexual orientation and had such experiences, organized opportunities for socializing and living grew. And as with any large group, subgroups began to form within the larger organizations. These lesbian and gay subgroups included the original "Castro clones," gay men in the Castro district of San Francisco, California, who adopted ways of dressing and grooming that included short hair, mustaches, flannel shirts, and jeans. Over the years, as the full diversity of the larger gay and lesbian culture became apparent, other groups within groups developed, emphasizing similarities and common interests, such as lesbians with children, people who enjoy drag or dressing in leather, women living in communities without men, circuit or "gym boys," and "lipstick lesbians." The list goes on and on with subgroups within subgroups within subgroups.

Belonging to a group can provide many positive and life enhancing experiences. The members become your peer group and provide a place for bonding and sharing, a place to "fit in" especially after years of real or feared rejection or condemnation. As with most peer groups, however, over time these groups can become limiting and the same processes that led to the development of such a specialized group can lead to pressure to conform within the group itself. Socializing only with people from your group may in itself become confining, leaving you feeling as if you cannot express opinions that deviate from the group's norms or expectations. As you get older, move into different life stages, or change your views, you may find yourself feeling rejected, even if there have been no overt behaviors from group members to exclude you. You may find that you say things to yourself like, "My friends will laugh if I go out with someone his age," or "Even though I have a different view of that person running for office, I'd better keep it to myself at the party." The pressure to keep up with your peers can be immense and if your self-esteem is low, you may find it difficult to be yourself and have or express your own opinions, thoughts, and feelings.

It's easy to forget that there are other ways to connect socially, emotionally, or intellectually if your range of experiences is narrow. Just as people who subscribe to heterocentrist or homophobic thinking tend to stay within groups that hold the same beliefs they do, so can any other exclusive peer group, with both groups potentially losing many opportunities for growth. Finding a balance between having a group with whom you can identify, yet feeling free to follow your own path, takes time and effort but is an achievable goal. Learning to tolerate others with different opinions and to find peer groups with the capacity to tolerate individual differences can be immensely satisfying.

You may have learned to devalue, ignore, or repress your natural intuition and feelings based on the values of your family of origin, the community, and the larger culture around you but that doesn't mean your lifestyle has to suffer for it. Building self-esteem holds the promise of greater self-acceptance and it includes learning to value your own natural responses to people and events in your life. You must learn to make decisions based on how you feel, rather than what others expect from you and what your negative self-talk has led you to believe. The last section of this book will teach you to change negative self-talk, attitudes, and beliefs that are distorted or that keep you from feeling healthy, happy, and secure.

QUESTIONS FOR REFLECTION

- What were the early messages you learned as a child about using alcohol or other drugs? What were your family models for the use of alcohol and other drugs?
- If you drink or use drugs today, under what conditions do you do so? Are you usually in a social setting or alone?
- Do you drink or use to reduce anxiety or relax? To help you with performance?
- What messages do you give yourself today about when, how, and whether to drink or use?
- Do you take a short-term or long-term approach to your future quality of life? If you take a short-term approach, what negative or distorted messages do you give yourself that keep you feeling pessimistic about the future?
- What messages are activated when you go to a lesbian or gay bar or other social gathering?
- How has AIDS affected your life? How has the stigma of AIDS had an impact on you directly or indirectly? How have your thoughts, feelings, and behaviors been altered because of AIDS?
- How does your sexual orientation, your ethnicity, and your gender interact to affect your self-esteem?
- How would you describe your personal circle of friends? Are

they diverse in gender, sexual orientation, race, socioeconomic status? If not, how does the lack of diversity affect your freedom to make choices?

- Do your friends share common interests, activities, and goals? How easy is it for you to choose to change the way you dress or look in terms of how your friends might respond?
- How much do you consider what your friends will think when you are making decisions about clothes, hair, who you will date, etc.?
- What advantages are there to having the friends you have? What are the disadvantages?

Part III

Healing:

Doing the Work

NINE

Feeling the Feelings

THOSE WHO DON'T KNOW HOW TO WEEP WITH THEIR WHOLE
HEART DON'T KNOW HOW TO LAUGH EITHER.

—*Golda Meir*

n Chapter 1, I explained the central cognitive behavioral concept, namely, that *thoughts lead to feelings*. An event occurs in
your life that, in itself, has no meaning. Then almost immediately you have a thought about the event that leads to feelings.
Sometimes, you actually feel the emotion before you recognize the
thought that preceded the feeling. Because thoughts usually happen
first, and are essentially based on your particular pattern of thinking,
sometimes, the feelings you are having are the result of a personal
bias. Your running inner dialogue (or automatic thinking) is there to
help you interpret the everyday events in your world as a form of protection. Sometimes you're aware of the constant chatter in your

head, and sometimes you aren't. Many people react to minor failures in their daily lives with, "That was so stupid of me!" We are like sports commentators, evaluating and commenting on every move, every decision, and every event in our lives.

If you aren't completely aware of this self-talk, then you may only feel the emotional consequences of it. It's like seeing the aftermath of a tornado without having actually witnessed the tornado itself— you still feel the devastation and the fear of something powerful having been there. Unfortunately, if you're not aware of this talk, or if you're aware of it but have no tools for challenging or altering it, you've left yourself at the mercy of the distortions, irrationality, and even maliciousness of your past.

A major goal of CBT is to assist you in becoming aware of your self-talk so that you can evaluate it in a more rational and objective fashion. Negative self-talk will then begin to lose its power to cause feelings of sadness, anger, doom, or despair. You can learn to challenge the negative voices that may put you down and cause you to feel, or anticipate, rejection. Chapter 10 provides some techniques that are commonly used to challenge automatic thoughts as they occur. Before we get there, however, let's talk about the *emotional* path to healing.

Digging Deeper

Uncovering your automatic thinking is the first step in raising your self-esteem, and you may have already felt some good feelings about yourself by reading the preceding chapters and recognizing the flawed early influences in your life. Then again, you may also have experienced an increase in negative feelings while reading the early chapters, given the breadth of issues that were covered—from early neglect, to abuse, rejection, and abandonment. These memories, and what they meant then and still mean to you now, are likely to be painful or uncomfortable at best to remember. Uncovering family rules about feelings will be helpful in the process of learning to be more authentic.

What were your family's rules about emotions? Which emotions were okay and not okay to express? How did your own family handle their feelings? Did your parents model alcohol use when they were tense, or screaming when they were angry?

Our larger culture values certain feelings over others. Some feelings are considered acceptable for men to express and while others are only tolerable in women. For example, males are often encouraged to feel anger and to act aggressively at times (e.g., "Make my day!"), while women are often trained to respond passively. And in a patriarchal society, masculine characteristics are often viewed as signs of strength, while feminine characteristics are devalued as weak.

As you begin to recognize and challenge negative self-talk, you will begin to feel some of the natural emotions you would have felt as a child had you been allowed to feel them. You may feel anger toward the systems that taught you that you were powerless, inferior, or worthless. You may find that you are angry with yourself for perpetuating this negative and distorted self-talk. You may also feel angry at the sources of the harsh and negative messages who methodically taught to view yourself as weak, ignorant, and ineffective (i.e., parents, family, role models). You *may* feel uncomfortable having some feelings because you have no experience allowing yourself to have them. Sometimes, giving yourself permission to have feelings that you've never allowed yourself to feel leaves you feeling vulnerable, weak, or immature. If you did not have good role models for how to process feelings appropriately, the problem is one of a *skill deficit* (meaning you did not learn how to deal with feelings in a healthy way). Luckily, something you did not learn as a child is learnable now.

DON'T DO IT ALONE

It's important to give yourself time to feel feelings as they come up so that they can resolve more naturally, without cutting yourself off from them or putting yourself down for having them. It will also be important for you to have adequate support in your life while you are resolving intense feelings. You can get this support from close

friends, family, or other loved ones who can provide a caring and listening ear, can allow you the freedom to feel your feelings without
having to make suggestions, and can listen non-judgmentally.
Sometimes, the people you love may not be able to provide this type
of support for you because of their own discomfort with having
intense feelings. In this case, it might be important for you to find a
trained professional who can allow you to express your feelings in a
non-judgmental environment (one in which you feel you can safely
and honestly express yourself).

Peer support groups can be helpful, particularly if the group has
clear, safe rules for how to respond to a member's expression of emotion. The goal is not for someone to fix you by helping you suppress
feelings, or to distract you from them, but to support you in how you
really feel about things, rather than how you think you *should* feel.
With experience, guidance, and non-judgmental support, you can
build your skills for handling feelings of different types and intensi-
ties. The important thing to remember is not to invalidate or minimize your natural feeling processes. If your feelings are scary, or you
think you might not be able to rein them in once you let them out,
consider enlisting the aid of a psychotherapist who can help you navigate this process safely.

Jane came from a family that did not allow direct expression of emotion. She learned early on that it was not ok for others to see you have
feelings. By age ten, she clearly understood that "big girls don't cry"
and that if you did, you were seen as weak and different from the rest of
the family. She learned to suppress her feelings about many things—
anger and loneliness, even unbridled joy or passion. Emotional control was valued and honored in her family. Her father seemed proud
that he did not weep at his mother's funeral when Jane was fifteen and
he believed that not missing a day of work after her death was an
accomplishment.

Jane internalized the family rules quite well and others saw her as
quite "unflappable," often relying on her strength and calm during
crises. She was the "strong, silent type" in her relationship with her
partner of fourteen years, Marga. They managed to do quite well for

themselves over the years, building a network of friends, developing independent and successful careers, and living in a home that they built themselves.

When Marga died suddenly after a brief bout with breast cancer, Jane's world seemed to come crashing in. She immediately felt an overwhelming grief that was paralyzing in many ways. She had never experienced an emotion this intense and unrelenting. She did her best to choke back the tears and go on with her life as quickly as possible, much like her father did when his mother died.

At first, Jane found some solace in her work. She found that the more involved she became with her job, the less she thought about Marga. When being at home alone became too difficult, she took work home with her and made sure that she had very little quiet time to herself. She kept going at this pace for almost two years, getting special recognition and advancement at work for her extra effort, and she found that she thought very little about Marga and their past together. Eventually, she began to find herself feeling worn down, exhausted, and unhappy. She started having trouble sleeping and she felt lonely but could not bring herself to go out on dates or to social events with her couple friends.

Jane's story is a classic example of unresolved bereavement. Jane did not have the family modeling or emotional tools necessary to allow her to process her grief over losing the love of her life. She took the only path she knew: suppress the emotion and distract from the thoughts as long as possible. I often see patients in my practice who have not given themselves the opportunity to process the genuine emotions that have arisen in their lives.

Healthy Feelings

Not all, painful emotion is a result of distorted thinking. Grief was a healthy and normal emotional response to this loss. Getting angry when someone abuses you or violates your rights is also an appropriate emotional response. But many people have trouble dealing in a healthy way with these honest emotions. Anger can be as valid as any other feeling—it has no more nor less value in your repertoire of feelings. What you *do* with your anger or grief is very important, however. Unhealthy ways of dealing with emotions include long-term *suppression* (trying to ignore uncomfortable feelings), acting on impulse through activities with short- or long-term negative consequences (such as fighting or drinking excessively), and setting up situations that perpetuate your intense emotional experience (giving yourself a reason to continue to feel sad or angry). The last behavior is often referred to as a *self-fulfilling prophecy*, where you cause your worst fears to happen simply because you are so focused on them.

As you begin to tell the difference between emotions based on bad information or negative self-talk and feelings that would be appropriate based on the situation, you will find yourself feeling moments of sadness or anger. It's important to give yourself some time to feel and process these natural emotions. Some of my clients use these opportunities to begin keeping a journal of their feelings. A journal doesn't have to be fancy. It can be simply a notebook in which you vent your feelings safely, review them later for insights, and keep track of them for future discussions with a therapist or close friend. I often encourage my clients to keep track of their feelings at the same time that they are keeping track of their thinking. Keeping a document of your growth can be nice to review later to see how far you've come in your journey to better self-esteem.

Giving yourself permission to feel emotions that come bubbling up, without judging them or resorting to old ways of avoiding them, may be easier said than done. Often people who do not have much experience with processing emotions feel awkward and uncomfortable attending to their feelings. They may even feel frightened of taking the lid off of intense emotions and imagine that if they do begin to open up, the feelings will never end. Many of my clients tell me that they sense that their feelings are bottled up inside, but they fear losing control of them if they begin to look at them directly. I often introduce them to the idea of *controlled release* of feelings, in which they designate a specific time and place that they feel safe opening the door and letting the feelings come out. For example, you tell yourself that you will attend to the feelings when the time is appropriate, like after dinner at home in your study. It is important to keep this contract with yourself. Using this technique without following up is like promising a child that you will take them to the movie and then canceling later with no explanation.

Create some opportunities this week to be alone with your thoughts and feelings. Take a walk, sit in silence, or try a mindfulness meditation exercise as an opportunity for awareness.

While feelings themselves are not to be feared, the behaviors that they lead to can be dangerous or harmful. If you are not experienced at allowing yourself to feel great sadness, fear, or anger, you may have developed powerful ways to distract yourself from the overwhelming depth of your feelings. This includes using alcohol or other drugs, and harming property, yourself, or others. If you have a history of acting in potentially destructive or impulsive ways when feelings become overwhelming, or if you have a fear of this happening, don't attempt to process these feelings alone. Feelings that seem overpowering should be processed in a setting that will be safe, where you will be protected from harming yourself or someone else. A qualified psychotherapist's office is the best setting to learn to deal with powerful feelings more effectively.

Mining for Gold

In the course of this book, you are learning to have a better relationship with yourself, which includes both listening to and validating your *emotional self*. As an adult, you have the capacity to change the voice in your head from a harsh, punitive, and authoritarian one to a more reasonable, validating, and nurturing one. This means not ignoring, punishing, or avoiding the emotional side of you. Healthy parents do not punish children for the feelings they have, but help them understand their feelings by validating them, helping them see that their interpretation of an event may be inaccurate, and then teaching them how to handle feelings responsibly.

Your feeling side is rich with opportunity. Learning to listen to how you feel, to stay in touch with your response to an event that you have realistically appraised, helps you to get to know the real you. After years of being told that your feelings are unimportant or that your desires are "wrong," you now have the opportunity to let yourself have authentic reactions and then handle them effectively instead of pushing them aside or "acting out" as a distraction. The more authentic you can be with yourself, the better chance you have of learning to value who you are as a person, rather than constantly striving to be the person others wanted you to be.

By learning to listen to your feelings, and not fear or invalidate them, you can also more carefully determine the thinking patterns behind those feelings.

But sometimes, your feelings are in response to an interpretation of an event that you made, rather than the event itself. Assuming that a critical remark by a coworker about your department's performance was *really* directed at you individually, without getting other corroborating evidence of this, can lead to hurt feelings and tension in the office. Your interpretation in this situation may be colored by past experiences or core beliefs about how others see you generally rather than by an accurate perception that you were being targeted. In the next chapter, you will learn how to challenge immediate, but potentially inaccurate interpretations of events that can lead to feelings that may be unjustified but keep you feeling low. The good news is that learning to challenge automatic interpretations can have a dramatic and positive effect on your mood.

Ten

Modifying Self-Talk

WE WANT TO MAKE OURSELVES CLEAR: OUR FIRST JOB IS TO
FREE OURSELVES; THAT MEANS CLEARING OUR HEADS OF THE
GARBAGE THAT'S BEEN POURED INTO THEM.
                                        —*Carl Wittman, A Gay Manifesto*

Recognizing your self-talk is the first step in raising your self-esteem. The next step of changing it involves learning to evaluate and respond to both the *content* of what you are saying and the *type of distorted thinking* you commonly use.

TRACKING THE BEAST

Most people find that when they are beginning to try to pay attention to their thinking, it's easier to analyze an event that led to a thought and then the feeling after the fact. Learning to catch yourself at or near the exact moment that you are saying negative things to yourself feels awkward or unnatural when you first try it. Over time, and with practice, it becomes easier to catch yourself making negative or even punitive self-statements that in turn lead to feelings of anger, stress, or fear. Try to avoid saying things to yourself about the process like, "I'll never learn this technique . . . it just confirms my worthlessness!" The key is to keep practicing.

Automatic Thoughts: A Review

Once you get more comfortable with recognizing when you're having automatic thoughts, you'll be ready to implement the second step in building your self-esteem: evaluating the accuracy and usefulness of the thinking. But before you begin learning how to change them, it may be helpful to examine some key points about automatic thoughts.

1. They are usually experienced as *brief self-statements,* sometimes in the form of just a few words like, "Stupid!" or "I can't handle it!" Or for some people they are experienced as quick, negative images, perhaps from the past or of an anticipated negative consequence. Both the automatic words and images are usually experienced as having popped up spontaneously and can be so fleeting that you don't notice them unless you're trying to.
2. You experience most automatic thoughts or images *as if they were true* since they arise out of childhood, a time of your life when you did not have the capacity or freedom to question them. You also experience them like reflexes, happening so quickly when a trigger event occurs that you feel as though you have no power over them or as if they can never be changed.
3. Automatic thoughts are often extreme and include rigid rules hidden in the words *should, must,* or *have to* as in, "I must always be perfect (happy, young, clean, responsible)."
4. Because these thoughts pop up so quickly, *you often do not*

*challenge them and may forget about information that
contradicts them.* They happen so naturally that you may
forget that the automatic thinking is learned and not
something you were born with.

5. While automatic thoughts are usually specific to the
situation you are in, there are deeper levels of beliefs that
represent common themes. After you begin to recognize the
specific types of automatic thoughts that you have regularly,
it will then be important to start to recognize themes or
patterns of underlying beliefs.

INGRAINED HABITS

Not only do you have automatic thoughts and underlying beliefs
about yourself, but you also have patterns in the ways that you think.
People who tend to see the glass half full or half empty or the concept of seeing the world "through rose-colored glasses" would be a
good example of a particular style of thinking.

In the next section, we'll review the most common types of negative or distorted thinking. One of the first things you'll notice while
reading them is that you may not fit neatly into just one of these patterns, but use a different style for each unique situation. All of the
patterns tend to take a distorted view, either overemphasizing the
negative aspects of a situation or person or de-emphasizing the positive. They all are missing balance or perspective and tend to stir up
intense and negative feelings. Another common feature for all of the
styles of thinking is that they are learned and can be "unlearned"
through practice.

Polarized or Black-or-White Thinking

People who think in a polarized way tend to limit their perspectives
of a situation to two alternatives: yes or no, good or bad, right or
wrong. They often cannot see the gray areas of life. People who use
a lot of *musts*, *shoulds*, and *have-tos* fall into this category and can

become quite harsh and punitive when they don't perform perfectly in a situation or on a task.

Example: "If I make a mistake on this project, I'll be fired," likely leads to ever-increasing anxiety, which may in turn lead to the very error that you had hoped to avoid.

Filtering, Discounting the Positive, or Tunnel Vision

These people tend to see life through a *filter* or lens that distorts their perspective. A form of filtering called *selective abstraction* refers to the process of paying attention to only the negatives in your environment rather than seeing a situation more realistically or in its entirety, including the positives. This type of thinking leads to feeling overwhelmed in a situation because you are focusing only on the downside and not to the resources you may have to help you out of the situation. Filtering self-talk includes words like *horrible, awful, unbearable,* and *overwhelming.* Such words suggest that the situation has *no solution* and that you have *no control* over it. Someone with low self-esteem might, for example, interpret going out to a social gathering and not meeting anyone as a sign of being "completely alone and unlovable," forgetting the fact that she has family or friends that love her and dismissing the past relationships in which she felt loved.

Example: "Since my lover left me, I have nothing left," prompts strong feelings of loneliness and heartache.

Catastrophizing or Fortune Telling

People who *catastrophize* tend to predict (or expect) the worst possible scenario for any anticipated event, regardless of the likelihood of this actually happening. Although the worst-case scenario may be highly unlikely, a *catastrophizer* will focus on negative future outcomes, leading to a perpetual state of anxiety and worry.

Example: "Because I failed this first test, I'll probably fail the whole course," which in this situation may create enough anticipatory anxiety to actually interfere with performance on the test.

Overgeneralizing, Magnifying, and Labeling

These styles involve taking a single event and make larger conclusions about life based on this one time event. Often people who have this style of thinking believe that they absolutely *cannot* make mistakes or that they *have to* be perfect. When they do make a mistake, they feel like a failure or as though they are destined to repeat the same mistake in the future. Words that are often reflective of *overgeneralizing* include extremes like, *all or none, everybody or nobody, never or always.* People who overgeneralize tend to make global, labeling statements that are inflated and overreaching about themselves, other people, places, or aspects of their lives, often based on a single encounter. A senate majority leader's ignorant remarks about lesbians and gays leads you to think, "All Republicans are ignorant," or when you make a mistake balancing your checkbook, you think, "I'm so stupid," as if one mistake reflects your entire worth.

Magnifying happens when you elevate the importance of an event beyond its actual importance, such as forgetting something on your grocery list and then putting yourself down as a homemaker. You can also minimize the positive in a situation, downplaying the good outcomes and overemphasizing the bad with self-statements like, "Even though the boss liked my work today, it doesn't mean that I am a strong employee."

Example: "Because I was hurt in my last relationship, I'll never be able to trust anyone again," which makes you seem aloof and distant.

Musts and Shoulds

These are absolute rules for living that you routinely apply to yourself and others, sometimes without even being aware of them. When you don't follow the rules, by mistake or intentionally, it can make you irritated, angry, and judgmental. Often, the expectations you have in the form of rules are irrational or unreasonable, but because you learned them as a child, you accept them without question.

Also, since you're not always aware of these *should statements,* you respond emotionally to them automatically and don't have the opportunity then to challenge them. Having unrealistic expectations for yourself or others can make you feel constantly like a failure or irritated with the people around you when you (or they) don't meet the unreasonable standards.

Example: "Everyone should always like me," leading to chronic feelings of stress and worry.

Personalizing

This style refers to making everything always about you. One way you can personalize a situation is by always comparing yourself to others, with such self-statements as, "She's so much more intelligent than I am," or "My body is hideous compared to his." You tend to make value judgments about yourself on a continuous basis, ultimately devaluing yourself if your self-esteem is low. Another way you can personalize is by always assuming that you are the source of other people's problems or the cause of a negative event. For example, you may blame yourself for the failure of a team project even though the outcome was most likely related to a number of problems throughout the process.

Example: "That cashier is scowling because he doesn't like me," may be a completely incorrect assumption that sends you down the path of distress and self-criticism.

Other Styles

Other types of errors in thinking include *emotional reasoning,* or making decisions based solely on your feelings rather than rational consideration of all information; *mind reading,* or anticipating what you believe others are thinking about you or a situation and but failing to consider other alternatives; *blaming,* which involves finding fault in any situation and making yourself or someone else responsible, even when there is no one clearly to blame; *entitlement falla-*

cies, which involve the irrational belief that you should *always* win, get what you want, and have a positive outcome from every endeavor, leading to extreme disappointment and blame when the outcome is not in your favor; and *control fallacies*, where you expect yourself to have control over a situation that is uncontrollable, like the weather or an illness.

Many people start to change negative patterns of thinking simply by increasing their awareness of when and how they happen. Some of my patients feel excited as they become aware of negative self-talk and then go on to then recognize patterns of distorted thinking. I hope you have begun to feel a greater sense of self-awareness at this point in the book and even a greater sense of control as you begin to understand why you sometimes think or feel as you do.

Problematic Non-distorted Thinking

Sometimes, you may identify an automatic thought that doesn't appear distorted or irrational, but that leads to negative or immobilizing emotions.

By all standards, Jack was considered overweight at close to four hundred pounds. As Jack's weight increased over the years, he found himself becoming more and more depressed and socially isolated. He recognized that he clearly had developed distorted ways of thinking about himself that sabotaged his plans. For example, about three years ago he decided to try to change his life by seeing a weight loss professional and following a sensible weight loss program that included moderate exercise, a change of eating habits, and emotional support. He began the program with considerable enthusiasm and followed the plan perfectly for the first five days. On day six, however, Jack woke up to a phone call from his mother about his father's recent hospitalization with chest pain and shortness of breath. Worried about his father and living too far away to get there quickly, Jack spent the day catastrophizing about the outcome of the doctor's tests, imagining that his father was dying and even that he himself was likely going to die from obesity.

Jack completely abandoned his careful weight loss plan that day, finding himself eating more than normal as he struggled to deal with the anxiety of his father's symptoms. His thoughts not only turned to catastrophizing about himself and his father's future, but he also then began to blame himself for ruining his weight loss plan.

What really seemed to bother him the most, however, was what he saw when he looked into the mirror—*fat*. He couldn't ignore the scale that registered 389 pounds, just two pounds down from where he started five days ago. He found that all he could think at times was, "I am fat. I am not a normal size and I am slow." Then he would immediately feel sad and lonely. Jack had learned how to recognize his distorted or unreasonable thoughts and had relatively good success at challenging and replacing them with healthier thinking. But he always seemed to stumble when he looked in the mirror and began the repetitive self-statements about his size. In fact, he felt as though he deserved to be depressed when he tried to find the distortions in the mirror statements and couldn't disagree with the content. He felt that it was true that he was fat, his weight was outside of the "norm" for males his size, and he did take longer to climb stairs or walk down the hall than most people. He didn't know what to do about these powerful thoughts that elicited strong depressing and de-motivating feelings.

There are times when negative feelings such as depression or insecurity are triggered by thoughts that are true and accurate. One could argue that for gay men and lesbians, some of the frightening cultural messages we receive like, "If you are gay, you are at risk for harm," are also true since we live in a relatively homophobic society. The key in this case then is not whether the thoughts are distorted, but whether they are useful or helpful. Repetitive thoughts that may be true, but serve to undermine your confidence, enrage you for hours, and depress your mood, are also problematic and can be challenged.

Don't Just Sit There: Change It!

Several techniques have been shown to be helpful in learning to change negative self-talk. *Evaluating Your Thoughts, Developing the Nurturing Side,* the *ABCD Model,* and *Thought Stopping* are the most effective.

Evaluating Your Thoughts

Take a minute and review some of your Daily Thought Records from Chapter 1 so that you can look for patterns. For each event that triggered an emotional response, see if you can identify an automatic thought that preceded the feeling. Not only is it important to evaluate the content of the thoughts, but you must also pay attention to the tone and images associated with the thoughts. You'll recognize that at times, what people say with words and what they mean can be very different.

For example, someone can say the words, "Don't you look nice today!" but even a slight alteration in the delivery, with a scowl or smirk, radically changes this from a compliment to sarcasm. It's important to not only determine the words that you say to yourself, but also to consider the tone with which you say them. I've had some patients tell me that they actually "hear" the words or phrases they heard from parents during childhood with the same tone of voice that their parents used. If you find that the actual content seems reasonable but you still feel put down or insecure, try digging a little deeper for the sarcasm or implicit threat that you may still be using on yourself.

The next step is to identify the distorted thinking pattern. Is it an example of filtering, polarized thinking, or personalization? Or is it non-distorted, but problematic, as in the example about Jack?

Once you've identified the pattern, the next step is to come up with a healthier *alternative* to the negative thoughts, making a conscious effort to think about the event in a more reasonable or objective way, as if you were a bystander observing the event rather than experiencing it. The accompanying list of thinking distortions and ways to refute them may be helpful.

For these and the other styles of negative thinking mentioned but not covered here, the key is to recognize that each systematically distorts the way you view yourself, a situation, or another person. Counteracting your negative thoughts may take some practice and you may need to use the Daily Thought Record regularly at first to get the hang of it.

Developing the Nurturing Side

When counteracting a distorted thought, it's helpful to imagine responding to the distorted self-talk as if you were responding to a close friend in a gentle, compassionate voice. One strategy that has been helpful to some of my patients is to imagine that your counteracting voice is that of an *ideal parent*, one who is totally accepting, unconditionally loving, and nurturing. Some have even found it helpful to imagine how they might speak to a child who was feeling shamed, inadequate, frightened, or alone, since it is often easier in the beginning to feel compassion for someone else (an innocent child for example) rather than yourself. You then gradually learn to immediately recognize the negative self-talk as soon as you begin to feel uncomfortable feelings and then quickly counteract it with a new, self-nurturing voice. I will expand on the use of these techniques later in the self-nurturing chapter.

The ABCD Model

Another more structured method for understanding your self-talk is called the ABCD model and is commonly used in Cognitive Behavioral Therapy. Each letter stands for a step in recognizing and disputing negative self-talk.

A stands for the *activating event* that triggers the negative self-talk. An example might be reading the newspaper and

THINKING: DISTORTIONS AND REFUTATIONS

STYLE OF THINKING	SUGGESTIONS FOR COUNTERACTING
POLARIZED THINKING	POLARIZED THINKING
Example: If I make a mistake on this project, I'll be fired.	*Think about options along a continuum and appreciate the complexity of the situation.* *Example: I may make a mistake on this, but I'm human and sometimes things are beyond my control. My boss may be disappointed, but probably won't fire me.*
Filtering, Discounting the Positive, Tunnel Vision *Example: Ever since my lover left me, I have nothing.*	Consider the positives, the good things you are still grateful for. *Example: It hurts that she left, but I do have wonderful friends who still love me. I am not alone.*
Catastrophizing, Fortune Telling *Example: Because I failed this first test I'll probably fail the whole course.*	*Remind yourself of the realistic likelihood of your prediction actually happening.* *Example: Failing the first test doesn't mean that I can't learn this stuff. I'll just have to find a different way to study.*
Overgeneralizing *Example: Because I was hurt in my last relationship, I'll never be able to trust anyone again.*	Put the specific event into a larger context. *Example: It will take time to heal from that relationship, but I'll learn from this and eventually find someone I can trust.*
Musts and Shoulds *Example: I can't believe I didn't see that problem coming. I should always anticipate every potential problem.*	Allow mistakes to happen, be more reasonable and flexible with yourself. *Example: I'm upset about the problem, but I can't expect myself to anticipate every potential problem.*
Personalizing *Example: That cashier is scowling because he doesn't like me.*	Don't make unproven assumptions without checking them out in real life. Recognize that all humans have positive and negative qualities. *Example: That poor cashier is having a bad day.*

seeing a story about a hate crime toward a lesbian or gay
person.

B   stands for the *belief* (or negative thinking) that is triggered.
After seeing the story about the hate crime, you may think,
"The world is a dangerous place for me," or "I will probably
be attacked soon."

C   is for the *consequences* of having that thought—the feelings
you have, such as anxiety, insecurity, or rage, and the
behaviors that these feelings lead to, such as avoiding going
out, dating, or trusting someone you care about.

D   stands for the *disputing self-talk* that you use to counteract
the negative distortions. In this case, you might say
something like, "I'm generalizing a specific event (someone
who was attacked) to myself ('The world is a dangerous
place'), which is a form of personalizing, and I'm expecting
the worst ('I will probably be attacked soon.'), which is
catastrophizing." Even if it is true that violence against
lesbians and gays happens, it is not helpful to ruminate about
it. Your disputing thoughts could be, "It makes me
angry/frightened/sad to read about violence against gays, but
I can learn to protect myself and remind myself of the fact
that the vast majority of gays and lesbians are not victims of
violent attacks."

Write this model down and go through it regularly until you
reach a point of quickly identifying and disputing distorted thinking.
With practice, most people can learn to do this without writing each
step down and find that they feel a sense of emotional relief almost
immediately when they dispute the negative thinking.

Thought Stopping

One of the most basic and effective techniques for dealing with distorted or harmful thinking is called *thought stopping*. Self-talk
occurs quickly when you are in a triggering situation. The moment
you interpret the event, even if it is objectively vague or ambiguous,

and begin the self-talk, you will immediately feel an emotional reaction to the self-talk. The more negative the talk about your value, your abilities, or your potential, the more likely you have low self-esteem. This pattern of thinking can set up a self-perpetuating cycle that leads to more negative feelings and more negative self-talk. The first step in interrupting this cycle is learning to recognize the negative self-talk immediately, *while you are still in the moment.* This process involves first concentrating on the negative or unwanted thought for a short time, then quickly stopping it and clearing your mind.

Before you attempt this technique, you must first prepare yourself to respond with healthy self-talk when you need it later, after you recognize and stop the negative self-talk. Make up a list of healthy responses that are counter to the typical thought processes you have observed in yourself while reading this book. Some general, but positive self-statements that you can use might include the following: ("I am not worthless, stupid, or evil. I am worthy, intelligent, and good."

- "I do not have to be perfect. All human beings make mistakes."
- "Relax and breathe. I can cope with this situation."
- "It is not helpful to think like this. I do not deserve to treat myself like this. This self-talk is just an old habit."
- "Even if she rejected me, I know that I am lovable."
- "I have value, regardless of what anyone else says."
- "It's okay to have feelings about this situation, but I will not let the feelings trigger the old habitual self-punitive thinking."

These statements may feel forced or unnatural at first. The next chapter will address some of your core beliefs that may make saying anything positive to yourself feel artificial or faked. Construct your own list of positive self-statements that feel more comfortable to you, but try to avoid self-statements that are blatantly *untrue* such as, "I am a math genius," if you have trouble balancing your checkbook.

Try to make the list balanced, realistic, and believable. The specific words are less important than the attitude of self-acceptance and encouragement. Imagine what you would say to your own child, as a responsible parent.

Make your own list of pleasant, encouraging, or positive thoughts.

Occasionally, I find that people have difficulty saying more positive or encouraging things to themselves because they don't believe the statements. They have spent so many years repeating the same negative self-statements that they believe them to be true at their core. If this is the case for you, it will take time and practice to chip away at these core beliefs. Changing the way you think is just the beginning of building your core sense of self-esteem. The final chapters of this book delve into other ways that you can begin to change core beliefs and, essentially, your relationship with yourself.

Practice stopping the negative thinking and replacing it with something encouraging or more positive.

Interrupting the Loop

Sometimes, a downward spiral of thinking feels like it plays over and over like a broken record. This type of loop is most obvious at night, particularly when you're trying to sleep, but your mind keeps replaying a negative event from the day. A well-known behavioral treatment for stopping smoking in the 1970's suggested that smokers get caught in a downward spiral of thinking from, "A cigarette would taste great about now," to a more frantic, "If I don't get a smoke right now, I'm going to lose it!" and the anxiety that these thoughts create pushes them into taking a puff. The smoker in this program learned to interrupt the craving for a cigarette (and the sense of urgency created by the spiraling thoughts) by wearing a rubber band around his wrist and snapping it when necessary. The pain from the "snap" of the rubber band distracted the smoker from this spiral, allowing him to substitute more anti-craving messages like, "A cigarette would be nice, but I won't die if I don't get one." This technique has been used in many other behaviorally oriented therapies from dieting programs to the treatment of phobias.

It is not necessary to use physical force to interrupt the downward cycle of negative self-talk. You may be able to simply say to yourself "Stop!" vigorously enough to interrupt your automatic thinking spiral. Others have found that at times, the thinking pattern feels so strong that they have to say it out loud, yell it, or even clap their hands or snap their fingers. I recommend that you practice thought stopping when you are alone until you can reliably interrupt the process either by thinking it to yourself or using some silent reminder like clenching your fist or tapping your forehead (something less likely to draw attention to yourself in public).

If you find that your frustration builds with repeated unpleasant thoughts and images, you can create an angry "talk back" statement as a form of combating the negative self-talk. For example,

- "Stop the blaming and catastrophizing!"
- "This negative garbage is not helping!"
- "These old messages are wrong and unfair!"
- "Enough is enough!"

Come up with your own angry rebuttal statements. You can be as colorful with your language as necessary. Just remember that you are rebutting the old, negative messages, not speaking to yourself in a self-punitive way.

Write these angry rebuttals down in your journal or on a blank piece of paper and keep it with your other lists.

After you have interrupted your undesired thoughts, you're ready to insert the more positive self-talk. You also can substitute pleasant scenes at this point, including your favorite and most relaxing images. Think of the most relaxing place you've ever been . . . a beach . . . beside a mountain lake . . . your grandmother's house when you were a child. Or, if you can't think of a specific spot, use your imagination to create the perfect, relaxing and safe spot for you. The more vivid you can make your image, recalling the sights, sounds, smells, and tastes of your place, the better able you will be to break the negative thinking spiral.

If the negative thoughts come back within thirty seconds, keep saying "Stop!" to yourself, counteracting the negative thinking and substituting the same or another pleasant scene. Practice pleasant imagery at other times, especially when you're not upset, so that you can be more prepared to use it to interrupt negative thinking.

Take a moment and describe a scene now for yourself that makes you feel relaxed and comfortable.

Make sure you include as many of your senses as you can. What are the sights you can see from where you are? Is there a pleasant scent in the air? Can you feel the sun on your skin or a cool, comfortable breeze? Do you hear birds or ocean waves in the background?

Beaches are common relaxing scenes for many people. If this is the case for you, you would want to imagine the feel of the warm sand, the sounds of the tide, the smell of the ocean air, and maybe even the taste of salt as you swim or float in the water. In your journal or on a piece of paper, write down your own relaxing scene. Be sure to include the location, sights, sounds, smells, and tastes. It might be helpful to use a relaxation CD or music as a form of distraction when those thoughts are just too intense or repetitive.

We will discuss the use of imagery and visualization for building self-esteem in more detail later in the book. For more information about thought stopping and other cognitive-behavioral techniques, I highly recommend the book *Thoughts & Feelings: Taking Control of Your Moods and Your Life* by McKay, Davis, and Fanning.

At this point, it might also be helpful for you to revisit the Daily Thought Record from Chapter 1 and add two new columns on the right side of the form. After the "Automatic Thoughts" column, make a column with the heading "Counteracting Arguments." This column will be where you record an adaptive, *alternate* way of thinking that will help reduce the negative feelings. To help with this column, ask yourself the following questions adapted from the book *Cognitive Therapy: Basics and Beyond* by Judith Beck:

1. What evidence do I have that this thought is true or will happen?
2. Are there other ways to think about this situation or explain it?
3. What is the worst (and best) thing that could happen in this situation? Will I live through it? What is the most likely, realistic outcome?
4. How could changing my thinking affect this situation or my reaction?
5. What should I do about the situation that will help me cope?
6. If my friend was in this situation and had this thought, what advice would I give him or her?

After you have come up with a counteracting argument to the irrational or maladaptive thought, make another heading beside it to the right and call it the "Results" column. Here, you will record the effect of changing your thinking on your feelings and behavior. See the revised Daily Thought Record for an example.

REVISED DAILY THOUGHT RECORD

TIME/DAY/DATE	EVENT	AUTOMATIC	FEELINGS THOUGHTS	COUNTERACTING THOUGHTS	RESULTS
5:02 pm. Monday 7/15	Copy Store(1) closed.	(1) "What if I get fired?"	Fear, anxiety.	This is a mistake that anyone could make. I'll find a store that's open later or go first thing in the morning.	Less anxiety
		(2) "I'm so incompetent."	Despair, sadness.	This has nothing to do with my competence. I could not control the traffic	Less sad, more reasonable thinking. traffic.

RESPONDING TO CRAPPY MESSAGES YOU HEAR IN THE MEDIA

It's currently the rage in American politics to use social issues as political wedges between people. Nowhere was this more evident than in the presidential election of 2004. George W. Bush, bogged down with questions about the war in Iraq and a struggling economy, seemed destined for only one term in office when his fortunes were changed by shifting the debate to "saving marriage" by advancing an anti-gay marriage agenda. Other politicians at all levels, both before and since this election, have discovered that using complex social issues to divide the electorate and "fire up the base" can be a successful strategy for the moment in the U.S. It is not unusual these days to wake up to headlines proclaiming the "sanctity of heterosexual marriage," or the looming threat to society of allowing two same sex adults to make a spiritual commitment to each other.

If you find yourself responding emotionally to public statements made by people in the media such as politicians, religious figures, and others, take a few moments to do the following:

- *Consider the source.* Does this person represent a radical constituency? If the speaker is speaking as a representative of a larger organization, is this person speaking from his or her own personal biases rather than as a true representative of the views of the entire membership of his or her total organization?
- *Consider the speaker's motivation.* What does the speaker have to gain, personally or politically, from making the statement? If the person is speaking from a personal standpoint, did she have a negative interaction with a lesbian or gay person in the past? Is he struggling with his own sexual identity issues and is threatened by gay men or lesbians who are out? Is he or she responding to social stereotypes and misinformation? Does the speaker get paid to make false and inflammatory statements by the media or an organization? If

the speaker does represent the views of a larger organization, is this a way to divide or unite political constituencies? Is this a calculated "hot button" statement meant to stimulate fund-raising based on fear-mongering?

- Ask yourself if the statements are distorted. Do statements by such an individual make them true just because he or she said it? Could the person be using unscientific or unproven data? Is the speaker manipulating or misinterpreting the results of a legitimate study? Is he egocentric in his or her approach to interpretation of the Bible, Torah, Koran, or other religious materials? Or does she take the material out of context?

- *Consider whether the media has biased the story by selecting controversial people to discuss the issue.* Did the producers of the show seek out a public figure who would make inflammatory remarks to boost ratings? Did they create an oppositional tone between two conflicting perspectives instead of including a full range of perspectives? Are you allowing yourself to be manipulated by the media for their own gain?

These are questions that may be helpful in getting yourself to de-escalate your feelings. It may be the case that the opinions of the speaker are distorted in the way that your own thinking may be at times. Hearing someone else say negative things about you can be enough to trigger the negative thought spiral that we discussed earlier. It would then be appropriate for you to begin the process of stopping the negative thoughts you are having and begin substituting healthier ones.

I'M MAD AS HELL AND I'M NOT GOING TO TAKE IT ANYMORE

I also believe that on a larger level, building self-esteem includes taking action. Political activism can take many different forms, including staging a "kiss in" protest with ACT UP; writing letters to your congressperson, the editor of your local paper, or the producers of a show with unbalanced perspectives; or even refusing to do business with companies that discriminate against lesbians or gay men. Other forms of social action include helping friends and family understand gay and lesbian issues more completely, marching in a pride parade, calling your cable company to complain about programming that is offensive to you, and doing business with lesbian/gay-owned or gay-friendly companies. There are many levels of action with which most people can be comfortable no matter how bold or timid they feel. Everyone can turn off the television or change the channel when a zealot or intolerant viewpoint is given airtime and everyone can learn to turn off the residual effects of hearing such talk.

You can't change the world overnight, but you can teach yourself to feel less powerless in a complex and sometimes overwhelming world. As you change the way you think and take action to change the world when you can, you will find a growing sense of personal power and greater self-esteem.

Recommended Audio

For help with distraction from repetitive stressful thinking, I created the audio CDs, *Drifting Downstream: Guided Relaxation for Stress Reduction* and *Drifting into Sleep: A Step by Step Guide to Falling Asleep*, available through amazon.com and iTunes.

ELEVEN

Self-Nurturing and Forgiveness

"THERE, THERE LUCILLE," SAID LUCILLE HERE. I TRIED REMEM-
BERING WHAT WORDS MY MOTHER USED WHEN I WAS SICK. I
NEEDED ME A NICE SOOTHING NICKNAME TO GOO-GOO AT MYSELF.
WHO ELSE WOULD?
    —*Alan Gurganus, Oldest Living Confederate Widow Tells All*

Overcoming years of ignoring your true feelings will take time and patience. You may never *completely* erase all traces of negative core beliefs learned as a child. But you can begin to spend less time suppressing feelings, and harshly judging yourself, and more time feeling the same compassion for yourself that you would show most other human beings. Imagine a world with less anger and judgment.

Encouraging Care

The word *nurturing* refers to the act of caring, protecting, and encouraging, and is used most often to describe the loving way good parents interact with their children. Most of us have an understanding of what it means to nurture someone or something, even if you were not well nurtured as a kid. Part of the journey towards building a healthy sense of self-esteem requires that you begin to *treat yourself with respect and encouragement regularly.*

Important keys to self-nurturing include learning to revise old negative core beliefs, learning to listen to and validate your feelings, reconstructing a more balanced picture of yourself (with both positives and negatives instead of just the negatives), protecting yourself from harm or abuse by constructing healthy boundaries and making smart choices, and appropriately asking for what you want and need.

Changing Your Core and Conditional Beliefs

A common core belief for lesbian and gay people with low self-esteem is that "Gay and lesbian people are morally inferior to straight people." This belief is reinforced in many ways, through some religions who preach that anything gay is evil, the culture we live in that tells us we are not worthy of "marriage," and families who reject anyone that doesn't conform.

Aside from negative core beliefs about your sexual orientation, you may also have core beliefs that are harsh and critical about your value as a human being. Some of these core beliefs may make you feel like you are "bad, evil, unworthy of love, or likely to be rejected."

A helpful first step is to articulate your core beliefs and then intentionally create more objective, realistic, and nurturing beliefs as goals.

The following exercise can help you be prepared to deal with your thoughts and feelings when you recognize a core belief that might be influencing your thoughts or behaviors.

REVISING YOUR CORE BELIEFS

OLD CORE BELIEF	REVISED CORE BELIEF
I am inferior to others because I am gay. I must always be perfect to be accepted.	Gay people are humans and thus equal to all others. No one is perfect.
I am evil/sinful/bad because I am lesbian, gay.	Sexual orientation is not a moral issue. Mutually consensual sexual and emotional relationships between adults are my right and choice.
I am unworthy of love/joy/peace.	All human beings have worth, even if we don't understand the specifics (i.e., how you fit in).
I am stupid.	I have been smart enough to survive, learn, and change.
I am helpless.	I am not helpless. I am an adult with a brain and supportive friends.

In your journal, try writing down some of your own *core beliefs* and then some revised, healthier ones. The same strategy will also be helpful for changing the conditional beliefs, or rules that you live by, that may be extreme, irrational, or maladaptive.

Try listing some of the *rules that you make yourself live by* and rewriting them to make them less extreme. Make a column on the

THE RULES YOU LIVE BY

OLD RULE	NEW RULE
I must always be slim/buffed/on a strict diet.	I will try to stay healthy and in shape, but gaining a few pounds here and there is normal.
If people make a mistake with me in a relationship, they are to be avoided.	Making mistakes is completely human. I will communicate how I feel and work through the conflict.

left side that you call "Old Rules" and a column on the right that you call "New Rules." For each old rule on the left, write a new, more reasonable rule on the right.

Occasionally, I find that even when my patients do the exercises faithfully, and they feel significant reduction in anxiety, insecurity, anger, and despair, it does not always mean that they experience an increase in happiness, peace, joy, and satisfaction with their lives. Beyond challenging the dysfunctional thinking, you must develop an *emotional connection* with yourself by developing a sense of self-nurturing.

Great spiritual belief systems have arisen from the need to understand our place in the universe—to understand our meaning and purpose. Ideally, you would have been raised to believe that you were highly valued from the moment you were born, simply because you existed. Yet, many of us grew up with the distinct impression that what we felt, thought, or wanted didn't matter and therefore, we didn't matter.

Truth be told, your existence affected every decision that your parents made, from the moment of your conception. The place you hold in the universe is important, even if you do not yet understand why. The next chapter is designed to help you with finding your own answers to these questions. Each person's search for meaning is unique and holds the keys to developing a more nurturing relationship with yourself.

SELF-NURTURING: BEYOND THE COGNITIVE

Imagine that dealing with your self-talk is like living in a barracks with a loudspeaker blaring things like "You're stupid!" "You'll never succeed!" "You're worthless!" every time you made a mistake. Imagine the anxiety, irritability, and ultimately despair you would feel if you never heard a word of encouragement when you accomplished something. You would eventually learn to expect nothing from yourself and see yourself as worthless and inferior. You would also likely begin to feel as though you could not make important decisions without guidance. You might become passive, trying to avoid making mistakes that would lead to more verbal abuse.

Consider the overall quality of your self-talk and your typical emotional responses to it. Is the self-talk something you would say to another person? In most cases where the self-talk is predominantly negative, people would almost never want to say to someone else what they say to themselves. For example, you might say to yourself, "You deserve to be punished because you are so lazy," in an attempt to motivate yourself to do something you are not looking forward to. However, most people would be reluctant to say those words to a stranger, out of a sense of respect and propriety. You would probably choose to motivate someone in a more generous way with, for example, "I know you must be tired of doing this work, but there's only an hour left and I know you can get through it."

The second statement is obviously less punitive and more encouraging. Imagine now that you live in a barracks where there is a loudspeaker that shouts words of encouragement when you make a mistake or you are tired—"That's okay, everyone makes mistakes! You'll get it eventually," or "Keep trying. I know you can figure it out." This voice might also comment on things you have done well—"That was great! Keep up the good work!" and/or "You're a model employee!"

Obviously, it's not a simple task to move from a negative, de-motivating basic stance to an encouraging, nurturing one. Ask yourself: "Do I deserve compassion?" The correct answer is "yes," regardless of what your feelings tell you. *Everyone deserves compassion*, no matter who you are, the color of your skin, the amount of money you have, the religion you follow, your past behaviors, or the *gender of the person you love*. Only through compassion can people trust enough to make changes.

But some of you still say things like, "How can I feel compassion toward a murderer or child molester? Don't they deserve to be punished? Aren't they evil?" All good questions with a simple answer: All people have value and deserve compassion; it's *behavior* that's problematic. Blaming an addict, condemning a criminal, judging another person's value, all fall into the punitive camp that creates a hierarchy of human beings. And once you buy into the belief that some humans are "better" than others, it's a short jaunt to the perilous path of making judgments about people's worth based on factors that have no bearing on anything—the shape of their eyes ... the sophistication of the words they use ... the money in their bank account.

Some prominent leaders think they are being compassionate when they draw a similar distinction between being lesbian or gay and the act of having sex with another person. You've probably heard the saying, "Love the sinner and hate the sin," used by some right-wing leaders in this country. This distinction is a deception in many ways, implying that adult consensual sexual activity is equal to murder or rape and that hating a person's behavior is somehow not a part of that person. And it presumes that the hater is qualified somehow to judge the actions of another person. Political types, always sensitive to possible political fallout, often tone down that rhetoric a bit into, "Love the sinner, but their acts are an illness (or addiction) that must be treated," which appears superficially "conservative but compassionate."

Parallels between *adult, consensual sex* and *harming* another person are totally inappropriate. Many religious and political figures continue to view gay and lesbian people from outdated and disproved models, namely that homosexuality is an "illness" or a "sin."

Say to yourself, "I am gay. I have value. I am healthy."

These words are the foundation of developing self-compassion, self-encouragement, and self-esteem. They will help you fight the negative messages that are all around you in the media, the workplace, and sometimes in your family. Sometimes, this means confronting the lawmakers about their attempts to deprive you of your civil liberties. On a deeper level, it's important to understand your absolute right to love, acceptance, and freedom. The following is a list of core principles to use as a guide for developing your own beliefs.

The Seven Queer Truths

1. You are not responsible for your family's ignorance or mistakes. They bear at least some responsibility for their own ignorance and misjudgments even if they did not intend harm.

2. Society is the problem, not your sexuality.
3. There are many spiritual paths and religious systems, only some of which are anti-gay and homophobic. There are plenty of other belief systems that are gay-affirmative. No one has a monopoly on God or spirituality.
4. You deserve (and are worthy of) love, acceptance, and respect exactly as you are. Your feelings and opinions are valid and deserve a chance to be considered regardless of what others want.
5. You are perfect in your imperfection. No one is perfect and, therefore, when you make mistakes, you are enjoying a common bond with all other humans.
6. You have inherent worth simply because you were born. Your value does not come from what you accomplish or who you please. You hold a place in the world for a reason, even if you haven't figured out exactly what that reason is.
7. You can give yourself permission to let go of the past. You have the capacity to adhere to higher values such as forgiving others even when they do not seek it. Forgiving yourself for mistakes you have made is essential to your future growth.

Forgiving and Moving On

If you have a lot of guilt and remorse for past behaviors, it's time to feel the regret and begin to forgive yourself. You have likely paid your debt for behaviors that you regret and it is now time to begin a new relationship with yourself; a more compassionate one. If you don't believe your debt is paid, consider constructive ways to give back to your community or the people you may have hurt along the way. You may consider attempting to repair old relationships if the people you harmed are willing. Although direct apologies can be healing, it's not always possible to do so for several reasons. First, the people from your past may be unable or unwilling to accept your apology. Second, if they are particularly uninterested in repairing the relationship, they may take the opportunity to continue the cycle of abuse rather than opt for healing. Third, if you feel you cannot control yourself should they take the opportunity to mock you or "push your buttons," it is better to protect yourself and them by foregoing such an interaction.

If you cannot heal the old wounds in a relationship directly because of the other person's unwillingness or instability or your fear of your own reactions, you may find healing through alternative rituals. Here are some suggestions:

Letter Writing Ritual

Write a letter to the person who hurt you or whom you have hurt. Write the letter with the expectation that you will *not* send it so that you can express yourself more freely. Explain exactly how you believe you hurt them and how they may have hurt you. Ask this person to forgive the hurtful behaviors and make an effort do the same. Express why the person is important to you and why you would like to have the connection repaired. Let yourself feel the feelings that come up— anger, grief, or fear—and put all of this down in the letter. When you have finished, put the letter aside for a day or two to let your feelings subside. Then choose a time and place to destroy the letter and let go of the issues and feelings you've written about. Tear it up, burn it in a fireplace, or find another creative way of disposing of it. As you see it disappear, allow yourself to put the unsettled issue to rest.

Empty Chair Technique

Another way to heal old wounds is to use the *empty chair technique*. This is a simple but powerful way for you to have a "conversation" with someone (or even something) when the other participant in the discussion is not physically present. Essentially, to begin a healing conversation, you need to sit across from an empty chair, imagining that the person with whom you would like to have a dialogue is sitting in the empty chair. The advantage of this method is that you can imagine the person under your complete control, forced to listen to you and to let you finish your thoughts.

In this scenario, you might explain to the person in everyday language what the problems were between the two of you, how you were hurt by the person, and what led to your lashing out or running away. You might then switch to the other chair and become the person to whom you are speaking. What might this person say in response? Remember that you have the power in this exercise to have the person respond appropriately, rather than defensively or with hurtful rage. This is your opportunity to have the kind of dialogue you have always wanted to have with the person who has hurt you, or whom you have hurt. If you are trying to let go of your own hurtful behavior, it is your opportunity to apologize and ask for forgiveness. If the person hurt you, it is your chance to take the high road and make peace.

If you find that you cannot forgive someone else, particularly when that person is not actually in dialogue with you, you may need more time to heal. It is especially important then that you learn how to self-nurture now so that you can provide an environment for yourself that encourages healing. Constructing a life for yourself that is based on support and nurturing will give you the strength you need to move beyond painful episodes from the past.

The empty chair technique has been used in many other ways that can be helpful in your daily life. For example, you can practice conversations you might have with someone in your life now. You also can use this technique to begin a dialogue with parts of yourself that seem anxious, afraid, or confused. I will discuss this type of internal dialogue a little later in this chapter.

If you do choose to attempt peacemaking with family or friends, and you feel psychologically ready to do so, here are a few pointers:

- Make sure that you will be safe from the other person's feelings as well as your own. Choose a public place or take someone with you if you have a real fear of the other person's response. Your safety is paramount.
- Don't apologize for being lesbian or gay. Only apologize for your behaviors that were unnecessarily hurtful.
- Don't expect them to apologize to you. Sometimes those

same people may have been hurtful to you but are not ready
to admit their own responsibility.

- Be prepared to leave if old tensions start to brew. You must
  be in control of yourself and be prepared to protect yourself
  by leaving.
- Understand that by making the first move, you have made
  restitution regardless of the outcome.

If you find that you need more time with the issue of forgiving
yourself, I recommend that you read *The Self-Forgiveness Handbook*
by Thom Rutledge.

What Self-Nurturing Is and Is Not

Some people believe that they are great "self-nurturers" because
they treat themselves to dessert occasionally or they get a massage
once a month. While those behaviors can be a part of learning to
self-nurture, just doing things that are pleasurable does not constitute a self-nurturing attitude. Self-nurturing means providing yourself with an environment that encourages your health and growth
physically, emotionally, cognitively, and spiritually. Getting an extra
dessert now and then is physically rewarding. Unfortunately, having
an extra dessert regularly as a form of self-reward can be damaging
in the long run as you gain weight, watch your cholesterol rise, and
learn to substitute sugar for emotional intimacy.

Self-nurturing is not just about rewarding yourself for a job well
done or a task accomplished on time. It is also not just rewarding
yourself with immediate gratification as with desserts, alcohol, drugs,
or other quick fixes. Self-nurturing is about doing the right thing for
yourself in the big picture. A short-term hedonist is someone who
lives for the moment, grabbing every ounce of pleasure she or he can.
Too much immediate gratification, however, can lead to problems
down the road that can make life more miserable. It is much more
rational, and self-nurturing, to consider the long-term consequences
of immediate gratification and to attempt to care for your body, mind,

and spirit in ways that will keep you feeling good over time. Think about the attitude you might adopt if you were caring for a child. Would you feed the child candy every day? Or would you teach the child to have a balanced diet and make healthy choices?

Think about your life priorities.

What would you say is the most important thing in your life? Take a look at the following list and rank the items by placing a number from 1 to 10 (with 1 being the most important and 10 being the least important) by each. I've added two "Other" categories for any issues I may have omitted that are important to you. Then take a minute and roughly estimate what percentage of time you spend per week on each of these (your total should equal 100 percent).

When you look at this list, are there any discrepancies between

LIFE PRIORITIES

Priority	Rank	% of Time
Job/Career/Money (time spent working, thinking about work, paying bills, etc.)	☐	☐
Home (cleaning, decorating, remodeling, gardening, etc.)	☐	☐
Taking care of others	☐	☐
Spirituality (meditation, prayer, religion)	☐	☐
Health (exercise, medical, dental)	☐	☐
Sex	☐	☐
Education/Growth (not job related)	☐	☐
Building relationships (partner, friends, family)	☐	☐
Entertainment (TV, movies, recreation)	☐	☐
Other	☐	☐
Other	☐	☐

the amounts of time you spend in an activity and where it falls on your list of priorities? Many people find that what they would *like* to be emphasizing in their lives and what they actually *are* doing are out of sync. If you have low self-esteem, you often place the needs of others before your own, feeling as though you don't deserve special attention or somehow have to make yourself indispensable to others in order to have value.

Building good self-esteem will involve attempting to redistribute your energy in ways that place your personal needs higher on the list of priorities. Ultimately, you are in the best position to listen to what you need emotionally, physically, and spiritually and then become your own best caretaker. Imagine how much more enjoyable life would be if you felt attended to, acknowledged, and nurtured. I encourage you to begin placing yourself higher on your list of priorities and to spend more time in self-care activities. If necessary, add another column and redo your rankings or percentages to reflect your long-term goals.

Learning to Nourish the Self

Let's now get even more specific about how to live day to day in a more self-nurturing way. The goal is to develop an attitude toward yourself that is *encouraging* rather than discouraging, *forgiving* rather than condemning, and *respectful* instead of belittling. You have learned strategies for changing your attitude and monitoring your thoughts and feelings. What about putting these strategies into day-to-day practice?

In this section, I will make some specific suggestions about living a more self-nurturing life from three perspectives: cognitively, emotionally, and behaviorally.

Cognitive Guidelines for Every Day

Once you have mastered the techniques in Chapter 10 and can more easily recognize negative, distorted, or harmful thinking, your cognitive daily living goals are simple.

1. When you find yourself feeling insecure, sad, angry, or confused, search your thoughts for self-talk that is discouraging, frightening, or otherwise irrational.
2. Evaluate the self-talk for accuracy or usefulness and begin using thoughts that dispute this type of thinking. For example, "Where's the proof that this thought will actually happen?"
3. If you find that negative thoughts are repeating and creating a negative spiral, use thought stopping techniques followed by pleasant imagery.
4. Think about what core beliefs are being activated by the situation and if the belief is negative, try to respond with a revised, more accurate core belief. For example, "I am a responsible adult" in response to "I am an irresponsible child." (You can do this one later when you have time for a break if you are trying to finish a task.)
5. When you are disputing a negative thought, remind yourself that you are your own best guardian or the parent you always wanted. Your new voice (or self-talk) is respectful of you, is wise and understanding, has endless patience, and believes in your absolute value to the world.

Emotional Nourishment

Many lesbian and gay people have spent years being told what they can and cannot feel and then teaching themselves how to disregard feelings that are "unacceptable." Men are taught that they can't be emotionally sensitive and also be masculine, while women are taught that showing too much strength makes them unfeminine. Years of these types of messages make a very simple process seem quite complicated. It no longer surprises me when patients come to see me who are confused by their feelings, alienated from themselves emotionally, and convinced that they cannot handle their feelings directly.

To give yourself emotional nourishment, you must learn to work your way through all of these negative and distorted messages about emotions. Feelings are a natural part of every human being. You have them for a reason—to guide you in your everyday life. They are like reflexes in response to your brain's interpretation of an event. Feelings happen automatically in reaction to a perception. For example, you do not need to tell yourself to feel frightened when you hear a strange noise late at night that awakens you from sleep. Your brain picks up a sensation from your ears and then takes the available data (darkness, the fact that you are supposed to be alone in the house), and your emotions immediately responded appropriately with fear. The fear then motivated you to get up quickly (and quietly) and check your surroundings. It would've been strange to have been awakened, perceived danger, and then felt sad. When your perception of an event is distorted, you will have the response that is appropriate for the perception, but it is based on inaccurate data. When you learn to correct your self-perception or interpretation of an event, the emotion that follows will more accurately reflect the situation you are in.

As a lesbian or gay child, you were told from many sources that your feelings and attractions were inappropriate or just plain wrong. You then grew up not always knowing when to trust certain feelings. This self-doubt translates into insecurity and thereby affects self-esteem.

Chances are, if you learned not to trust yourself emotionally, you also will have a difficult time allowing yourself to feel more positive feelings like happiness, joy, excitement, and calm. If you do have fleeting moments of happiness, you may find that you talk yourself out of feeling good, as if you were waiting for the other shoe to drop. Self-nurturing involves not only doing things for yourself that make you feel good feelings, but it also means making room for you to have all of your feelings.

There are several ways to begin allowing yourself to have feelings more directly. First, if you are particularly concerned about how to begin the process—or if you fear your feelings—you may want to consider getting into counseling. A good psychotherapist can help you learn to process feelings in a healthy way. You may need some instruction in how to process feelings such as anger and grief if your family did not handle these feelings well. Chapter 13 is all about how to find a good psychotherapist.

STARTING THE EMOTIONAL JOURNEY

I highly recommend keeping a daily journal of your feelings. The goal of the journal is not necessarily to track specific events of the day but to keep track of what you felt at various points during the day and what you feel as you write. Allow yourself the freedom to go off on tangents, keep track of dreams (and the feelings in them), and observe unusual feelings that seemed to pop up out of nowhere. Try not to judge yourself for the feelings, but accept them as is. Later you can go back and evaluate whether the feelings were in reaction to distorted thinking or a misinterpretation on your part. There are structured forms of journals available that may provide you with more direction, but if you have no trouble writing down your feelings, a plain spiral notebook will do. One client who had spent years suppressing her feelings began journaling about three years ago and is now up to over a dozen volumes!

Another excellent way of learning about feelings is to try to talk to someone you trust with whom you can share your feelings. A partner might be a good choice. A supportive family member or friend might also be willing to listen and give you some validation. It's important that this person remain non-judgmental and supportive of your feelings. She can give feedback about your perceptions that led to the feelings when you are ready, but she's not allowed to make judgments about the feelings themselves. Take your time. Acknowledge to yourself, and your listener, that this is a new, and sometimes scary experience. Begin by talking about something you know you've been avoiding such as old anger, hurts, fears. Stop when you need a break and ask for a hug or to be held.

Again, the goal of getting to know your feelings is so that you can begin to use them as a guide, a form of *intuition*. You can think of your feelings as tools that you have been hesitant to use in the past and were actually warned away from. You are an adult now and can train yourself to use your feelings confidently and proudly. You can start today by not judging yourself when you have feelings, but by listening to them, honoring them, and using them to help you decide what to do in any given situation. And if this is too hard to tackle alone, don't hesitate to seek professional help.

Giving Yourself Permission

Feeling affection for yourself when you need it might sound like a strange concept, especially if you feel at some deeper level that you don't deserve affection. The empty chair technique, which I described earlier in the chapter, could be of some value here. If you are having a difficult time feeling self-compassion or self-nurturing but you know you need it, imagine that a child about six or seven years old, is sitting in the empty chair, feeling the way you are currently feeling—perhaps alone, scared, and confused. What are your natural impulses? Would you sit there and let the child cry? Would you tell her or him to shut up?

Hopefully, you would be able to find some compassion for the child and would try to say something soothing like, "You'll be okay," or "I'll protect you." Some of my clients have learned to practice a form of visualization in which they imagine taking the child onto their laps and hugging or soothing them. In the beginning, you may need to imagine the child as a neighbor or stranger, but eventually, as you become more self-compassionate, you can imagine the child as the emotional part of yourself or the child version of you who needed hugging and unconditional love when you were growing up. Many of us have no problem being self-critical or harsh when we make mistakes. People with good self-esteem however have a healthy, compassionate voice that helps them through the hard times. It's never too late to create this nurturing self.

GETTING TO KNOW YOU

It's important to develop an appreciation for your good qualities, strengths, and efforts. Make a list of your best qualities. Add to that list any qualities you have received recognition for by family members, peers, friends, employers, or teachers. The list can include anything from intelligence to personality characteristics (such as kindness, calming, trustworthiness, caring, and so on) to special abilities and talents (for example, musical or artistic skill, an ability to put people at ease, or to listen attentively). Allow yourself to enjoy any compliments or praise you've received recently or in the past and dispute any negative thinking or self-talk that won't allow you to hear the positive feedback. If you've had difficulty seeing yourself as having any positive attributes in the past, try to construct an image of yourself now that is more balanced. You might want to include the things you like and the qualities about yourself you hope to change. Put this list in your journal or on a piece of paper. Here are the categories you should include: Things I Am Good At, Personal Characteristics I Have Been Complimented For, Abilities or Talents I Have, Accomplishments I'm Proud Of, and Evidence That I'm Liked or Valued.

Easy Self-Nurturing Activities

Aside from the emotional work, there are behavioral ways to nurture yourself. Finding activities that bring you pleasure and reward you when you have worked hard or withstood something difficult to bear are a part of what it means to take care of you. I've certainly indulged in a gift to myself here or there, like saving up for a professional massage occasionally when I feel tired, or treating myself to a good meal when I've had a busy week of quick, but not-so-nutritious meals. Treat yourself as you would a friend who deserved or needed cheering up.

The important thing to remember is to find a range of things that you can use to treat yourself for a job well done, or even when you wake up feeling irritable or lonely. Behavioral rewards can include treats like special meals, desserts, professional massages, and vacations. But they can also include things that don't cost money like a slow walk through the park, intimate time with a partner or close friend, playing with a pet, taking a hot bath, meditating or praying, scheduling time to relax, and not work on a project or job task, or even listening to your favorite music or reading a great book. Try not to rely too much on rewards that may have other long-term negative consequences, like too many fattening pieces of pie or an excessive amount of alcohol. If you can only think of a few ways to reward yourself, you may need to do some exploration to find new ways to treat yourself. One particularly creative person I know took herself to the largest music store in San Francisco to try to discover more about her music preferences. She, in fact, spent the afternoon there at each of the store's numerous listening stations until she found new music that she enjoyed. This is the kind of homework assignment we could all use!

Protecting the Self

Anyone who nurtures also protects. Learning to protect yourself from harm is also a type of self-nurturing. Setting firm limits in relationships is an important skill that you may or may not have learned as a child. If your self-esteem is low, your rights were likely not always respected when you were growing up. In some cases, parents who have low self-esteem themselves often don't have a concept of what constitutes a healthy boundary as described in Chapter 2. As an adult, it's important that you learn to construct healthy boundaries to keep yourself from being hurt needlessly. Consider the figure on the next page, which represents a person with healthy boundaries.

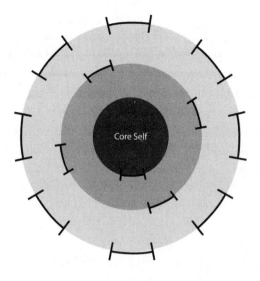

Figure 2.

The inner circle of the diagram represents the *core self* where you are most vulnerable. This is the place where you can most easily share intimacy. Around this circle is a strong fence with only one door, one entrance. A person with strong boundaries knows how to keep the door closed as a form of protection against intruders, only allowing the most trustworthy partner or family member in. The entrance standards to the innermost circle are high. Anyone allowed to enter into this level must have shown you enough evidence that they will not use information you share against you.

A second, larger fence around the first one has a few more doors. The entrance standards are less stringent, but people who get to enter here have shown you that they have an interest in being close to you and that they do not intend to hurt or manipulate you. You are still selective, but they have to earn your trust to learn more about you.

Finally, the largest circle represents the outermost boundary, with many gates. People you meet whom you find interesting but have little history with, or friends you only socialize with in groups, usually enter here. Outside the largest fence are the strangers, acquaintances that make you a little nervous, and people who you know have the potential to hurt you. If you build your boundaries effectively, you have some control over who enters at each of the outer levels and complete control over whom you choose to be emotionally intimate with or vulnerable to at the innermost level. As you grow to understand and appreciate yourself more, you will find that it becomes easier to keep your boundaries strong without locking all the doors to the healthy people in your life who provide a sense of love and belonging.

Becoming Assertive

One way of protecting your boundaries is by learning to speak up for yourself when you feel someone is taking advantage of you. Sometimes in families with dysfunctional systems, self-protection takes the form of acting aggressively or passive-aggressively. *Assertiveness*, an appropriate alternative to any forms of aggression, can be learned just like other skills you may not have been exposed to before. The keys to learning assertive behavior include learning how to stand up for yourself and getting what you want without feeling guilty, acting and communicating with reason instead of emotion, and avoiding feeling resentment that turns into disparaging self-talk when your rights are violated. If you'd like to read about becoming more assertive, I recommend the classic book *Your Perfect Right: A Guide to Assertive Living* by Robert Alberti and Michael Emmons.

You have the power to choose whether you will continue the negative self-talk you likely learned when you were a child or whether you will begin to transform your relationship with you to one of self-compassion and affection. It's my hope that through the skills you learn in this book, you will see the choices more clearly and choose the latter.

Twelve

Spirituality

LOVE THY NEIGHBOR AS THYSELF.
—*Leviticus 19:18*

Given the huge amount of damage done to lesbians and gays over the years by people representing organized religions, it is not surprising that many have severed their ties to religion and become suspicious of religious people. People who have felt condemned, ostracized, or abused in the name of God often become skeptical about religious groups who purport to be gay-friendly, gay-tolerant, or even gay-centered. Even if you weren't raised in a religious family, you probably understood the major religions' positions on sex from peers, school, and the media. Unfortunately, because of the painful association you may have had with organized religion, you may have also actively avoided cultivating a personal sense of spirituality.

"Why is it important to have a spiritual life when I've done just fine without one?!" you may ask. Some gays identify as atheist or agnostic and leave it at that. For these people, even the word "spirituality" may have associations that are distasteful to them. Occasionally, when I use the word *spirituality* in conversation, some people think I must be referring to spirits or other divine entities that shape our world, such as angels, wood nymphs, fairies (no pun intended), or the Holy Spirit. When I use the term spirituality, however, I am including both the external representations of God and the *internal resources of the human spirit.*

All humans have a need to understand the larger questions of living, including, "Where do I fit in?" "What is my part in the world or universe?" and "Where do I find meaning in living?" Regardless of whether you believe in a God that is larger than, or exists outside of you, or if you believe there is no larger force than what you have within, I use the term *spiritual* to describe the search for answers to the questions.

Big Picture Thinking

Many people have a highly personal, yet organized system for attending to their spiritual needs. Some people find that organized religion provides the best answers to these questions of why they exist and what their role is on this planet. They find comfort and a reduction in anxiety (or angst) by relying on their faith in their concept of God or in their religious organization's teachings. By practicing the rituals of the organization (such as daily prayer or meditation, religious ceremonies, reading religious materials or texts), they find peace and satisfaction, a closer relationship with "God," a feeling that they are not alone, and answers to everyday problems.

Others find that the explanations provided by religious doctrine or dogmas don't feel right or comfortable. They find that using their own reason or logic, rather than faith in a religious institution, fits them better and provides just as much peace. They feel an added boost to their self-confidence when they solve a problem on their own. Some have developed a heightened sense of intuition as a guide to navigating daily hassles and dilemmas. I find that most people who consider themselves atheists have a well-developed sense of how the world is organized and a spiritual sense of their own power to change themselves and their environment.

Many gays and lesbians actively avoid acknowledging their spiritual side or assume that spirituality *must be* connected to organized religion. Who can blame them when many religions have been *at best* silent on the spiritual concerns of lesbians and gays and *at worst* both condemning and rejecting? Being rejected is particularly painful for those who were raised to believe that a specific religious organization speaks for God. If the organization rejects them, they are made to believe that God has rejected them as well. Even if you were not directly rejected or harmed by religion, the fear or *anticipation* of rejection may have led you to reject religion or anything remotely associated with it, including a personal spirituality.

A healthy, well-constructed, and active spiritual life can be a great source of peace, strength, and growth when confronting life's struggles. Your views on spirituality may be central to core beliefs about your place in the world and your ultimate sense of self-esteem. One purpose of this chapter is to provide some direction for improving or developing your own personal sense of connectedness.

MAKING TIME TO BE SPIRITUAL

One of the most important parts of developing your spiritual self is simply *making time for it,* just like making time to brush your teeth, groom, and dress before work or taking time to work out, run, or nap. The following diagram illustrates the areas of healthy living that need your regular attention. By ignoring any one or more of these areas, life may be out of balance.

As you make time for developing your spiritual life, you'll find that your perspective begins to change about yourself and others.

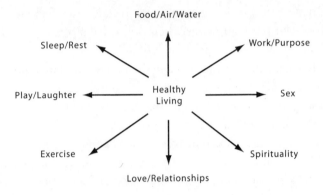

Figure 3. Aspects of a Balanced Life

Keep in mind that creating a balanced life is a lifelong process that waxes and wanes. If you find that it is difficult for you to maintain consistency in your practices, don't be hard on yourself or give up! Give yourself a break and start again where you left off.

SPIRITUAL SCARS

If religious people or their teachings hurt you, the spiritual side of you may be wounded or scarred. It can be difficult to separate the harmful effects of religion from the spiritual ideas that religions attempt to express. By understanding the differences between religion and spirituality, you may be able to reconnect with the part of yourself that needs healing. An important key to begin healing is for you to remain in control of the process and not allow yourself to be guided by other spiritual or religious people whose agenda is to make you conform to their particular beliefs. If you had a particularly traumatic experience with religion in the past, I recommend that initially you *avoid* placing yourself in a religious context until you feel spiritually stronger and can reject doctrinal ideas that don't feel right to you.

Here are some suggestions for developing your own rituals:

1. *Set aside a regular time every day to allow yourself to attend to your belief system.* Taking some quiet time for reflection first thing in the morning can help set a positive and relaxed tone for the rest of the day. Take five or ten minutes to calm yourself at the end of the day before going to bed. Stepping back and taking a larger perspective on your life can help you let go of minor daily worries and get a better night's sleep. The important thing is not whether you take five minutes or an hour initially, but to practice self-reflection on a regular basis. If you can manage to practice at the same time every day, you will find yourself beginning to relax as that time approaches in anticipation of your quiet time.

2. *Pick a comfortable place to practice your daily ritual.* Find a spot that feels quiet, private, and free from distraction. Inside the house, you could pick a favorite chair, room, or window with a view. Outside the house, you could pick a spot in the park, in a garden, or by a favorite tree. Sit quietly while you practice your ritual, or practice as you are taking a walk, running, or cycling. One of my patients practices her spiritual ritual as she walks on the treadmill in the morning. She finds the repetitiveness of the activity soothing and calming.

3. *Experiment with various ways of enhancing feelings of self-acceptance and self-nurturance.* Some people use a ritual that was effective for them from the religious tradition in which they were raised, like prayer. Some find the repetition of a formal prayer relaxing and empowering while others prefer to pray as if they were having a conversation with a nurturing God, higher power, or themselves. Meditation is helpful for becoming more centered and mindful of the values that are most important to you. Imagery or visualization can be a powerful form of ritual, using only visual or auditory images of healing, self-nurturing, or growth. Actively visualizing yourself performing a dreaded task or handling a difficult situation successfully, or modeling yourself after a respected

spiritual leader can actually enhance your performance in
real life.

4. *If you do believe in the existence of God or a higher power, you
may initially need to work on reshaping your image of God,
from angry and condemning to unconditionally loving,
forgiving, and accepting.* Some of my gay and lesbian clients
have come from such emotionally abusive backgrounds that
they were constantly told, "God despises you," or that they
were "sentenced to hell" for having an attraction to someone
of the same sex. These messages became a deep-seated scar
for many of them, making them feel that they did not deserve
spiritual nurturing or even to feel joy at all. The empty chair
technique, as described in the previous chapter, may be a
useful exercise if you've been exposed to these types of
messages. Begin by imagining that God is in the chair across
from you. How do you feel? Are you afraid? Ashamed?
Angry? These feelings are keys to understanding how your
thoughts were shaped about your role in the spiritual world.

Next, you might try imagining the God-image becoming
more approachable, willing to listen to your feelings and
answer your questions. Give your image the qualities of an
unconditionally loving, ideal parent or grandparent. Express
any old feelings that you may have left over from years of
rejection, such as grief, confusion, or even anger. The entity
you imagine is wise enough to accept your feelings without
judgment. Ask the image to begin a new relationship with
you, leaving behind the old messages you were taught.
Continue with this image as long as you like, taking it in a
positive and inclusive direction.

If you do not believe in a God entity or higher power, you
can substitute a conversation with yourself for the times when
you feel alone, using your revised core beliefs from Chapter
11 as guides for words that might feel soothing. You can
imagine the "child" part of you that is feeling emotional or
alone sitting in the empty chair and the "adult" you taking the
child into your arms for a hug and comfort.

Some of my patients have taken this exercise further in their daily spiritual practice by calling upon the image that they developed whenever they feel alone or vulnerable to hold them, nurture them, or support them. Others visualize a real adult figure from their childhood who was unconditionally accepting of them and nurturing.

5. *Don't be afraid to try other creative forms of spiritual reflection like giving yourself a special self-nurturing or restorative retreat now and then.* Some find that planning a professional massage or a trip to the mountains, beach, or river helps them let go of extraneous worries and focus on what's important—the positive things or people in their lives and the things they have to be grateful for. Some people have built altars in their homes that included items such as pictures of loved ones, candles, incense, and flowers so that they would have a special place to open up to inner reflection and spiritual practice. Some find that they can augment their experience by listening to music or by doing something artistically creative like playing an instrument, drawing, painting, or doing crafts.

6. *If you find that you need more guidance in your spiritual search (as I found I did along the way), it may be helpful for you to speak with a religious or spiritual figure about some of your questions.* It's important to find someone who will discuss with you your beliefs, but will not attempt to force you to conform to his or hers. I recommend that you try to find someone who comes from a tradition that is known to be gay/lesbian affirmative or at least is known to respect the traditions of other religions as well as his or her own. You may need to do some homework about the reputation and position of the person before you actually meet them. If you need assistance with finding such a person, you may want to try the following:

- Call a local lesbian or gay switchboard (if one is available) to ask for lesbian/gay spiritual resources in your area.

- Ask your lesbian or gay friends if they have had positive experiences with a local religious leader.
- Look for an interfaith agency or chaplaincy program in your area since these agencies would be more likely to respect a wide range of religious views.
- Attempt to locate a school of theology or divinity school at a larger state or private university where a diversity of views is represented.
- Contact national offices of organizations like Dignity (for Catholics), Integrity (for Episcopalians), and the Metropolitan Community Church for names of local groups that may have suggestions.

These suggestions are meant to be general and don't begin to explore the many ways you could foster or improve your own unique spirituality. You may already have well-developed spiritual practices and find these suggestions too elementary. In that case, you might want to continue your growth by reading about other spiritual practices or by finding a group of people with similar spiritual interests to explore with and learn from. Everyone in the group need not have the exact same beliefs as long as everyone respects the rights of others to believe as they choose. Some find that by trying to understand and respect the beliefs of others, they gain new insights into their own belief system that expand and enhance it.

INTERACTING WITH ESTABLISHED RELIGIONS

While developing your spirituality does not require association with a particular religion, the advantages of doing so, such as the social support it provides to members and the charitable activities it may perform, may outweigh the disadvantages for you. Some religious organizations, in fact, are attempting to resolve some of the contradictions within their own teachings regarding gays and lesbians. For example, while the Presbyterian church recently voted not to extend leadership positions to gays or single heterosexuals who are not celibate, the fact that the issue was debated within the church for several years, and that there are a significant number of people within the church who supported the ordination of lesbian or gay people, signals that further change may be ahead. Officials in the United Methodist Church acquitted Rev. Jimmy Creech of charges that he disobeyed church rules by performing a unity ceremony for a lesbian couple in September of 1997, although his bishop later fired him for other reasons. Many Reform and Reconstructionist Jewish groups also tend to view homosexuality as a state of being into which some people are born and is therefore not in the category of being moral or immoral.

If you have a strong connection to a particular religion, and wish to continue practicing the basic traditions and teachings of the religion, look into whether a gay or lesbian subgroup within your organization exists and contact them for support and assistance with maintaining religious ties with a gay or lesbian-affirmative focus. Despite the stance of the national organizations, it is possible to find individual congregations within the larger religious organization that do not accept the anti-gay rhetoric of their governing bodies. Many lesbians and gays find comfortable homes within such local groups and are able to pursue their spiritual needs with dignity, respect, and acceptance. My partner Brad is a devout cradle Catholic, who continues to go to Mass regularly. One of the ways that he has been able to integrate his sexuality with the Church's teachings is by attending gay Catholic meetings from time to time and meeting individually with an openly gay spiritual advisor.

The more accepting of yourself you are, the more easily you will be able to maintain connections with mainstreams religions, recognizing them as complex systems that have both healthy and unhealthy qualities.

NON-WESTERN BELIEF SYSTEMS

Many gay and lesbian people have moved away from Western-based belief systems to more Eastern-based ones, such as Buddhism.

Buddhism is fairly neutral on the issue of sexual orientation, thus making it an attractive alternative for spiritual exploration by gays and lesbians. While individual practitioners of Buddhism may exhibit culturally prevalent homophobic attitudes, the institution itself does not discriminate with regard to sexual orientation, allowing openly gay and lesbian practitioners the opportunity to become ordained.

There are billions of non-Christians in the world and many thousands of formal religious systems who do not discriminate against queer people. The key is to trust your feelings and your ability to use reason. Use the same type of strategy to evaluate the appropriateness of the words of the religious leaders as you do your own thinking: dispute the irrational, distorted, and hypocritical.

FINDING YOUR OWN PATH

Regardless of the path you choose for exploring your spirituality, whether it be completely or partially within established religious practices, or outside of organized religion altogether, the key is to recognize that the spiritual side of yourself is a part of who you are as a normal human being. Starting your own path does not have to be difficult. If you can do nothing more than take time to reflect on day-to-day experiences and allow yourself to place them in a larger perspective, you have begun the process of spiritual healing. Allowing yourself to feel your feelings—both the negative and the positive—is another part of the spiritual experience. Learning to listen to negative feelings like anger, sadness, and frustration provides you with an opportunity to expand your view of a situation and perhaps teach yourself to take a different stance next time in a similar situation. It also gives you the chance to practice some of the cognitive skills you have learned in the book, including evaluating negative thinking and disputing irrational or distorted self-talk.

Developing your sense of spirituality will help you feel connected to the world, see life as an ongoing process, and begin to understand that you have value simply because you exist. If you can give yourself permission to enjoy the positive feelings, your spirituality becomes a part of the self-nurturing process you read about in the previous chapter.

It is important for you to remember that spiritual development is an ongoing process that will continue for the rest of your life. No one is perfect, and life is not predictable. How you take care of yourself—emotionally, cognitively, physically, and spiritually—will affect how you will experience life. If you begin to understand that you are as entitled to joy and peace as much as anyone else and you learn how to love and respect yourself completely, the journey will seem more than worth it.

PART IV

Expressions:
New Topics
and Currents

THIRTEEN

Transgender Self-Esteem

Am I gay? Am I bisexual? Am I a girl or a boy? Who decides? How do I decide? Based on society's input? My feelings?

There is no doubt that the journey for most transgender people is hard. Rejecting the social norm for sexual orientation was difficult and scary enough for me, and I can't even imagine how complicated it is to find, on your own, your truth despite the overt and covert social messages about the "right way" to be and then learning to understand your gender identity in a biological body that tells you constantly that you're something else. We're talking layers of identity development that often require self-awareness, facing your fears, and standing up to the harshest of criticism and rejection. There is also no doubt that in a society that prefers simple choices and puts people into neat categories (whatever the issue!), it's threatening to have what you know (or what you think you know) to be called into question. What do you mean, that this person who looks female is actually male inside??! This concept can be overwhelming, especially to people who may have perhaps had their own issues with identity and struggled to define themselves.

Growing up for everyone, regardless of gender or sexual orientation, means creating an identity, a definition of who we are—what we like and dislike, what turns us on and off and what rules we follow or reject. Most heterosexuals use social criteria as guidelines in defining themselves. In the 1960's, with huge social changes happening everywhere, the phrase "I'm trying to find myself" was coined as young people experimented with image and rebellion, drugs, and music. For the average straight person, born into a body that "fits," the answers are hardly a blip on the radar screen. Most children and teens have tons of images of how to be a man or a woman, from their families and maybe even more importantly, from the media. Most heterosexual children have the benefit of a large group of others, going through similar phases of sexual development and practicing mating rituals (like holding hands in public and pimply, pubescent flirtation). For a lesbian or gay person, who typically struggles with why they have feelings of attraction to someone of the same sex when society tells them this is not "normal," figuring out where you fit during the hetero hormone rush can become a battle. You may want to fit in, you may have enormous pressure to fit in, but maybe the best you can do is stay quiet and avoid notice.

Now imagine trying to identify your sexual orientation in a culture that leaves little room for deviation from the norm, *and* feeling like you live in a body that doesn't feel right. Imagine trying to "find yourself" with no support, advice, or personal role models. Imagine in some cases, routine harassment, criticism, and even physical abuse as you try to put all the pieces together.

As rampant as homophobia remains in the world today, I would argue that *transphobia* or the irrational fear of, and hostility towards people who are transgender, is even more intense. Transphobia is widespread among heterosexual Americans, and although not often discussed openly, exists even within the lesbian, gay, and bisexual population as well, although hopefully to a much lesser degree given our own experiences with discrimination and oppression.

What is really behind this irrational fear and disdain? *Genderism*, a term coined to describe the belief that one's gender always does, and should, match their biological sex, may be one of the more important factors behind prejudice and discrimination towards people who are transgender. Because we all construct a personal identity as we grow, and find a sense of safety in fitting in and being considered "normal," often people who do not fit the normal rules we've adopted are scary and anxiety-producing. The existence of someone whose biological sex does not define their gender identity in itself can threaten the very foundation of someone who has rigid beliefs about how the world works.

Genderism may in fact be just a variation of old-fashioned *sexism* as well. Cultures who are dominated by men have a need to place people in strict gender categories in order to justify and maintain control. A sexist way of thinking might involve the beliefs that traditionally, men are superior to women as leaders; therefore women who assume leadership roles are somehow "manly" and therefore strange or suspect.

Trans Terminology

Before I delve deeper into the self-esteem specifics, I thought it might be useful to discuss the current state of trans terminology. As we learn more about the varieties of people and what labels (if any) are preferred, it is clear that within the trans community, there is a continuum. My search for the most current and most accurate terminology led me to a wonderful conversation with sexologist, Dr. Michele Angello, a professor at the Institute for the Advanced Study of Human Sexuality in San Francisco.

According to Dr. Angello, the word *transgender* has become an all-encompassing term to refer to people whose gender identity and/or gender expression differs from conventional expectations based on the physical sex they were born into. In other words, transgender includes everyone from *cross dressers*, people who choose to dress in opposite sex clothing for comfort or erotic purposes with no desire to alter their body, to *transsexuals*, people who desire to live in a body more consistent with their gender identity, but may or may not choose surgery to accomplish it. Dr. Angello finds that many, in fact she believes most, transsexuals do not have surgery for a variety of reasons including the medical risks of the surgery itself, the high cost of the surgery, career, or relationship concerns, and may or may not choose to take hormones instead.

For this chapter, in an effort to be as all inclusive as possible, I will use the terms transgender or trans, which also includes people with experiences or identities that include MTF (male to female) transsexuals, FTM (female to male), drag kings, drag queens, gender queers, and others.

The Reality of Transphobia

There is little question now that transgender people experience tremendous social hostility. The National Coalition for LGBT Health in 2004 called violence against trans people an "epidemic," particularly for trans women (male to female) of color. A 1997 GenderPAC anti-violence report found that 27% of transgender people had been victims of violence, which may be an underestimate given high levels of distrust of police and the criminal justice system among transgender people.

In a 1999 National School Climate Survey in New York conducted by the Gay Lesbian and Straight Education Network, almost 74% of transgender youth reported hearing homophobic remarks "sometimes" or "frequently." A 1995 study by the Massachusetts Youth Risk Behavior Surveillance found that GLB youth were four times more likely to report being threatened with a weapon on school property than heterosexual youth.

As I've mentioned before in the book, we are not immune to the overt and subtle messages from our society about our status and our worth as we grow up and form our identity. It's challenging to form a healthy sense of your self amidst all the negativity, prejudice, and discrimination. We may have buried deep these sexist, homophobic, and genderist beliefs that later affect our choices and threaten our very survival. My personal beliefs that transphobia is even more widespread than homophobia arises from several observations.

First, in the few studies that have been conducted with transgender people, the numbers of self-destructive behaviors and impulses that these groups have endorsed are alarmingly high. Suicide rates are consistently high, with suicide attempts ranging from 16 to 37% and suicidal thoughts in an estimated 64% at some point in their lives. Several studies in large cities have found that transgender women are at high risk for contracting HIV, for living in poverty, to be or have been incarcerated and having an addiction problem. In a 1997 study, the San Francisco Department of Public Health found that out of 392 MTF participants, 80% did some type of sex work, 65% had a history of incarceration (31% within the past year), while only 13% had college degrees. The median monthly income was $744, 47% were homeless, and 2/3 of African-American transgender participants had HIV. In the same department's study, there was a lower prevalence of HIV in FTM than MTF, although significant portions still engage in survival sex, intravenous drug use, and sex with men.

Sex work is apparently common for survival, particularly in young transgender people in urban environments, as is rejection by family, and difficulty finding gainful employment. Because it's often hard to find gainful employment for many transgender people, there is also a lack of health insurance, and relatedly, a lack of medical and mental health care. Even if access to health care services is available, many trans people report being afraid of health care provider hostility or insensitivity. Studies of HIV infection rates for transgender women range from 14 to 47% and are even higher for transgender sex workers who are unable to find other forms of employment and may be forced or induced with money to engage in unsafe sex. Other health concerns include the lack of FDA approval for transgender hormonal therapy, the apparently widespread use of black market silicone injections, as an alternative to hormonal therapy to enhance appearance, administered under non-sterile conditions with industrial grade, rather than medical grade, silicone.

Some experts, including Dr. Angello and transgender activist Nancy Nangeroni, question the generalizations that can be made from the data from these types of studies. First, they both mentioned independently that most transgender people are in the closet, so to speak, and therefore the samples are more representative of only a small segment of the much larger continuum of trans people. The groups represented in this study likely represent those who are suffering the most. As young people, they come out about their gender and sexuality issues at home, are often kicked out, and then turn to the only visible role models, often sex workers, that they can find in the urban environment for support and help. Their lifestyle quickly turns to basic survival in a world where they may have not completed an education and have few marketable skills.

They were both also quick to point out that while confronting transphobia does lead to common experiences, regardless of one's background, the full spectrum of transgender likely includes people from all ethnic, cultural, socioeconomic, and educational backgrounds. We often have trouble ferreting out people for studies who do not wish to be ferreted out!

There is no doubt that society can be cruel, especially to people who don't fit the mold. Surviving cruelty requires adaptation and sometimes compromise as these studies reveal. People who challenge the "norms" of what society says is acceptable pay a price in the real world, but also internally. Fighting for change is a theme I mention throughout this book. Political activism, in whatever small or grand way you can muster, is important to supporting your identity and potentially leading to change in social realities. In this chapter I encourage you to tend to your internal landscape as well, identifying sources of self-sabotage and automatic self-criticism.

Coming Out Trans

Dr. Aaron Devor at the University of Victoria, BC, proposes that there are fourteen stages of transsexual identity formation in his 2004 article entitled *Witnessing and Mirroring*. Appearing in the respected *Journal of Gay and Lesbian Psychotherapy*, Dr. Devor builds upon the theories of lesbian and gay identity development that I discussed earlier in the book by Dr. Vivian Cass, but proposes that transsexual and transgender people have unique issues that they encounter along the way to healthy self-concept. A summary of Dr. Devor's proposed stages is shown in the accompanying table (*see pages 214–215*).

Dr. Devor, himself an open, FTM transsexual and professor of sociology, explores in great detail, the subtle and various shifts in self-perception that occur throughout the transsexual/transgender process of self-acceptance. While Dr. Devor's model was designed with FTM transsexuals in mind primarily, Nancy Nangeroni felt that they were "pretty much right on" for her, except for Stage 13, describing a stage of "mostly invisible" transsexuality, which she feels may not be the case as often in MTFs, especially later in life.

It is clear, however, that social beliefs and mores can play a huge role in the ease with which a trans person moves through these stages. Cultures that have less rigid ideas about what is male and what is female may be more open to people with identities that fall outside the "norm." On the other hand, cultures that have very strict assumptions about what makes a man or woman (i.e., genitalia defines one's sex) can make self-discovery harsh and complicated. Exploring your identity in a neutral environment is difficult enough with few role models or mentors; now add criticism, transphobia, and threats to the mix! It makes sense then that the era and region in which you were raised, whether or not you were raised in a rural or urban environment, and your family of origin's belief systems and relative dysfunction all make a difference in your ability to success-fully negotiate the challenges of self-acceptance. Dr. Devor likens

STAGES OF TRANSSEXUAL IDENTITY FORMATION

	STAGE	SOME CHARACTERISTICS	SOME ACTIONS
1	Abiding Anxiety	Unfocused gender and sex discomfort.	Preference for other gender activities and companionship.
2	Identity Confusion About Originally Assigned Gender and Sex	First doubts about suitability of originally assigned gender and sex.	Reactive gender and sex conforming activities.
3	Identity Comparisons About Originally Assigned Gender and Sex	Seeking and weighing alternative gender identities.	Experimenting with alternative gender consistent identities.
4	Discovery of Transsexualism or Transgenderism	Learning that transsexualism exists.	Accidental contact with information about transsexualism.
5	Identity Confusion About Transsexualism or Transgenderism	First doubts about the authenticity of own transexualism.	Seeking more information about transsexualism.
6	Identity Comparisons About Transsexualism or Transgenderism	Testing transsexual identity using transsexual reference group.	Start to disidentify with women and females. Start to identify as transsexed.
7	Identity Tolerance of Transsexual or Transgender Identity	Identity as probably transsexual.	Increasingly disidentify as originally assigned gender and sex.

the process of developing who you are to looking into a mirror. He finds that we all deeply wish to be seen by others as we see ourselves and that this constant witnessing and feedback is how we successfully come to know and like ourselves, if this feedback confirms what we feel inside and reinforces the sense of "self."

On the other hand, when the messages that we receive from society do not match what we feel inside, he feels that this is when psychological distress and self-destructive behaviors result. When especially harsh or severe, he believes that even suicidal impulses or psychosis can be the result. Challenging society's rules and cultural assumptions, and even confronting the potential loss of family and

STAGES OF TRANSSEXUAL IDENTITY FORMATION

	STAGE	SOME CHARACTERISTICS	SOME ACTIONS
8	*Delay Before Acceptance of Transsexual or Transgender Identity*	*Waiting for changed circumstances. Looking for confirmation of transsexual identity.*	*Seeking more info about transsexualism. Reality testing in intimate relationships and against further info about transsexualism.*
9	*Acceptance of Transsexual or Transgender Identity*	*Transsexual identity established.*	*Tell others about transsexual identity.*
10	*Delay Before Transition*	*Transsexual identity deepens. Final disidentity as original gender and sex. Anticipatory socialization.*	*Learning how to transition. Saving money. Organizing support systems.*
11	*Transition*	*Changing genders and sexes.*	*Gender and sex reassignment.*
12	*Acceptance of Post-Transition Gender and sex Identities*	*Post-transition identity established.*	*Successful post-transition living.*
13	*Integration*	*Transsexuality mostly invisible.*	*Stigma management. Identity integration.*
14	*Pride*	*Openly transsexual.*	*Transsexual advocacy.*

Reprinted by permission from Haworth Press from Devor, A.H. (2003). "Witnessing and Mirroring: A Fourteen Stage Model of Transsexual Identity Formation," *Journal of Gay and Lesbian Psychotherapy,* 8 (1/2), 41-67.

support systems, requires enormous courage, self-examination, and honesty. According to Dr. Devor, becoming a transsexual or transgender person is "never easy." Learning to respect and admire yourself for taking this incredible journey is a part of the road to healthy self-esteem.

NOTES FROM THE FIELD

Sexologist Dr. Michele Angello describes the budding awareness of trans identity as simply "feeling different," which most of her clients reported began for them around the tender age of 8. She finds, however, that the beginning of puberty often becomes the most challenging part of development for transsexuals who begin to see their bodies change in ways that feel like a betrayal. In her extensive work with transgender adults who have come to her for help, most report that their adolescence was the most tumultuous, as puberty confirmed their worst fears—that they were indeed living in the wrong body as they confronted the ultimate societal rule: that your sex and your gender must be the same. Dr. Angello describes the experience of puberty as a "betrayal" of the body after years of hoping that the pre-pubescent body would still develop in the direction that the trans child hoped it would go. Watching their worst nightmares occur, developing unwanted breasts or coarse body hair where you didn't want it, confirms the child's worst fears—that they are living in the wrong body. Add to that, the growing social pressure to fit in at school, to date and to explore sexually, few of us escape the adolescent years without some emotional scars and stories of rejection or feeling like an outcast at some point.

Dr. Angello has heard many stories of MTF transsexuals who struggled to fit in by adopting hyper-masculine behaviors or career paths like becoming a Marine or a firefighter, perhaps even as a way to convince themselves that what they felt would go away if they just tried hard enough. In her observation, FTM transsexuals tend to choose a different path, often assuming a "lesbian" identity initially because of the sense of greater flexibility and acceptance in adopting more traditionally masculine behaviors and identities in lesbian communities. She also finds that the "coming out to others" process is particularly challenging for a trans person who also identifies a same sex sexual orientation, a situation she refers to as a "double whammy."

There are obviously many potential barriers to the coming out process, both for the LGB person and the transgender person as I have identified earlier in this book, but deserve a brief mention again here. Acceptance of gender and sexual orientation differences varies according to your cultural and ethnic background, your religion (which Dr. Angello says is most frequently cited by her clients as one of the most difficult barriers to self-acceptance), family support (or lack thereof), barriers to compassionate and effective health care, and your peer group acceptance.

TAKING ACTION

As I have recommended elsewhere in this book, I believe the development of a positive and healthy self-esteem involves fighting the good fight within against the internalized negative social messages, but also involves taking steps toward political and social action.

Help Others Who Are New to the Process

While going through the process on your own may be exhausting, don't forget to do what you can for your peers and your community. Obviously, we are missing significant opportunities to help our young transgender people at important milestones as they struggle to understand themselves at important junctures in their lives. Volunteering with a transgender or LGBT youth organization can help provide others with badly needed role models and mentors, if you feel ready and healthy enough to do so. Imagine how different your own life would have been if someone that you trusted and respected had been there to guide you through the process of self-acceptance.

Most LGBT youth organizations are badly in need of financial support, but could also find a way to use other contributions as well, such as donations of old clothes or books. Find a way to give back in honor or memory of people who treated you kindly along the way.

Make Time to Work on Positive Self-reflection Every Day

As I have argued in the first portion of this book, even if you have freed yourself from the external barriers to full acceptance, by moving to safer ground and by organizing a healthy support system and living a more authentic lifestyle, it will still be important to challenge the vestiges of old condemnation and self-criticism that may be hanging around in your head. Taking on the negative internal messages and replacing them with more compassion and encouragement is a place to start this process.

Work on challenging the negative thinking, about your body, about your emotions, about your abilities, and replacing them with a compassionate, realistic voice. Spend time recognizing the parts of you that you have come to love, the strong parts that stood up to society's assumptions. Forgive yourself for mistakes that you may have made along the way or the people you may have hurt. Forgive yourself for hurting and doubting yourself when you were tired and felt afraid or alone.

Find Yourself a Support Group

Study after study has strongly supported the effect of social support on mental health, on physical health, and on general happiness and life satisfaction. We are social creatures and when isolated, we go a little bonkers!

When I was a new psychologist with a private practice in Baton Rouge, Louisiana, in 1993, I was one of only three openly gay mental health professionals in a town with a population of over half a million. I still remember a phone call from a desperate young man who needed to complete the "required" two years of psychotherapy, recommended at the time by the sex transitions medical clinic in Texas, where he had been seen in consultation. He was absolutely terrified to face the changes alone, was living at home with his parents and had never shared his feelings with anyone other than at the Dallas clinic. A novice myself to the struggles of someone dealing with transgender issues, I cautioned him that I had little to no expertise in this area and that it would be better for him to see someone who did have experience and training in this issue.

There was a pause on the other end of the phone and he finally quietly stated, "But there is no one else here, you're my last hope." We agreed to meet—me with little trans counseling experience, and he with no money and a broken-down car. I finally found a transsexual counselor in Atlanta who agreed to supervise me by phone as my lonely client and I started down the path of helping him build a more positive self-concept. We eventually did find him a support network and he moved to a much more trans-accepting city, Minneapolis, rooming with new transgender friends who were also living his experiences.

I wish that I could say that things had gotten much better, but recently, in writing this chapter, I went to my local Barnes and Noble (here in the SF Bay Area!!) to find whatever books were available on the latest trans issues. Amazingly, on the four shelves labeled "Lesbian and Gay Issues," I found one single, solitary book on transgender issues—a memoir by Kate Bornstein. It made me realize how lonely, even in a crowd, life can be at times.

Today thank goodness, we now have the Internet, which has become a place to shop for books that our local bookstore doesn't carry, magazines that we can subscribe to, online chat groups we can join, and community resources that we may have been unaware of or have trouble finding on our own. At the end of this chapter, I have listed resources that I thought were particularly helpful, some of which include resource lists of their own.

Nancy's Story

In 1999, I was fortunate enough to be asked to appear to discuss the topic on a radio show called *GenderTalk* with the hosts and life partners, Nancy Nangeroni and Dr. Gordene O. Mackenzie. Both stood out as interviewers for me—sincere and thoughtful, intelligent and open.

When I asked Nancy to help me with this chapter, she was again cooperative, candid, and articulate as she shared her story with me.

Born into a large Italian family, with three brothers and four sisters, Nancy recalls, as many transgender people do, being aware that she did not fit at a very young age, although at this point she can't recall specifics. She described her family as fairly homophobic and that there was "lots of anti-sissy patrolling going on" to try to make sure she conformed to the gender stereotypes that they assigned to her based on her genitalia. She recalls flashes of awareness of a larger social bias as well, to follow rigid "gender appropriate" roles of the "little boys should play with trucks and girls with dolls" variety. By ten, however, Nancy began to understand that these roles were not appropriate for her.

"I was not more than ten when I realized that I, undeniably a boy, fervently wished I'd been born a girl," she remembers. Her clearest memory, however, was around that time, when she developed an intense interest in her two older sisters' clothing.

"I felt such tremendous guilt during that time, for looking at pictures of ladies' underwear in catalogs, and sneaking opportunities to try on their clothes while they were out." Nancy feels that her biggest challenge of all in learning to feel good about herself has been the guilt, from a variety of sources but internalized at a tender time.

Not all the messages were subtle about her budding fetish for cross-dressing. Discovered by her sister and reported to her mother, Nancy remembers her mother sitting her down for a discussion during which she equated transvestitism with "perverts."

Her father, on the other hand, she describes as "gentle, but clear about being a man." She fondly recalls that he attempted to encourage her to find more masculine pursuits, rather than to punish her interests in more feminine things. Sadly, she recalls no adults in her life in whom she could confide honestly. She spent much of her young adult life cross-dressing in secrecy and feeling huge amounts of shame, all the while earning a degree in electrical engineering from MIT and establishing an enormously successful professional career in the field.

It was after a terrible motorcycle accident in 1981 at age 28, that Nancy, who had previously been closeted to her family, decided to "come out." She decided then to tell her family that she was a crossdresser and possibly a transsexual. She believes that they were so relieved that she was still alive, her disclosure about her gender status paled, specifically stating that they cared less about the cross-dressing than about having her around.

While her family relationships have had their ups and downs since then, Nancy is clearly happier to be "out" of the closet than suffering the confinement of being "in." She recalls her first, "off-putting" contact with an Orange County trans support group in the mid-1980's after they responded to her initial inquiry with guidelines for how to transition and obtain surgery, neither of which she felt close to being ready for. In the late 80's she started electrolysis and attended her first trans event, Fantasia Fair, in late 1990, where she met another trans person for the very first time. Inspired by the event, she came out as "possibly TS" at work upon her return home.

At age 39, in 1993, Nancy made the transition to living full time as a woman. The same energy that she used for holding the closet door shut seemed to burst forth as she became a writer and activist for transgender issues, leading eventually to the show, *GenderTalk*, which includes listener forums, resources, and connection.

Today, Nancy identifies herself as "transgender, transsexual, and cross-dresser." She refuses to accept the labels of other people and her passion for justice is evident in her tone as she speaks.

"Over the years, Gordene and I have received hundreds of e-mails from people who not only thank us for providing a forum, but a few have thanked us for saving their lives" she says, minimizing her own personal impact on the listeners.

When I asked about the biggest contributors to her own self-esteem, she immediately replied that her study of other cultures where transgender people are "respected, honored, and included" had made the biggest impact on her. "Native American and other indigenous cultures often viewed trans or intersex people as spiritually gifted or shamans," she remarked.

It is also clear however that even as she recovers from a recent neck injury, she is eager to return to the studio and her work with *GenderTalk* and transgender activism. She finds that social and political activism reinforces the inner work that she's done over the years to learn to love and respect herself. "If we don't push back a little, in a society that tells us we're second class, we may find ourselves in an ever-retreating position," and, she says, "If we don't contest it, our silence means consent."

Almost in the same breath, she goes on to say that her relationship with Gordene over the past 8 years has been another big influence on her self-esteem. She describes Gordene as, "the person I had always hoped to love," who remains a constant source of strength, support, and integrity. She readily admits that they have had their ups and downs, but their willingness to work through it all, to talk openly and frankly, and to not run from a challenge, has helped them continue to grow over the years instead of breaking or drifting apart.

Before I could say good-bye, Nancy made me promise not to make her sound like a role model despite my distinct impression that she is one. She wanted me to be clear that she's had her share of struggles and her thoughts still turn dark at times. Her modesty is sincere, and her point well taken— good self-esteem is something we have to continually strive for in a trans/homophobic world, not something we achieve and then move on to the next conquest. I'm not sure I've ever met someone so honest about it all. Perhaps I can call her a *roles* model?

QUESTIONS FOR REFLECTION

- How old were you when you first knew that you were different? Did you talk about it? What was your family's response if you did?
- How did you choose to handle your feelings as a child? Did you stay quiet and try to fit in? Or did you actively follow your heart? Or both?
- When did you first become aware that your body was different from how you felt?
- How did you first become aware of the existence of other transsexual or transgender people? What was the context of the discussion? Positive or negative?
- How did you cope with transphobic remarks as a child and adolescent? How do you cope now?
- List some hard times in your life that you faced with courage.
- What are the physical things about yourself that you like?

What are some of your best emotional features?
- How has your journey made you stronger, more flexible?
- In what ways can you give back to your community that will make you feel like you're making a difference?

RESOURCES

GenderTalk Radio: Includes an all-inclusive, carefully screened guide to resources for transgenders, www.gendertalk.com

International Foundation for Gender Education, www.ifge.org

International Journal of Transgenderism, www.symposium.com/ijt

LGBT Education Resources for Students, Faculty, and Staff, www.lgbt-stlearning.org

Medical Therapy and Health Maintenance for Transgender Men: A Guide For Health Care Providers, www.nickgorton.org

National Coalition for Transgender Equality: Social justice organization dedicated to advocating for the equality of transgender people, www.nctequality.org

National Gay and Lesbian Task Force: Organization that promotes civil rights for gay, lesbian, bisexual, and transgender people. www.thetaskforce.org

National Transgender Advocacy Coalition, www.ntac.org

Trans Family and Friends Support, www.transfamily.org

Transgender Resources by a Psychologist, www.genderpsychology.org

World Professional Association for Transgender Health, Inc. (formerly known as the Harry Benjamin International Gender Dysphoria Association), www.wpath.org

Fourteen

Aging and Self-Esteem

LIFE'S TRAGEDY IS THAT WE GET OLD TOO SOON AND WISE TOO
LATE.

—Benjamin Franklin

As a middle-aged gay man, the topic of how to cope with getting older has become of increasing interest personally. Funny how that happens. Over the years, I have had clients, both straight and gay, who came to therapy for other reasons, but the topic eventually drifted to aging in a society that values youth and beauty over wisdom and experience.

My premise though, that our society is increasingly youth oriented, is based on nothing more than my opinion, so how do I verify it?

Last week, I picked up a local gay newspaper, which I tend not to do so often anymore, and I flipped through the sections about theater, politics, and other issues of note to our community and ended up at the back of the last section. You know the one, full of pictures of hot, buff guys just waiting for your call. Most were young, all were definitely physically attractive (in a variety of ways), and the emphasis of course was on sexuality and muscles.

I then flipped through an old *Genre* magazine, a national lifestyle publication for gay men, lying on the coffee table. It is there for a reason, which I'll mention later, but for purposes of my "research," I scanned through the visual images, without really digesting the text. On the cover, hard to miss, were rock-hard abs, a perfect chest, and little noticeable body hair. The model's haircut was perfect, as were his teeth and even his eyebrows—he couldn't have been over 25. The cover model had an entire section devoted to him in the middle, decked out in the latest fashions, looking adorable and chic. Other models in the back stood there with super tans, rippling biceps, and square jaws, tempting me to buy euro-cut underwear—uh, *no!*

The Advocate, which I read for the excellent articles, is a bit more inclusive. There were images of people of all different kinds and genders. There were signs of crows-feet and neck laxity intertwined with pictures of slim, hot young things of all genders. There were still pictures of buff, swim-suited guys enjoying their vacations and adorned by unique jewelry but these were minimal and subtle. Someone there is paying attention to inclusiveness and diversity I think.

Finally, I grab the glossy and slick *San Francisco* from the table, the magazine for those in the "know" about our fair Bay Area jewel. It is not "gay" per se, but there is certainly a gay sensibility about it— fashion, style, and socialites abound in the pages. Style probably best describes the images. There was a range of colors and ages represented among the people, although I must say, they all look well-to-do and could all be considered very effective and attractive representatives for their respective ages.

My little research project hardly proves anything. But my experience tells me that our culture as a whole is still very focused on youth and beauty. Our favorite actors and actresses are skinny and perfect for the most part. My clients still stress about "getting older," and I notice that people I've just met react slightly differently to me in my middle age than in my twenties. My gray hair—or what's left of it, my wrinkled forehead (even when I'm not surprised), and my slightly sleepy eyelids when I'm wide awake suggest that age occurs on the outside—even if I still feel 30 on the inside.

Lately, I find myself wondering more and more about what retirement will look like. Occasionally, I wonder about the day that I will face the same age-related problems that my parents now face: loss of independence and the need for assistance or a different type of housing. This topic has become very personal for me.

AGEISM IN AMERICA

I have mentioned ageism once or twice throughout this book, but how does one prove that it exists and if so, to what degree? Most people would agree that there is bias against seniors, evident even in sarcastic birthday cards with pictures of coffins, or parties with black balloons or the grim reaper favors. Clearly, there is a scarcity of older characters on TV shows and in movies, despite the active careers of actors like Helen Mirren or Judi Dench. And despite the fact that both Ms. Mirren and Ms. Dench are vivacious and attractive women in real life, recent roles for both portrayed them in somewhat unflattering ways on screen (see *The Queen* and *Notes on a Scandal*).

There are some cold, hard facts to support the notion of ageism apparently as well. The US Equal Opportunity Employment Commission receives an average of 19,000 age related complaints per year, although age discrimination is often hard to prove in court. Health care for older adults is another area where ageism apparently surfaces frequently. The Alliance for Aging Research, the nation's largest nonprofit organization dedicated to supporting and accelerating the pace of medical discoveries to vastly improve the universal human experience of aging and health, presented to the US Congress in 2003 a report that suggests that the elderly are less likely to receive preventative care and have limited access to doctors with training in the needs of seniors. The American Geriatrics Society, for example, reports that there are only 7,600 physicians in the U.S. who are certified as geriatric specialists, when they estimate the need is at least 36,000. The American Association for Retired Persons (AARP) says that while over 50% of consumers are over 50, only 10% of advertising is targeted towards seniors.

Some estimates of the number of older lesbians and gay men range from 1.75 to 3.5 million "gay and gray" people in the U.S. and these numbers are likely increasing as baby boomers move into their senior years and medical advances extend our life spans. Our seniors will face many of the same issues that all seniors face as they slide into new, sometimes invisible, roles in society.

The Way It Used to Be

There are cultures today that maintain a high regard for aging people within the community. Native Americans rely on the elderly for preserving traditional values and knowledge. Cheyenne legends, for example, contain stories of older women who wield power, as in the story of the "Old Woman of the Spring" who has the knowledge and power to restore the waning numbers of the buffalo.

Koreans believe that family loyalty is one of the utmost values. Children are instructed to respect and care for parents, and to bring no dishonor to their families. In South Korea, elderly parents typically live with their first married son, although there is concern that as industrial development and westernization occurs, these traditions will be lost.

The *abuela*, or grandmother, in Mexico is highly respected and often cares for her grandchildren so that both parents can work outside the home. In other Latin cultures, the elderly continue to occupy a key role in the family and are often treated with status, authority, and respect.

In Japan, there is a national holiday on September 15th called "Respect for the Aged Day" and many Japanese continue to follow Confucius' dictum to respect and obey the elderly, often turning to them for advice and counseling.

In the U.S., there was a time when, not only were the elderly

revered, but even emulated! The practice of wearing white, pow-
dered wigs in the time of Washington and Jefferson was actually an
attempt by community leaders to appear older and perhaps wiser
because of it. Fashions of the day were cut to imitate the sloping
shoulders of the elderly!

So What Happened?

Many experts believe that the changes are related to the great industrial revolution of the 1800's. Just as it appears that urbanization and
the decline of the family farm led to the development of a gay and
lesbian "identity," as people moved to cities for jobs, it also led to the
mobilization of our society. People left those family farms where
they had large, extended families, to form smaller nuclear families
and over time, the wisdom and value of the elderly was lost. Other
experts believe that there were other cultural factors as well that contributed to the devaluing of our elderly and placing emphasis on the
young. The physical demands of factory work led to recruitment of
younger workers who could handle these demands and the devaluing of older workers. Evangelical religious movements began to
preach the value of youth, self-improvement, and progress, with
chances for redemption, versus the view of the elderly, whose lives
were seen as past their prime without promise. Western medicine
began referring to aging as the "incurable disease," which also
shaped the public's consciousness in a negative direction.

It's not too much of a stretch to see how, over time, stereotypes of
people getting older have arisen and the cultural awareness of aging
is at an all time low.

QUEER AGING

Ageism exists in the greater culture, but what about specifically in
the queer world? Is it different for gay men than it is for lesbians? Is
there more ageism in the queer community than in the hetero
world?

Appearance and Youth

My search for actual studies or data on this topic was relatively fruitless. Relying on my clinical (and personal) experience, however, I do get the feeling that getting older as a gay man can be scary. If one were to only visit the obvious gay hangouts in urban environments, one might get the impression that youth is pretty and that attractiveness is reserved for the "A-list," that is, gays who dress well, work out, and are perennially tan. And, given the obvious ageism in the society at large, it would be reasonable to assume that we picked up on the messages about appearance and youth as we grew up.

Because so much of our energy is usually tied up during adolescence with "fitting in," while simultaneously hiding blossoming same sex attractions, we often miss the opportunities to explore ourselves in a sexual or intimate way like our heterosexual peers did. In my opinion, many queer young people don't have the freedom to explore their independence because of the homophobia at home or school, or they don't end up coming out to themselves until years later. Coming out to yourself can happen at almost any age, sometimes after attempts to live "in the closet" were unsuccessful, or when something in our unconscious mind finally clicks and we realize that we have feelings for the same sex.

When we do finally come out to ourselves, and then feel ready to start acting on it, many of us go through a delayed or second adolescence of sorts. While we don't have to worry about the acne and what to wear to the school dances, we do still experience a lot of the insecurities as we learn about ourselves in a new way, make sense of ourselves as lesbian or gay, and try to understand our attractiveness level within this new peer group. Often I find that the first queer peer group that people join after they come out becomes the group that they continue to identify with, sometimes for the rest of their lives. Does this initial peer group then have some special power to affect our self-image as we age? Do we compare ourselves to the group that we've felt closest to first, after years of feeling alone and isolated? Maybe our first peer group is where we first felt free enough to explore our sexuality, to be who we always wanted to be, and felt accepted.

Because of this usually initial important time of your life, it may be a little frightening to think about aging out of this group and into the next phase of life.

The Gay Agenda Myth

Now is probably as good a time as any to mention the myth of the "gay community" and the problems inherent in making generalizations about us. Although the anti-gay forces in our culture would prefer to label us with stereotypes and false agendas, the truth is that we are an incredibly diverse group of people who have only one sure thing in common—namely, the shared experience of oppression. Having said that, this common experience makes many of us feel as though we indeed are a part of a larger social community. Keep in mind that the era and culture in which we were raised, and the then present levels of homophobia, sometimes make the experiences of older LGBT quite different from the perspectives of our younger gays.

Until recently, for example, sodomy was illegal in every state in the U.S., punishable by prison and/or imposed "medical" treatments including electroshock, lobotomy, and aversion therapy. A gay person raised under these repressive conditions might have any number of reactions to these real threats including marrying for appearances' sake or even chosen celibacy. Yet, there are still pockets of extreme homophobia in the U.S., particularly in areas outside of the urban environment where queer youth still feel threatened and too afraid to come out, despite the political and social gains and support groups.

On the other hand, for queers who were actively engaged in early gay liberation movements, proclaiming your sexuality proudly and rejecting many social conventions became the norm. Just as heterosexual youths in the 60's explored "free love" and "finding themselves," young gay men in the 70's came roaring out of the closet to the tune of Donna Summer in gay communities like Christopher Street in New York and the Castro in San Francisco.

Your coming out experience, at whatever age or era, likely

remains a factor in later development of self-confidence, and self-esteem.

Are We Doomed?

One could argue that given the obvious cultural homophobia and heterosexism, how could we not experience feelings of lower self-esteem in general and particularly while aging and possibly facing (or fearing) rejection by our younger peers?

On the other hand, it has been recently suggested that having to deal with the stigma of homosexuality may actually prepare us to deal more positively with the stigma of aging. When facing ageism in the larger culture, we already have experience at evaluating who we are in the face of stereotypes. Dealing with discrimination and stereotyping successfully then leads to greater self-acceptance and self-confidence, which in turns prepares you for other life challenges as you age!

Practical Challenges

It is challenging to face the slow physical decline that occurs in the body over time. Thank goodness that we actually do age relatively slowly so that we have time to psychologically adapt to the changes a little at a time rather than all at once. Can you imagine feeling and looking like you were 25 years old for 50 years, then suddenly waking up in the body of a 75-year-old? We might die of shock in that moment, even if we knew it was coming! One might argue that staying young is important in a society that equates youth with beauty regardless of sexual orientation. One could also argue that once you have come out and found an accepting peer group, perhaps for the first time in your life, that it would be difficult to age away from that group and the activities that your first peer group enjoyed. There was a time in my life when dancing and clubs were very important in my social life. Eventually, however, my interest waned (although a good dance club is fun once in a while!) and I now prefer other types of socializing. Transitioning into middle age has had its bumps and bruises, but I actually feel more comfortable in my own skin now more than ever. This is not to say that other practical issues don't loom somewhere in my consciousness.

I think about retirement like everyone else, but I also think about financial decisions with my partner, like how to protect him if I die first or visa versa. I also think about my health as I get older and, at the end of life, what kind of care will I need. As my own parents age, and I become directly involved in their decision-making about it all, I think about my own situation of course and the special circumstances we have as a gay couple. As I become more successful professionally, and I watch the amount of federal and state taxes I pay increase, I do get a bit angry as I think about the services that George W. deems appropriate to dole out at his discretion; yet Brad and I are not afforded full equal rights by the same government. I wonder, at times, if the administration understands the hypocrisy of taxing us at the full rate while not providing us with equal access. The sad fact is that they probably do.

There are at least four issues that appear to be of practical concern to older lesbians and gay men. First, our health care system is biased toward heterosexuals and is not always conscious of this bias or the need to adjust for this. Many lesbians, gays, and transgenders are hesitant to talk to their doctors about their sexual orientation and effectively create a barrier to good communication necessary for quality health care. And good health care becomes even more important as we age.

The second concern for many older gays and lesbians is the lack of social or legal recognition for our partnerships. We have made some progress since the first edition of the book came out. Marriage is legal in Massachusetts, and a few other states have added civil unions or domestic partnership rights that are close to marriage. Federally, however, gay marriage or domestic partnership is not recognized at all, resulting in the loss of hundreds of financial and social benefits associated with heterosexual marriage. We cannot file our taxes jointly or take the marriage tax credit. Without special legal maneuvering, we may be left out of medical decisions for our spouses and may lose custody of our children or the remains of our loved ones. For senior couples, they may not be allowed to live together in retirement facilities or nursing homes.

Another concern that I share with others is that if I must live in a nursing home or other medical facility at some point, will it be predominantly queer or at least senior LGBT-friendly?

Things are looking up apparently. The Gay and Lesbian Association for Retiring Persons, Inc., a 501(c) nonprofit public purpose corporation whose purpose is to enhance the aging process of members or couples in the GLBT community, lists three predominantly LGBT-only facilities currently operating, with five more in development. In California, the nonprofit Gay and Lesbian Elder Housing Association is about to break ground in Hollywood on an $18.6 million building that will have 104 affordable apartments and a community center for anyone LGBT or LGBT-affirmative.

The other major concern identified by senior gays and lesbians are the limited resources available to them, in terms of support groups geared toward people who come out at later ages, or avenues for meeting other gay seniors socially. Isolation is a problem for many seniors as their spouses or friends die off and biological families may be alienated over sexuality.

There is apparently hope on the horizon as groups such as SAGE (Senior Action in a Gay Environment) are working tirelessly to improve conditions for our seniors. According to their Web site, "professional social workers advocate for individual seniors in areas such as medical and legal services, home care, housing, and help with government and other benefits. SAGE is further committed to fostering a greater understanding of aging, to promoting positive images of life in the later years, and to supporting and advocating for the rights of senior gay, lesbian, bisexual, and transgender people in both the gay and straight communities."

Retirement may actually have a very positive side effect for queer seniors. Some researchers have found that lesbians and gay men were more likely to have a network of close friends than heterosexuals (possibly because heterosexuals tend to focus more on immediate family interactions rather than building outside friendships) and when work life is over and the kids are grown, there is more time for socializing. Another benefit for queer seniors may be that as we become freed from living with the threat of harassment on the job, or being fired because of our sexual orientation, we can become more socially and politically active without fear of financial consequences.

Grrrrrrr!

In many ways, lesbian and gay people have also resisted social stereotypes of "youth equals beauty" and clinging to traditional standards of attractiveness. Many lesbians, confronting both sexism and homophobia, choose to create their own standard of attractiveness that does not conform to these views. In some ways, the absence of visible role models for an openly gay person may have helped us find our own notions of who and what is hot.

Early out gay men sometimes intentionally assumed more feminine characteristics for a variety of reasons, but most probably because the first obvious gay men in the public eye shared these characteristics (think Oscar Wilde), and because they may have assumed that if they weren't like heterosexual men, they must be more like women. Similarly, the stereotypical "butch" lesbian may have taken on the characteristics of men, who were the only other models for people who were sexually attracted to women, and as a way to reject the traditional role of women in a sexist society. This, of course, is an oversimplification of the possible factors that may have contributed to early stereotypical behaviors, which may have also included biological or genetic factors as well.

The pressure to conform and fit in, at whatever age you are, is enormous. Typically we associate this pressure with adolescence and there are plenty of TV shows, books, and movies addressing this conflict, one of the best of which is *The Breakfast Club*, where the school jock, rebel, popular girl, nerd, and outcast in detention together, confront the layers of social strata that keep them separate during regular school hours. What is less obvious, however, is the continuing social pressure to conform as adults, to look and act like the community in which we live and work. Adult outcasts are treated perhaps even more viciously at times than teens, particularly if they are perceived as threatening the norm or tradition.

In some segments of the gay world, this pressure to conform exists as well today. The idea that you are "too old" to go clubbing, or that only the young or buff are beautiful, is something feared by many as they age and don't conform to what the magazines tell us is valuable.

In reaction to this enormous social pressure, however, there are subgroups within the larger gay world that openly challenge the notion that young is beautiful and buff is best. One of these groups, referred to as the bear movement, took the bull by the horns and created new standards of sexuality and beauty for men who felt that the mainstream gay culture was not welcoming to men who weren't hairless, firm, or young. Bears are typically mature gay or bisexual men, many with hairy bodies and facial hair. Some are heavy-set, but some are not. Some display hyper-masculine appearances, with flannel shirts, jeans, and boots, while other bears do not. The effort to avoid rigid definitions of what makes a bear is evidence of the attempt within this subculture to resist social pressure to conform. While some bears believe that you must have a hairy chest or face to qualify, others feel that anyone who identifies himself as a bear is one! Since its beginning in San Francisco in the 1980's the bear movement has grown to include many clubs and organizations, like the Gay Leatherbears and Big Musclebears, some of which unfortunately identify with their new standards so rigidly that men who do not fit in are excluded! Magazines that specifically cater to bears as sexy and desirable people have developed huge followings worldwide.

Lesbians too have created their own places of comfort and safety that include a large variation in appearance and behaviors. Some women, who prefer to dress in feminine clothes and use makeup, are alternately referred to as "lipstick lesbians" if they are attracted to other women who dress and act more feminine, and "femmes" if they are attracted to masculine women. Within some African-American and Hispanic lesbian communities, a term known as AG (for aggressive) lesbians, draws its influence from the rap world, complete with baggy pants, baseball caps, tattoos, diamonds, and language of the hip-hop scene.

One might argue that many younger people are also resisting gay and lesbian stereotypes, by virtue of refusing to even identify a specific sexual orientation or label, preferring instead to use the term "queer," meant to reflect the fluidity and continuum of sexuality without the need to categorize or define specifically what this includes for each individual.

Gender Differences in Aging

Some experts suggest that while there are shared similarities for older gay men and lesbians, there are issues that are unique to each group.

Gay men were, and are, significantly affected by the HIV epidemic in large numbers. Having lived through the hysteria around AIDS in the early 1980's changed my perspective on life. It changed the way I thought about the future and about the value of life in the moment. For some, the future seemed uncertain, even bleak because of the viral threat, and it became important to grab as much gusto as you could, since life would likely be short, and aging wasn't a realistic possibility in their worlds then. Today, AIDS still affects us and our young people, despite advances in treatment and a significantly extended lifespan. Some studies have suggested that an alarming rise in unprotected sex and drug use may be related to the idea that aging is frightening to some young people, and they see the probability of contracting HIV as inevitable, so they choose to die young and leave behind a beautiful corpse rather than coping with a bleak looking future. Much energy in the gay male community has been devoted to HIV, some suggest to the point of reduced focus on aging and retirement.

Lesbians, on the other hand, who were less directly impacted by HIV, may be more prepared to deal with the life changes associated with aging, since they didn't have as much stress associated with the epidemic and could focus more energy on preparing for retirement and beyond. One struggle for many lesbian couples is the financial impact of sexism in the workplace, namely that women continue to make less than men on average, about 80 cents to the dollar earned by men. This has real life consequences for a household with two women wage earners, versus two men. Until this disparity is corrected, through political activism from both men and women, lesbian families must plan for their futures carefully.

Reducing Stress with Planning

Suze Orman, financial guru and TV personality, who recently admitted during an interview that she is a lesbian, recommends signing a cohabitation agreement that sets forth your mutual rights and obligations with respect to joint and separate property, as well as stating any other financial or general obligations or expectations you wish to agree upon preferably in advance of, or even after, moving in together.

Because we do not have the automatic rights granted by federally recognized marriage, and only limited rights in states who allow same sex marriage or unions, we must take the extra step of creating legal relationships with those we love to help protect our wishes as we get older. Equally important would be creating a will that clearly identifies your wishes for how your assets should be distributed after your death, even if those assets are currently minimal.

In addition to recognizing our financial wishes, Brad Leary, my partner, who works as a hospice social worker with people facing a terminal illness, recommended that I address the other ways that same sex partners can take control of important parts of their lives. He is acutely aware of the family struggles that can occur over who is entitled to make important decisions for a person whose health or independence is declining. He recommends regularly to our friends that by thinking ahead, many of these problems can be avoided. For example, power of attorney (POA) is a legal instrument that is used to delegate legal authority to another person that you choose. The person who signs the POA can legally make property, financial, and other legal decisions for you should you become incapacitated.

There are different types of POA ranging from very broad to very specific and limited, for example, to situations where medical decisions need to be made for you.

Brad also recommends completing an advance directive form that tells your doctor what kind of care you would like to have if you become unable to make medical decisions (if you are in a coma, for example). These forms can be obtained from physicians, attorneys, health departments, or state departments on aging. Another practical form to consider is a disposition of remains form that can help you state what form of ceremony you wish (if any) after you have passed away and what will happen to your remains (burial, cremation, etc.). The last thing I would want to happen after my death, for example, would be a fundamentalist Christian funeral with a right wing minister with complete strangers clicking their tongues over the "pathetic, big city homo!"

Taking control over these issues by preparing ahead can go a long way in making the aging process more relaxed.

Confidence Throughout the Aging Process

My personal models for aging were from the South and from my family. The older people I saw regularly were from my large extended family and included tons of uncles, aunts, two sets of grandparents, and later, my own parents. Because I am from the rural South, the values around me were perhaps more old-fashioned about getting older. My religious upbringing did overtly teach respect for parents and for the wisdom of seniors. My favorite grandmother lived to be 99 years old and was an important force in my life and my perspectives on strength, love, and faith.

When I was younger, struggling within myself to identify the feelings that I had about myself and my sexuality, she was always there for me, even though I never shared with her these feelings. I like to think that if I had been brave enough to have talked to her about being gay, her personal wisdom that she accumulated from living through the Depression, her life of hard work and mothering 9 children, would have helped her understand. Regardless of her initial reaction though, I trust that her unconditional love for me would have been a constant. She provided a real life example for me of someone who was loving, sincere, and modest at every stage of life.

Given my own experiences as a therapist who has worked with many people across the lifespan, and the experiences growing up in a community rich with active and the rare studies that do focus on LGBT aging, there are a few common themes that emerge.

1. *Build a strong social support network.* Regardless of sexual orientation, developing and maintaining a strong social support network is of utmost importance. Whereas heterosexuals tend to focus on relationships within the family sustaining them into the senior years, it is likely that LGBT adults focus more on the created family of close friends that understand and accept them as they are. We must do better as a community in providing safe and supportive environments for our older adults and seniors to come out in and to socialize. Joining groups like SAGE and the Senior Pride Network, even before you feel the need personally, can help these groups continue their work to increase the visibility of LGBT seniors and provide more resources for those that may need it now.

2. *Coming out, come out!* A few studies of our older adults strongly support that the act of coming out leads to better self-esteem. Years of living in the closet can wear you down, keep you feeling edgy or anxious, and prevent you from making connections with others. If your job was a major reason for staying in the closet, make leaving the closet one of your retirement plans. Freedom to be who you are is priceless.

3. *Find a sense of purpose.* Many of us develop self-esteem that is built on our professional accomplishments or through our roles as parents. When the kids are grown and we approach retirement, the foundation of that self-worth can diminish, leaving you feeling alone and useless. People who find new

passions, new meanings, and new roles that keep them motivated tend to deal with the aging process better than those who continually mourn the losses but haven't found new outlets or interests. Meaning or purpose can take many forms, from volunteering with a school, to getting that degree you always wanted, to pursuing better intimacy with your friends or partner. Find something that makes you smile, feel needed, or look forward to the day.

4. *Stay active and fit.* Your mind and body are, and always have been, connected. Your mood and sense of well being is directly linked to your fitness level, no matter what age. Fitness has many benefits, including improved cardiovascular function, reduced stress levels, and greater physical mobility. Endorphins, produced during exercise, can both help you relax and can improve your sleep quality. Make exercising and eating right a priority now to enjoy better health across your lifespan.

5. *Formalize your plans.* Many people worry about the "what ifs" of the future—financial, health, and estate problems can come up for anyone. Lesbian and gay people often have additional worries about these issues given the inability to marry and other lack of legal recognitions for our rights and protection. While we can't predict or control for every possible issue that might arise, there are ways that we can avoid some of the potential problems through good planning. Your ideas about how you would like to spend your senior years, how to invest for your retirement, where you would like your money and assets to go when you die, where you would like to go if you need living assistance, and how you would like your remains to be handled are all important things to think about, but if you don't take steps to formalize these plans practically and legally, they may just remain ideas.

Take the opportunity sooner rather than later to protect yourself and your investments in formal, legally binding ways. An attorney sensitive to the needs of LGBT people is a good place to start and the National Lesbian and Gay Law

Association (an affiliate of the American Bar Association) can help you get started. Attorneys can help you with creating a legal relationship with your partner, can help you set up your will, and provide you with all the other paperwork that would be helpful in carrying out your wishes should you become incapacitated or die. Often, many firms who specialize in lesbian or gay legal concerns have a special package rate for helping you complete the basic will and testament, power of attorney, and other advance directive paperwork so that you can feel more secure about the future. The Gay Financial Network (www.gfn.com) provides an online directory of LGBT (or friendly) financial planners who understand the special needs and challenges of queer people and money, especially around your investments, retirement accounts, and taxes.

Anything you haven't written down somewhere in a legally binding form is essentially useless if you cannot speak for yourself someday. Give yourself some peace of mind by taking care of these things now.

6. *Challenge negative, ageist thinking.* By now, if you've read the rest of the book, you know that my thing is thinking. Just like I encouraged you to examine your own internalized homophobia, the negative messages about your self-worth from your family or upbringing, and the ways that you may be repeating these messages today, the way that you handle the aging process will have a lot to do with confronting negative thinking about age and self-worth. It is too easy to go along with "old people" jokes, with buying into the media images of beautiful young people as the only standard, and living your life as a stereotype that limits your choices and your satisfaction. Take some time to confront these internal messages and to challenge the "accepted" view of older people in this society. Hang around some older people who don't fit the stereotype, who are active, happy, and energetic, long after retirement, and you might just find yourself mesmerized.

I mentioned earlier in the chapter that I did some research about images of gay and lesbian people by flipping through some magazines. I also mentioned that I would come back to the *Genre* magazine specifically, so let me now share why this issue is on our coffee table.

After about a year into my relationship with Brad, we decided that we wanted some nice pictures of us together, just for the house and our desks at work. I found a gay photographer in San Francisco who agreed to give us a good price for one roll of film. We headed to the city, hoping that we'd get at least one good shot that we both liked. After we finished the shoot, the photographer offered to take them immediately to a photo lab that he liked so that we could get the results right away. While we were looking them over later, the photographer casually asked if we would be interested in reducing his fee by agreeing to put a couple of the shots in a stock photo agency as a "gay couple." With "fee reduction" flashing in our heads, we quickly agreed and signed the papers, thinking the request a bit odd and that our shots would sit in a file cabinet somewhere in Butte or Poughkeepsie. We took our prints home and lovingly placed them in frames.

One evening, while searching the Internet together in preparation for our commitment ceremony, Brad and I clicked on a gay wedding Web site and were shocked to see our own images looking back at us! Over the next few months, those shots that we signed away began popping up almost everywhere. Our friends, even more surprised than us, could hardly contain themselves when they would open a *Genre* magazine or click on a Web site and there we were. The high point was one night when my friend Mary called at 10:30 p.m. screaming into the phone, "Turn on Comedy Central!" Turns out, we were a background graphic on *The Colbert Report*!

Why tell you this story, you ask? Having never really thought of myself as a specimen of physical beauty, it reinforced the notion for me that this middle-aged, balding and graying, gay man is a part of the queer world. For whatever reason, for however brief the fifteen minutes, Brad and I were one of advertising's "real gay couples." Real is good. I am who I am.

Questions for Reflection

- Who were your role models for aging as a child?
- What was your culture's attitude about older people when you were growing up?
- How often did you spend time with someone elderly when you were a kid?
- What were the early messages you received about older lesbians or gays, if any?
- What is your gut reaction to the idea of getting older yourself? What are your reactions to senior or elderly people in general and older lesbian or gay people specifically?
- How do you see yourself in 5 years? Ten years or more?
- What are your plans for after retirement?
- What can you do to accept yourself and age more gracefully?

Resources

AgeLine, research.aarp.org/ageline

Classic Dykes, www.classicdykes.com

Gay and Lesbian Association of Retiring Persons, Inc., www.gaylesbianretiring.org

Gay and Lesbian Elder Housing, www.gleh.org

Gay Financial Network, www.gfn.com

Lesbian and Gay Aging Issues Network, www.asaging.org/lgain

National Lesbian and Gay Law Association, www.nlgla.org

Old Hags and Sagging Bags: A Forum for Ancient Crossdressers, www.geocities.com/WestHollywood/8938/ohsb.htm

Old Lesbians Organizing for Change, www.oloc.org

Services and Advocacy for Gay, Lesbian, Bisexual & Transgender Elders (SAGE), www.sageusa.org

Transgender Aging Network, www.forge-forward.org/tan

FIFTEEN

Queer Parenting
and Self-Esteem

According to Ellen Perrin, MD, professor of pediatrics at Tufts University Medical School in Boston, between 1 million and 6 million children in the U.S. are being reared by committed lesbian or gay couples with most either born to a heterosexual couple, adopted, or conceived through artificial insemination.

How and when queer people become parents is as diverse as the reasons that non-queer people become parents. Some become parents from sexual experimentation when they were young, without intending to end up with a child. A few are conceived through rape or coerced sex. Others who haven't become aware of their same sex attractions by the time they are adults follow through on societal and family expectations, get married to someone of the opposite sex, and do what typically happens next—have a baby or two.

More recently, in a growing cultural phenomenon, which likely parallels our society's growing acceptance of gays and their relationships and also reflects the technological advances in reproductive medicine, some of us are actively choosing to be parents. Lesbian or gay couples are discussing, planning for, and eagerly awaiting the birth or adoption of a child more than ever. Most queer couples that I know have approached the idea of parenting very seriously and sincerely, and have devoted countless hours and boundless energy to the process of being good parents, regardless of whether or not they actually go on to raise a child. There is always an awareness of potential legal and social complications that could imperil the process that were necessarily incorporated into their child-rearing. Contracts, agreements, and financial arrangements are often discussed openly between partners who don't have the legal protection of marriage in many areas prior to becoming pregnant or pursuing adoption.

Queer parenting remains a touchy subject for many heterosexuals—specifically the idea of a same-sex couple rearing a child, regardless of how the child was conceived or welcomed. Maybe the social discomfort is a result of old disproved myths suggesting all homosexuals are pedophiles. Or maybe at a deeper level, it is the idea that any non-traditional household that "works" is threatening to the people who cling to rigid views of how the world must be, in order to calm their own anxieties about life and the unknown. Or maybe we're just looking at plain old institutional sexism, misogyny, or religious intolerance. Homophobes suggest all types of reasons that we shouldn't parent, from the perspective of "marriage is for procreation only," to irrational anxieties about the psychological health of the child (e.g., "A child needs to have both a mother and a father to grow up correctly"), to concern for the child's socialization and safety (e.g., "Life will be so much harder for them with their school peers"). The last issue is of particular interest to me since homophobic solutions for social risk typically include limiting the ability of queers to parent, rather than focusing on reducing the cultural homophobia that makes society less safe for children in general.

Thankfully, the American Psychological Association's Committee on Lesbian, Gay, and Bisexual Concerns has been actively attempting to reduce stigmatization, prejudice, and violence for sexual minorities from a rational, science-based perspective since 1975 — *and hasn't found one shred of evidence that children raised by gays are at a disadvantage.* In fact, a few studies even suggest that children raised by queer parents may have some advantages over children raised by a traditional heterosexual couple! In their 2005 summary of available research studies, the CLGBC, along with the Committees on Children, Youth, and Families and the Committee on Women in Psychology, finds that many criticisms of early research in this area, namely small sample sizes and limited diversity in terms of race, culture, and gender of the subjects, have been addressed as more research has been focused on this topic, and methodology has been improved. If you'd like to see this very comprehensive summary of exactly what the research says, please visit APA's Web site listed at the end of this chapter.

As the evidence overwhelmingly suggests, there are no valid arguments against parenting, based solely on sexual orientation. Having said that, there are always ways that parents who are interested in promoting the best health and well-being of their children can facilitate this process.

There are two parts to this chapter that address a few of these ways of improving your parenting. First, we'll spend some time exploring your style of parenting and how self-esteem may impact your ability to parent. The second part will provide some suggestions on strategies for building good self-esteem in your child or children.

SELF-ESTEEM AND PARENTING

Most of us were raised by heterosexual parents who hadn't a clue as to how to intentionally raise a child with great self-esteem, regardless of their eventual sexual orientation or gender identity. They either had good self-esteem themselves, and, therefore, based their style of parenting you on what they must have learned from their parents, or they perpetuated child-rearing strategies that didn't always promote self-confidence or well-being. You are probably lucky if your parent or parents were raised by someone who had good self-esteem. So much of our styles are transmitted unconsciously, through role modeling and imitation, that we likely picked up at least a few mannerisms and values from our parents, even if intellectually we know that they weren't the best methods based on our experiences from childhood.

Your emotional impulses at crucial parenting moments are subject to the same internalized messages about behavior and self-worth that we've talked about in other chapters throughout the book. Given that most heterosexual parents assume that they are raising heterosexual children, and therefore selectively praise or reject behaviors or feelings that they feel are appropriate, it is highly likely that you picked up messages that you may or may not have confronted within yourself about what behaviors are healthy or praise-worthy in your own children. Add to your family's own specific beliefs and values that you've incorporated, the parenting styles in the community in which you were raised, for your specific generation, and you'll find even more beliefs about child-rearing practices that you may need to challenge or change. My own parents, for example, were from an era, in the conservative rural South, that supported the notion that sternness and physical forms of punishment were important and necessary ways to build character. Parents who chose not to spank a disruptive child in a public place would frequently be met with open scorn and disapproval from their peers! While not all parenting experts today agree on the use of spanking, most agree that physical force applied in a haphazard, emotionally charged or abusive way can be devastating to the child's developing identity.

As I explored in the early chapters of the book, I often find a parallel between how my clients were parented when they were children and their later, internalized self-talk. The more harshly they were treated as kids, the more negative and punitive the self-talk later. But before we take a look at your own unique internalized messages about parenting, let's take a look at a few "theories" of proper parenting strategies that you may have picked up along the way.

Parenting Theories

While the idea of learning to parent from a book or a class may seem strange to some people, many parents, particularly in an increasingly mobile society that moves from location to location and job to job, have chosen over the years to try to improve their parenting through parenting education materials. In some cultures, parenting advice comes from having a large extended family, with tons of uncles and aunts and grandparents, who actively participate in child-rearing and advising. I spent countless hours with my cousins, who were my closest friends and peers. Our lives seemed so similar in many ways that it took me a while to realize that the world didn't see things exactly the way we all did.

In the advent of the baby boom, however, with large numbers of WWII GI's returning home from war to start families, and the US economy growing with industrialization, books on how to raise children proliferated. One author, who literally became a cultural icon, Dr. Benjamin Spock, was a kindly pediatrician whose 1946 book, *Baby and Child Care*, became a huge best-seller with a lasting effect on the cultural conscience. In it, he encouraged parents to try to understand their children, a concept, believe it or not, that didn't carry much weight in the "children should be seen and not heard" era that preceded Dr. Spock. He often encouraged parents to understand what to expect from their children at every important developmental stage and to play an encouraging, supportive role. He emphasized being flexible as a parent, rather than adhering to hard and fast rules about things like when to feed a child or what kind of food they should be eating. Millions of young parents carried his books around for guidance and reference and it continues to be in print with an active Web site even today (www.drspock.com).

Dr. Spock's ideas about flexible, individualized parenting were criticized at the time as "too permissive," based on fears that overindulging a child could somehow make them demanding or narcissistic. Alternative parenting theories, some from more conservative ideologies like James Dobson of the intolerant Focus on the Family organization, promote their own approaches to child-rearing by closely tying parenting educational materials to right wing religious beliefs rather than on science. Dobson's empire currently, for example, includes recommendations for books such as A *Parent's Guide to Preventing Homosexuality*, written by Joseph Nicolosi, a reparative therapy advocate whose views have been rejected by the vast majority of mental health professionals in the U.S. today for his poor methodology and lack of scientific evidence. If Dobson and his organization are willing to recommend materials of this nature, it makes you wonder about the quality of his other recommendations regarding parenting! It makes me shudder to think of the harm that these supposed parenting authorities have wreaked on the children of their followers by attempting to shape a child's identity through parental will alone.

As I mentioned early in the book, there has been quite a bit of research that has examined parenting styles and the effect on the child. Excessively authoritarian or permissive parents often transmit messages, both directly and indirectly, that the child's feelings and needs don't matter, leading to the internalized negative messages that I've referred to throughout the book.

The recent controversy over parenting styles and how they may be related to the notion that there is such as thing as "excessively high" self-esteem arose out of a concern that by overly praising a child for attributes that they have no control over, like physical appearance, or praising them lavishly and constantly, even when they did not earn the praise through achievement or effort, that they become inflated with a type of falsely high self-esteem. Most experts would agree that children need structure and authority, but they need authority that is loving, firm, and respectful of their feelings even when they don't get their way—the authoritative model. Experts now are also recommending tying praise to actual achievement to enhance feelings of self-confidence, rather than producing children who are high in "self-like," who feel invincible and take unnecessary risks or are unable to take constructive feedback. Compliments are recommended for true accomplishments and making good choices rather than unlimited positives as a form of affection. Encourage your child to talk about feelings of disappointment and guilt and generally handling feelings responsibly; help them learn from their feelings and about the power and potential of mistakes to help them grow.

Again, regardless of the actual training your own parents received, or theory that they followed, the most powerful factor that likely shaped your self-esteem was the model that they provided to you in unspoken ways. If the model was harsh and self-destructive, you may continue to use this type of voice with yourself. Deconditioning yourself from this type of early training requires diligence and patience. Learning to counteract the inappropriate values that you picked up, or the unreasonable demands you place on yourself, can help you present a healthier role model for your own children. Watching you make mistakes, but then seeing you learn from them, accepting responsibility, and making healthy steps to deal with the consequences can go a long way towards instilling these values and skills into your own little ones. Even if your children are grown, you still may be a powerful role model for them in confronting aging and issues that will affect them later in life.

Your Self-Esteem Responsibilities

In order to build healthy self-esteem in a child, you must work on building it in yourself. Even if you understand what the current research says about good parenting styles, and you take workshops on parenting skills, children learn from us from watching our choices and our behaviors, as much as listening to what we say.

Your self-esteem level will be transparent to your children. They will learn from you, as you did from your own parents, how to handle disappointment, joy, success, and failure. Whether or not you actively teach these things to your child, they will observe it through your body language, your reactions, and your mood.

To be a good example for your children then, you must take an active role in taking care of yourself. You must learn to overcome your own self-abuse or criticism, to demonstrate the importance of actively treating yourself with respect and modeling the nurturing and accepting behaviors you may have wished that you had when you were a child. You have taken the first step by even reading this book and exploring some old, bad habits that affect the choices in your life. Becoming a role model by demonstrating realistic self-assessment skills and demonstrating healthy self-care around emotions is one of the most important things that you can do as a parent.

If you know that you have issues with your own self-esteem, make a plan to address them soon and regularly. If you have children now, will have them soon, or your self-esteem is particularly low, don't be afraid to seek professional help, specifically to develop a self-esteem building program and give you opportunities to explore how your childhood experiences shaped your own parenting style.

BUILDING HEALTHY SELF-ESTEEM IN YOUR CHILDREN

It's fairly obvious at this point that the most important piece of advice that I can provide in this section is a continuation of the previous section. In other words, your best opportunity for building healthy self-esteem in your child is by modeling healthy self-esteem within yourself.

Given that however, there are child-rearing experts who have studied the issue and have concluded that there are specific skills that can improve the chances of raising a child with a healthy, responsible sense of self-esteem. I will attempt to summarize some of the general recommendations here and will list resources at the end of this chapter for you to explore later for even more detail.

Infancy

Keep in mind that we are born without a sense of self, much less "self-esteem" when we are born. Children learn that they are lovable because parents care for them lovingly and smile at them regularly. Nonverbal communication is the only kind there is at this age, so gentle touches, being held, being changed and fed in a timely manner, and responsive interaction when there is pain or discomfort are all important ways to begin the self-esteem engendering process.

Toddlers

At this age, children still don't have a fully developed sense of self but see themselves through the eyes of their parents. They learn about who they are by exploring what they look like, the things they can do with their bodies, and whether they can count on a positive response from a parent when they are afraid or uncomfortable. Parents become the safe base to which they return after they've explored the world a bit. There is no ability to discern an unexpected reaction from a parent as related to them or related to another distraction. Everything is translated from a "me" perspective—how the world affects the child and how the child affects the world. There is little awareness that events can happen in the world that have nothing to do with them and along with that, events or objects that they don't see, don't exist!

Toddlers see themselves only through the messages that they receive from their parents. If these messages are that they are lovable and important, they will develop a positive sense of self. On the other hand, if these messages are that they are an interruption or pest, self-esteem will begin to reflect this sentiment.

Preschoolers

Around age 3, most children have established a basic sense of self as separate from Mom or Dad and can spend time away from the folks because they've established an inner sense of safety. Most of their information about themselves however comes from making physical comparisons to others their age, such as who can jump the highest or yell the loudest. As language develops, they begin to understand and use symbols for things, like pictures in a book or words that describe a color or size.

School Age (Pre-Puberty)

Starting school is often the first time a child has had to deal with life in a new environment, with new rules and new relationships all at once. Achievements include successfully fitting in with others, keeping up with learning new skills in the classroom, performing at sports during recess, and making friends. Problems at home or school can affect healthy development of self-esteem, especially if they distract from the tasks they are expected to be mastering.

Puberty and Adolescence

Just about the time a child is learning to feel pretty good about him or herself, having established some mastery over their world in some areas, the body begins to grow and change in ways that throw everything they thought they knew out of whack! Timing is crucial at this age, and maturing before or after the rest of your classmates can be traumatic. New identities are forming to match these new, more adult-looking bodies and another phase of identity development begins here as they attempt to establish their independence. Group belonging is especially important here as the teen attempts to feel good about him or herself.

Each of these phases includes crucial steps that the child must master on the way to the next stage. Frustration and anxiety about failure at new experiences is common, as are feelings of anger, resentment, and sadness as the child experiences limit-setting by you, the parent. Helping your child learn to cope with these feelings by owning, expressing calmly, and channeling them into healthy opportunities for learning can go a long way towards building confidence and resiliency in handling life later on.

Signs of Low Self-Esteem in Children

According to the experts at Kids' Health for Parents, an important Web site providing doctor-approved health information about children, signs of low self-esteem in children include:

- Not wanting to try new things.
- Frequently speaking negatively about him or herself, saying such things as, "I'm stupid," "I'll never learn how to do this," or "What's the point? Nobody cares about me anyway."
- Low tolerance for frustration, giving up easily, or waiting for somebody else to take over.
- Being overly critical of and easily disappointed in themselves.
- Seeing temporary setbacks as permanent, intolerable conditions.
- A predominant sense of pessimism.

Things You Can Do as a Parent

1. One of the most important things that you can do for your children is to accept them for who they are and help them do the same for themselves. Practicing self-acceptance will give you some tools for helping your child understand this concept and as I mentioned before, will provide an example for them to model. A good way to check their self-esteem is to observe how they handle mistakes. For example, if she misses a goal in soccer, she may choose one of several ways of dealing with this, including trying to figure out what went wrong to work on it for next time, or she might choose to blame the referee or herself. Children who have good self-esteem believe that their successes are based on what they do and that it comes from inside. Those with low self-esteem often pin their success on luck and failures on fate.
2. Keep your expectations reasonable and realistic. Children are very attuned to their parents' reactions to things and they need to know that people make mistakes sometimes and that no one is perfect.
3. Help your kids find things that they do well so that they can experience pride in a job well done. Give them chances to try new things that interest them until they find the one that they enjoy and are enthusiastic about, even if it surprises you.
4. Give your kids real responsibilities that they can be in

"charge of" so that they can learn that they make a difference and have something to contribute.

5. Allow your child to make choices and then be prepared to discuss the results of those choices, good or bad. Decision-making skills will be invaluable later in life when the choices get tougher!

6. Be supportive when they need you. Make time to listen to their joys, sorrows, guilt, and anger, without judgment or criticism. Teach them that it's ok to have feelings and to learn from them, but that the behaviors that follow the feelings are a choice. During times of disappointment or failure, sit down and process it with them realistically, while letting them know that your love and support are a constant no matter what.

7. Give them your time and spend time alone with them. This is one of the non-verbal ways that you can communicate that they are important to you and that time with them is of value.

8. Help your child learn to build healthy relationships with others by teaching them to communicate directly, but with sensitivity about how they feel and what they want. Help them learn healthy ways of dealing with conflict and how to compromise and share with others.

9. Be clear about your own family's values, such as respecting diversity and other belief systems, even when you don't agree.

10. Give them praise when they do well, but show them your appreciation for their interests and efforts. Appreciating an effort may actually go farther in building healthy self-esteem than empty praise for a performance that in reality falls short of praise-worthy. Keep your feedback positive, but accurate.

11. Teach them to identify and redirect inaccurate beliefs that they may hold (much like you are learning to do with yourself). Learning to test strong beliefs that make you feel insecure or angry or depressed and to look for supporting and disconfirming evidence is a skill that will be invaluable to them later. Teach them to practice making positive, but

realistic, self-statement such as "If I just keep trying, I can get this problem" rather than "I'm so stupid, I'll never get this!"

12. Normalize the struggles of adolescence and other hard times by letting them know that the teen years are hard for everyone, even you!

13. Support their schoolwork by taking an interest and offering to help, but without taking over. Get to know their teachers and make yourself available to the school when you can.

14. Be as consistent as possible with how you apply your parenting style. Children thrive when they know the rules, understand the consequences of bad behaviors, and can trust that the routine is reliable. Set clear and consistent limits.

15. Keep special mementoes of their achievements and milestones.

16. Develop special family rituals like bedtime stories, kisses good-bye, etc. that are traditions for your family. Physical expressions of affection, such as hugs and cuddles, are particularly important nonverbal ways of saying that you care about them.

17. Give unconditional love. This may be hard for you if you do not feel that you received this yourself. You may need to spend some time mulling over the difference between love that is tied to a specific performance or behavior (and could be snatched away if you make a mistake), and love that is there no matter what mistakes, accidents, or bad choices your child makes. Remember though, that unconditional love does not mean that you don't apply appropriate consequences for behavior that violates the family rules.

18. Resist comparisons between siblings. Comments like "Why can't you be more like your sister Kate?" only serve to remind your child of where he or she struggles in a way that may encourage envy, shame, and competition.

19. Avoid criticism that takes the form of ridicule or shame. Criticizing a child's actions when they make a mistake or bad decision is sometimes necessary and appropriate. But when it's directed towards the child's character (e.g., "You always

make the wrong choice!"), they can begin to feel inadequate and shameful. Try to use "I" statements such as "I would like you to wipe your feet before you come into the room rather than tracking it through the house" rather than "you" statements like "Why are you so filthy and disrespectful?" This may take practice, but also can be helpful in adult relationships as well!

20. Help your child develop several alternatives and possibilities when planning an activity, rather than putting all of their eggs in one basket. A child who only allows for one option experiences greater disappointment when it doesn't work out than a child who has made several "Plan B's."

Dealing with the "Gay" Issue

Frankly, good parenting is good parenting is good parenting, regardless of the gender or relationship status of the parents. As I mentioned before, the American Psychological Association has found no evidence that children raised by opposite sex parents are any better off than kids raised by same sex parents.

Yet, one of the unique issues often confronted by queer families is when and how to address the differences and potential challenges the child will face from a homophobic society in an effort to inoculate them when and if teasing or verbal assaults occur.

In an excellent publication by the Family Pride Coalition entitled *Talking to Children About Our Families*, authors Margie Brickley and Aimee Gelnaw address queer parenting concerns and provide some guidance for talking to kids about our families.

Their suggestions for babies under three fall in line with other good parenting suggestions I've discussed—showing them lots of affection, creating family rituals that include alone time with each parent, and celebrating a sense of togetherness. They go on to affirm the importance of using consistent language and names for family members like "Mimi" or "Papa." Having an extended family within the lgbt community, including people who will provide consistently positive messages to your child about your family is also important at this age.

For children ages 4 to 7, Brickly and Gelnaw suggest being careful to answer questions simply and honestly, but without providing so much information that the child gets confused. At this age, they'll be asking lots of questions about just about everything and the authors suggest that sometimes, responding to the deeper questions with a question, like "What do you think?" can help you understand more about what they're really wanting to know. Included in the article are examples of specific ways to have conversations about things like adoption, artificial insemination and surrogacy. Books can be helpful at this age that tell similar stories of nontraditional families, such as families that are "blended" (from previous relationships), multiracial, or just different from the other families in the neighborhood or school.

For children 8 and older, fitting in with others is one of the most important developmental tasks. Children may be reluctant to talk about families at this age, especially as they become aware that their families are "different" and may need to assume control of who they tell about their families. Having positive role models from you at this point is crucial, particularly about being proud and respectful of yourself and who you are. Helping them feel that you are safe, and not in danger, because of your sexual orientation is essential at this age as well.

Helping them learn and practice ways of handling questions from their peers can help them feel empowered. For example, when another child asks about mom's sexual orientation, Brickly and Gelnaw suggest answering directly "Yes, she is" rather than trying to keep it a secret, which can be a stressor in and of itself. Teaching them how to ask for help and support from adults like teachers or administrators if they need it can also enhance feelings of safety and reduce fear. Teaching them how to walk away from confrontation when necessary or being assertive when appropriate are important skills to learn early during this phase as well. Encouraging them to find friends who are accepting of their families or helping them participate in groups like Children of Lesbian and Gays Everywhere (COLAGE) can help them build strength through allies.

In sum, above all else, communication in both directions, regularly, is the key to educating your children about our lives specifically, but also about the full range of options for creating families, regardless of their eventual sexual orientation or family choices.

Professional Guidance as a Resource

One chapter is definitely not enough to address the issues that I've highlighted here. Being a parent is one of the most wonderful and challenging responsibilities of life. As a therapist, I admit that I am biased, but even if you've never considered going to a mental health professional or self-help class before, I urge you to take advantage of the myriad of resources that are available to help you with this journey.

Those options include parenting classes at local hospitals, social service agencies, and even community colleges or universities nearby. While you may have a good heart, full of love and good intentions, good parenting is a skill and there is plenty of information out there based on other parents' experiences and studies of methods that lead to healthier children, both physically and emotionally.

If you recognize specific issues that you have not worked through about your own childhood, and these threaten to affect your own choices, don't be afraid to get into counseling to identify and manage these issues so that they don't indirectly affect the little people you bring into your home. They are impressionable and sensitive and can see through "bad acting" quicker than Ebert or Roeper on their best day!

If you are co-parenting your child or children with someone else, whether it be your partner, your ex, your surrogate, or your biological donor, there are specific forms of co-parenting counseling designed to help improve communication between all involved parties and at a minimum, reduce any potential negative impact on the child. Be very careful not to use your child as a pawn over unresolved emotional breakup issues or feuds. There are therapists that also specialize in working with the entire family together, rather than singling out one member for individual treatment, which can help identify dysfunctional family communication or patterns and help the family adopt new ways of relating to each other.

Finally, don't be afraid to take your child to a child psychologist or therapist, especially when you identify problems that are affecting your child's school or home life and are not getting resolved on their own. A good child psychologist will make the experience more comfortable and will include you in the process of evaluation and treatment. Don't be frightened away from this resource by fears of "overdiagnosis" or "overmedication" if your child is suffering. If you feel that the therapist or doctor is not right for you or your child, don't be afraid to ask questions, raise your concerns, and if necessary, take your child to another professional with whom you feel more comfortable.

Resources

American Psychological Association Summary of Queer Parenting Research Studies, www.apa.org/pi/parent.html.

Child Development Institute, www.childdevelopmentinfo.com/parenting/self_esteem.shtml

Children of Lesbians and Gays Everywhere, www.colage.org

Gay Parent Magazine , www.gayparentmag.com

Kids' Health for Parents, www.kidshealth.org/parent/emotions/feelings/self_esteem.html

Parents, Families and Friends of Lesbians and Gays (PFLAG), www.pflag.org

Prospective Queer Parents Online Resources, www.queerparents.org

Talking to Children About Our Families, by Margie Brickley and Aimee Gelnaw, published by the Family Pride Coalition and available at www.familypride.org

Sixteen

Life on the Down Low

LIVING DOWN LOW, DOWN LOW
LIVING THAT DOUBLE LIFE
IT AIN'T RIGHT
—R. Kelly, "Down Low Double Life"

In 2004, Oprah had a guest on her show that viewers had never heard of before, yet his appearance changed the cultural dialogue on sexuality unlike any other. The man's name was J. L. King, an African-American publishing executive and author of *On the Down Low*, discussing his life of living as a heterosexual man, but secretly having sex with other men on the side. His basic premise was to link the rise of HIV in African-American women (and men) to this practice of sex on the "down low," claiming that the practice was much more common than generally recognized.

Although people were discussing this topic before Mr. King's appearance, the wider audience reached by Oprah's show prompted an explosive cultural dialogue about men who have sex with other men, yet identify themselves as exclusively or predominantly heterosexual, not gay or bisexual.

Many people have argued that some of the initial hysteria, particularly the assumption that "down low" behavior was primarily responsible for rising rates of HIV in African-American women was not actually supported by the epidemiological data. Keith Boykin, author and gay activist, followed J. L. King's book with his own, *Beyond the Down Low*, which actually takes a more thorough look at a complex issue and teases through much of the media frenzy that arose around this issue using facts and experience. Mr. Boykin helps us examine the social pressures that have created a need for black gay and bisexual men to feel like they must lead double lives. He also exposes the myth that the "down low" is exclusively a black male phenomenon. He rightly points out that while the term is a new one, the practice of leading secret lives crosses all ethnic and gender lines. Plenty of heterosexual white people choose to sleep around on their spouses, both men and women. It's the stuff sleazy novels and TV movies are made of.

The term "down low" has a thousand meanings, from a description of a man married to a woman who occasionally has sex with men, but identifies as a heterosexual, to cheating on a spouse, regardless of the genders involved. Sexual activity on the side has definitely been around thousands of years, so often the hysteria around this topic adds to the confusion, more than it helps the discussion.

In this chapter, my focus will be to explore some of the varieties of "double lives" and "down low" behaviors that affect gay men and lesbians, from gay-bashing politicians who later are outed involuntarily, to women or men in heterosexual marriages who come out to themselves only after they have created families. And of course, I will discuss the ways that self-esteem may manifest in the lives of these people struggling to survive in a sea of conflicts, pressures, and responsibilities.

AWARENESS

Despite a world of resources and information these days, on TV, through the Internet, and even visible community organizations (at least in urban centers), coming out to one's self and to others can still be difficult. Much of this book is devoted to just how hard it can be to confront direct and institutional homophobia. Coming out is a process. There are many factors that affect that process, from the era in which you were raised, the cultural attitudes toward sexuality and "differentness" of your community, to the religiosity and theology of your family. Much has been written about the coming out process, with attempts to be more inclusive of the diversity of experiences of people from all kinds of backgrounds.

Because of the complex interactions of many factors, it is still difficult to predict when someone will realize that they have same sex attractions, and once they do, if and when they will choose to act on those feelings. Society takes some of the blame for making it a hostile world for people who do not fit the accepted forms of sexuality. Even if some families have never uttered a homophobic word or action, it doesn't mean that the anticipation of rejection by friends or family, based on larger social messages can't exert pressure on one's psyche.

The pressure to conform, to fit in, is enormous. Studies of children, as young as 5 or 6, suggest that they are influenced by social pressure and will adjust their behavior in public to blend in. Advertisers capitalize on this knowledge by exerting intentional influences through TV commercials and product placement within youth-oriented programming.

So, even today, some people become aware of their feelings of being different early in life, for me at 12 or so, and others don't become aware until much later in their adult life. From a psychological perspective, the concept of *repression* may explain part of the puzzle of why people come out at such different phases of life. Repression represents the psychological act of excluding desires and impulses from your consciousness and attempting to keep them under wraps in the unconscious. Freud's followers referred to repression as a *defense mechanism*, which is a tool that your mind uses, of which you are likely unaware, to reduce anxiety when your impulses (*id*) conflict with your conscience (*superego*), where information is stored about what behaviors are "bad" and "good." Your superego of course is also your internal moral compass, formed by the messages from society that you were raised with. In this example, if your superego, therefore, was shaped by a strict religious upbringing that condemns homosexuality and parents who expressed openly hostile homophobia, you will experience enormous guilt and anxiety if repressed feelings of desire for someone of the same sex emerge.

Defense mechanisms, according to psychodynamic psychological theory, are necessary and healthy if used properly. An uncontrolled sexual urge would obviously be a potentially dangerous thing, in terms of disease and risk behaviors, but a sexual urge that is completely controlled can lead to problems of its own. It is possible that we can use defense mechanisms maladaptively, particularly if using them distorts our perception of reality. It's also possible that you can have an overactive superego that constantly makes you feel guilty and anxious, in which case you use too many defense mechanisms.

For example, other forms of psychological defense mechanisms include *projection* (accusing others of harboring your own unwanted desires), *reaction formation* (turning your unconscious, unacceptable wishes into the opposite wish), and *splitting* (seeing people as all good or all bad).

A defense mechanism becomes pathological when it is used in a rigid, inflexible, or exclusive way, or using the defense leads to significant problems in current relationships, work, or satisfaction in life.

Some or all of these deep-seated emotional processes may be responsible, at least in part, for determining when people are ready to identify sexual feelings for the same sex. Because these forces are largely unconscious, that means that generally the person may have no idea that these feelings exist until the defense system begins to break down, or the desires begin to creep into the conscious mind, forcing a different kind of mental gymnastic to keep it under control.

There are many thoughts about how someone who thought they

were heterosexual exclusively at one point in their life could later "discover" an attraction to people of the same sex. A psychoanalyst that follows the teachings of Freud might suggest that defense mechanisms were responsible for keeping those feelings from our awareness. A cognitive therapist might discuss this phenomenon as *dissonance*, the discomfort we all feel in learning something new, especially if it contradicts what we think we already know and believe in. A fundamentalist Christian might believe that the person succumbed to Satanic temptation. Some believe in a binary world of "either heterosexuality or homosexuality" with nothing in between, while others understand the complexity of human sexuality in all of its forms.

Regardless of your explanation, it is easy to see why it may take time to work through the layers of social expectations, family or religious teachings, and personal fears regarding change and disappointments to come to terms with your sexuality.

In an ideal world, once a child or adult became aware of an emerging sexuality that may not fit the majority practices, they would quickly begin to discuss these feelings with friends and family, who would then offer enormous support as the person worked through the feelings and exploratory behaviors. Real experiences, however, suggest that society has some catching up to do.

Patrick, a 50-year-old, gay man from the Boston area, with French-Irish roots, came from a working class, devoutly Catholic family with two older sisters. He remembers himself as much more outgoing and social as a small child than he was later as an adolescent or adult, but isn't sure exactly why or when the shift happened. He attended a small, local public school and although he wasn't especially feminine, he wasn't particularly interested in sports or typical boy activities he recalls. In the fifth grade, he was chosen for a citywide project designed to interest students in the arts and in drama. He remembers being very interested in the acting and having virtually no fear of rejection by the audience or his peers.

Things changed in junior high however when his family moved and he began attending a large regional junior high school next to a public housing project. He remembers developing some concern about the "tough kids" he saw there, given the fact that he was physically a very late bloomer. He quickly became a target for harassment by other kids for his size and lack of athletic interest. After begging his parents to send him to Catholic school, they finally agreed to allow him to attend a local Catholic high school, where he bonded with his eventual best friend, Frank, also a target and social "outcast."

From his first Communion in the second grade, Patrick wanted to be a Catholic priest. His devout family attended Mass regularly and he reflected on the safety that burying himself in the Church provided for him during those years. Part of his desire to go to Catholic school was driven by a desire to be an altar boy, since his local church did not allow non-Catholic school students to participate.

Patrick says he can't remember any overt same sex attraction to males until he was in college. He learned in CCD (Catholic Christian Doctrine classes) that it was a sin to act on bad thoughts, but that even bad thoughts themselves were sins. Now, he thinks that at some level, he learned to block potentially "sinful" thoughts from his mind back then and was so successful that he can't recall even having them.

In high school, he recalls that he woke up in a panic, having dreamed that he kissed his best friend Frank. He immediately turned to his church's rituals of confession and prayer.

As most boys his age, he began masturbating regularly, but Patrick's experience was constantly tinged with guilt and shame over the clear "sin" he was committing. A theme of setting deadlines and rationalization emerged during those years that Patrick recognized as having helped him cope with guilt around sexual feelings and behaviors many times later in his life. He remembers thinking, "I'll just masturbate until I get through high school and then I'll be able to stop."

In college, Patrick went for a visit to his friend Frank, who was at that point a sophomore and living in an off-campus apartment. One day, while Frank was in class, Patrick found Frank's gay magazines with pictures of naked men and became instantly very excited by them. He remembers thinking, "I'll jerk off, get this out of my head, and it'll be ok, I'll go back to being normal. As soon as I'm married, I won't do this anymore." Patrick felt at the time that his thoughts were something that he "could control" and for a short period of time, he was able to control the thoughts.

While very excited by those pictures of naked men, Patrick was also attracted to some women as well, which offered him some sense of relief that he probably "wasn't gay." He met Amy, was initially very attracted to her, and soon they were married and having children. He believes that he was successfully able to avoid confronting his deeper sexuality by throwing himself into the role of husband and father. He occasionally would still look at *Hustler*, would look at the males in the pictures, and would rationalize by saying to himself, "that's what I want to look like." Sex with his wife was good, but he remembers viewing the sexual act "from a distance."

It wasn't until he turned 30 in 1988, and his wife was pregnant with their third child and they began having discussions about a vasectomy, that he began taking a more introspective approach to his life. The thought of a vasectomy made him feel sad, like a part of his life was ending. It was during these journeys inward that he finally acknowledged his "gay" feelings to himself. For seven years, he remembers struggling internally with these feelings; with a sense of sadness and confusion. He often felt that he must be the only married man in the world with these feelings, and the thought of talking about how he felt was just too overwhelming. His Catholic upbringing continued to have a constricting affect on his fantasy life, as he worked hard to suppress his sexuality.

Finally, in 1994, while traveling for work in New York City, he was relaxing by watching a local public access channel when a show reviewing gay porn popped onto the screen. This prompted a trip to a porno video store and the first time he considered the idea of two men actually having sex. Soon, Patrick joined the millions of Americans subscribing to AOL, and quickly began exploring the m4m chat rooms while sitting in lonely hotel rooms when traveling for work. Initially, he says he just watched the conversations between others, having no intention of participating in the discussions or acting on sexual impulses. Eventually, however, he found himself chatting with other men who were also married, progressing from casual conversations to shared cyber and phone sex fantasies.

Patrick often felt extremely guilty about these conversations, but could somehow rationalize it because he was "away from home." As long as he didn't meet these men, he felt that he could, "get it out of my system," and go home on the weekend and be who he was "supposed" to be.

Around age 40, his marriage began to deteriorate. Amy was craving more intimacy, while he wanted less. He found himself becoming more attracted to men, both sexually and emotionally, and began having conversations with another married man who was in a similar place in his life. Initially, they were both determined to stay married and avoid relationships with men, but soon Patrick agreed to meet the other guy for coffee. A second meeting soon after Patrick's forty-first birthday led to sexual experimentation, during which he felt the most sexual excitement he'd ever felt in his life. After the meeting, Patrick was transferred to another project and he moved away, but he clearly remembers that an emotional line had been crossed. He resisted further sexual exploration for another year thinking that if he could just make it to his fiftieth birthday, his sex drive would diminish naturally and this struggle would end.

The Internet continued to be the one place that Patrick could talk honestly with other men who had similar feelings and explore the layers of programming in his head about who he was and what he wanted in life. He began working in a very isolated area, with lots of down time that gave him lot of time to think. It became increasingly clear to him that these feelings were not going away and he feared that his feelings might be something he couldn't handle. His relationship with his wife became more difficult and he began to have physical problems having sex with her. Amy was getting more depressed and Patrick found himself considering the value of his life insurance payout for his children.

His online friends Ted and Christian convinced him to see a therapist, a former Catholic priest, with whom Patrick could identify, who helped him for the first time in 2000 acknowledge to himself that he was a gay man. He could not imagine telling anyone in his real life about his revelation, but his marriage to Amy continued to deteriorate. He remembers the down time between sexual activity, and Amy's depression concurrently increasing during this time, and even secretly ordering Viagra online to help him perform with her.

By January of 2002, he realized that things were not going to get better physically and that he needed to explain why to her. This conversation did not go well. He had imagined that she suspected that he was gay, but in fact, her reaction was one of complete shock. Although they first talked about staying together, she was the one who began questioning the real feasibility of maintaining a sexless marriage. While at some levels Patrick now feels relief, and is more honest with himself and everyone around him, he sometimes wonders if he made the right choice since his family life changed so dramatically. Amy at times used her hurt and anger to punish him and to threaten to use his gayness as a weapon in divorce court. He knows some married men who are still in relationships with their wives and children but have occasional trysts with men and claim to be happy. He knows others who have come out to their wives, remained married, but are in open relationships so that they can act on their same sex attractions and are happy with this arrangement.

Things are better now with Amy, and his relationships with his children, all adults now, have continued to improve. After a few false starts, Patrick has met someone, Kurt, with whom he's now shared his life for two years. Loving a man in a committed relationship has been satisfying in many ways that he dared not imagine in the beginning of his journey. He still deals with family members who have not yet fully embraced him and his new life, but he is standing firm in his own self-acceptance and growth as a gay man.

Although Patrick's journey was sometimes rocky, as he learned to understand his emerging sexuality, he ultimately made it to a place where he felt more authentic as a gay man. Others who face this same challenge, namely deep-seated feelings of attraction to the same sex, that at some level they find unacceptable, are held at bay by other psychological processes that they may not realize are there.

Reaction formation, for example, is an unconscious defense mechanism which has been used to explain extreme homophobia in men (and women), who identify themselves as exclusively heterosexual. The thinking goes like this: Most men who are comfortable with their sexuality and find homosexuality, or the idea of two men engaging in sexual activity, not appealing or even repulsive, are successfully able to cope with these feelings in a socially responsible way (i.e. resisting homophobic expressions or threats). Some men, however, unable to cope with the idea of gayness, become anxious and overreact. Freud's theory of reaction formation, suggests that one possible reason that these men become so agitated at the thought of other men who are gay is because at some deeper level, they are conflicted about their own sexuality. Rather than admit this conflict, the nominal heterosexual adopts a very public anti-gay stance, both to strengthen his own internal resolve against acting on his own sexual orientation struggle, but also to throw off any possible suspicion of these feelings by others.

Interestingly, this theory was tested empirically by a team of researchers at the University of Georgia measuring penile blood flow in men who identified themselves as totally heterosexual when they were shown pictures of gay sex. Those who expressed the most negative and hostile attitudes toward homosexuals actually showed the strongest sexual arousal to gay porn. As Shakespeare may have put it best, "methinks thou doest protest too much!"

LIVING STRAIGHT, FEELING CROOKED

Other people who become aware of their interest in the same sex choose a different path from Patrick, both before, during, and after significant relationships with the opposite sex. Instead of the unconscious mind now holding back this information from consciousness, they actively use a process referred to as *suppression* to avoid dealing with uncomfortable feelings or thoughts. These are men or women who either have a long history of actively attempting to ignore feelings of attraction to the same sex and choose to marry as a way to prove their heterosexuality, or they only become aware of same sex attraction after repression begins to give way and these feelings emerge after they have already married or established a committed heterosexual relationship. Keeping uncomfortable feelings in a box, so to speak, requires an enormous amount of energy. Imagine the force fields in *Star Trek* that protected the ship from intruders ("diverting C deck energy to the shield Captain"). Day after day suppression of feelings or thoughts that are uncomfortable requires energy that has to come from somewhere else. Energy that could be used for professional, romantic, spiritual, or creative pursuits is drained away to keep these thoughts locked away.

Over time, keeping up this strict lockdown of a part of oneself can have devastating consequences. Family relationships suffer as a person begins to avoid intimate talks or time alone, for fear of losing control over the sensitive stuff inside. Laughing or totally relaxing is threatening as these times become moments when the guard might weaken. Long hours at work can turn into an obsession and taking time to explore feelings is minimized.

For some, living in this tense, exhausting place turns into clinical depression, complete with its own symptoms. Treatment may be avoided since acknowledging depression may mean that someone suggests you look inside for the causes. Exploring your inner life means opening up to the issues that may have caused you to close up in the beginning. Life starts to feel like a trap with no exits.

When a person actively trying to suppress same sex feelings begins to succumb to the exhaustion, inner resolve may weaken. Some choose to finally break vows of monogamy and act on these feelings in secret. Others drink or use drugs to blur the feelings of desire, guilt, stress, and shame. A few consider suicide and a few succeed.

SCANDALS AND SCOUNDRELS

Repression may explain why some men choose not to act on unconscious same sex attraction, but what about men who identify as heterosexual, express open homophobia, and who are in a relationship with a woman but have sex with men on the side?

This particular group of men has gotten a lot of press lately. Ted Haggard, founder and one time pastor of the evangelical New Life

Church in Colorado Springs, CO, made headlines late in 2006 when the man he reportedly was having sex with regularly, Mike Jones, outed him to the press. Jones, who claims that Mr. Haggard also was purchasing and using crystal meth with him as well, has implied that he felt an obligation to expose hypocrisy after he realized that Haggard was a conservative evangelist with anti-gay leanings who was married to a woman, yet meeting him for sex and drugs on the side. Mr. Haggard has admitted that he purchased meth, but claims that he didn't use it and also didn't have sex with Mike Jones. He was asked to step down from his ministry position by the board of the church he helped found.

The pressure to conform is enormous, regardless of your age or status in life. Reaching a modicum of professional success or esteemed position in the community carries with it the scrutiny of others. As difficult as it was for Patrick to come out, after having married and created a family, someone like Ted Haggard carries even more pressure (some of it self-imposed perhaps) to maintain an image of a role model. Sometimes, good old fashioned denial (e.g., "it depends on what your definition of 'is' is") or a meandering rationalization (e.g., "a massage with a full release isn't actually 'sex'"), are the ways that men who sleep with other men on the side explain away their behaviors.

Deep Closets

Other men, who may not be in primary relationships with women, but are publicly anti-gay, while privately they sleep with men, may use justification or rationalization to reconcile the opposing values they apparently hold. If these men know they are gay or personally aware, and at some level accepting of their same sex attraction, why then would they choose to support or proclaim homophobic positions?

Republican Congressman Mark Foley, who was forced to resign in September of 2006 after it was discovered that he regularly sent sexually explicit instant messages and e-mails to young male congressional pages, claimed in his defense that he had been abused by a Catholic priest as a child and later checked himself into an alcohol rehab program. While his homosexuality had apparently been an open secret in Washington D.C., and to the Republican leadership, his public response to speculations that he was gay before the scandal broke was that the question itself was "revolting and unforgivable." Which prompts the questions: *Did he mean that being gay was revolting and unforgivable? Or did he mean that reporters that ask questions about his sexuality were revolting and unforgivable? Was Mark Foley confused about his sexuality? Did the pressure of having power in a homophobic party cause him to compromise his own integrity? How could a man who was apparently widely known for his homosexuality bring himself to vote for legislation that was specifically anti-gay? Does the adage "absolute power corrupts absolutely" create these types of dilemmas?*

Jim West, former Republican mayor of Spokane, WA, had an equally troubled, double life apparently. After supporting legislation in his own home state to ban gays from working in schools and day care centers, Mr. West in the meantime was reportedly offering "internships" to young gay men, fresh out of high school. After his alleged use of the Internet, and the power of his position to attract young men surfaced, calls for his resignation began immediately. He defended himself for supporting anti-gay laws in office while living a closeted gay life by saying, "If someone hires you to paint their house red, then you paint it red. Even if you think it would look better green." He was eventually removed from office through a voter recall in December of 2005. Mr. West was diagnosed with colon cancer in 2003 and passed away from complications of the disease in July of 2006.

What explains the behaviors of Haggard, Foley, and West? Is there something about being in a position of power that leads to compromised integrity? Or were they just old fashioned hypocrites? Do they have underlying self-esteem problems? Targets of vengeful people? Not strong enough to confront the cultural homophobia that they have internalized? Some or all of the above? Perhaps we will never know the truth, but the facts remain that people who sleep with others of the same sex still face enormous social and internal pressures to maintain double lives, one that the public can adore, with another that dare not speak its name.

THE BISEXUAL SOLUTION

In a black or white, all or nothing world, it is easy to see how sexuality can be forced into the limits of dichotomous thinking. Before people began choosing to identify themselves as homosexuals, the idea that there was more than one option for sexuality was below society's awareness radar. As I've mentioned before, Alfred Kinsey, renowned sex researcher, was among the first to recognize that human sexuality lies on a continuum (i.e., the famous Kinsey Scale). The notion that a person was either heterosexual or homosexual was not supported by the data from his interviews with hundreds of "normal" males and females, and his 1948 book, *Sexual Behavior in the Human Male*, rocked the foundations of many people who had taken comfort in the notion that sexuality was fixed and unchanging, and you were either one way or the other.

The idea that sexuality could range from a one on his six point scale, meaning exclusively heterosexual, to a six, meaning exclusively homosexual, with most people falling somewhere in between the end points, radically changed the commonly held assumptions about the options that were available. Some historians have argued that we are progressing to past times when same sex behavior was considered a normal and appropriate part of life, such as in ancient Greece. The effect of dualistic ways of thinking , such as the existence of a heaven and a hell, God or Satan, Republican or Democratic, has entered the cultural consciousness, often forcing us to see complex issues as overly simplistic and categorized. Expanding the concept of sexuality as a fluid, changeable, and continuous phenomenon allowed the idea that one could be attracted to more than one sex to enter into the possibilities.

The notion that one could be bisexual, or have attractions to both sexes, added exploration opportunities for many teens and young adults in the "free love" era of the 1960's. It became more acceptable to "experiment" with sex play with both genders on the way to "finding yourself."

Bisexuality, as a viable alternative to an either/or mentality regarding sexual identity has helped solve the dilemma of finding the best fit for many people. One might argue that Patrick, in our example, could be considered bisexual, but now, in his own experience, he strongly prefers intimacy with men. Other people, who fall closer to the middle of Kinsey's continuum in terms of sexual orientation, may find themselves fairly equally sexually attracted to both sexes, yet find that their emotional affinity is for one sex or the other.

People who are aware of their desires for the same sex, and perhaps even fantasize about acting on those desires and enjoy the fantasy but choose not to step outside of a committed relationship with someone of the opposite sex, may also use a form of suppression to manage these feelings while remaining faithful to the committed relationship. But they also may choose to deal with the fantasies and behaviors in a more direct and honest way with their spouse. In nonmonogamous relationships, some open bisexuals have made arrangements with their affectional partner to allow bisexual expression or exploration outside the relationship in ways that both partners can accept. This choice can be difficult and challenging for many relationships, but does offer an opportunity to deepen the communication and deal more directly with issues of trust and vulnerability.

Today's constructs of human sexuality allow for the expression of many different dimensions or aspects of a person, including gender identity, sexual orientation, and affectional attraction, all of which can be dynamic and fluid over time.

THE INTERNET

One scarcely mentioned, but very important player in the down low phenomenon has to be the Internet. Before there were chat rooms, Web sites, and blogs, people who were interested in exploring their sexual feelings had to reach a critical internal pressure point in order to risk venturing out to a lesbian or gay bar, or a tea room, or respond to a personal ad. Summoning up the courage to even acknowledge same sex attractions can be a difficult, wrenching process. Acting on these feelings can be even more fraught with anxiety and intimidation.

When I was a teenager, coming to terms with my sexuality, I searched high and low for anything I could find on same sex attraction. One day, at 13, I accidentally stumbled onto the word "homosexual" in the *Encyclopedia Britannica* with the brief description "a person who is attracted sexually to people of the same sex." You may as well have hit me on the head with an anvil as I reeled from the first awareness that there was a term for what I felt inside, and that there must be others like me out there. Once I had a name for it, my search became a little easier, but was still limited to researching in a library (in a small, conservative town mind you) and in bookstores on the sly. It was by accident that I overheard a conversation in a high school hallway one day about an older alum's experience at a major state university "where they have homosexuals living in the dormitories." Right then and there, I knew that's where I would go to college! Once I arrived, I indeed finally found a formal student group for lesbians and gays on campus, and from there the pieces fell into place.

With the rise of the information superhighway, however, it has become much easier to read or learn about almost anything you have even the remotest curiosity about. You may not even understand why you feel like looking up some arbitrary bit of trivia; you just do it because you can. You might be surprised at some of the silly thoughts that have occurred to me to Google. I'm usually even more surprised when exactly the questions I am asking are answered with a few clicks of the keyboard.

Now, a person who is even mildly curious about sexuality issues can find almost anything on the Internet, from academic research on a topic to hard core, same sex pornography. A few people may even "accidentally" stumble on to a gay discussion group or blog, and find that their interest is piqued.

Aside from being able to read and explore topics from the largest library in the world in the privacy of your own home, the Internet also quickly became a place to connect with other people live, through chat rooms, and later Internet phones and Webcams. Chat rooms were established to provide places to send text messages instantly to others online at the same time and were typically set up around specific common interests or personal characteristics. America Online, for example, was one of the first and largest Internet service providers that offered many different types of chat rooms, for topics as broad ranging as gardening to automotive repair, all the way to gay or lesbian rooms.

Of course, these general interest chat rooms quickly became a place to meet others, first online and then sometimes, in real life. As the online chatting experience became more popular, more highly specific chat rooms were developed so that if your interest was dating, or quick sex, you could find a room where you could "listen" or participate in the discussions. Gay chat rooms therefore evolved into m4m (men for men), T4T (trans for trans), bisexual chat, leather and bear, lipstick lesbian, etc. By the mid-90's, it wasn't unusual to see mm4mm groups (married men for married men) and other highly specific types of discussion groups.

Chatting online, while psychologically risky (since it requires stepping into unfamiliar territory for some), offered a much safer alternative for many women and men to explore sexual identity than either isolated fantasy or taking the huge step of going out to meet someone in person. Many people found that creating an online identity allowed them to explore conversation and discussion in ways that they could have never mustered the courage to do in person. The relative anonymity of the Internet also allowed people to step out of themselves in ways that didn't present the possibility of a sexually transmitted disease or possible discovery and damage to reputations.

Adopting an online persona has expanded the ways that women and men with secret lives can try on new roles, without necessarily risking everything. Many men like Patrick, on the way to coming out, experiment with other men on the down low, and acknowledge the role that the Internet played in helping them find the courage to accept themselves and integrate a new identity. Meeting other men in similar positions, or adopting an online "gay" or "bisexual" persona in order to discuss feelings of same sex attraction before they are ready to act, creates an opportunity to educate, experiment, and explore. Later, once the decision has been made to move forward and to physically explore, the Internet becomes a premier way to meet others for activity on the down low, rather than in a bar or other public gathering place.

Today, many people use the internet as a forum for discussion of a variety of feelings, sexualities, theologies, politics, and—yes—even dating. Brad and I met through Match.com at the same time two of my close friends also met their heterosexual spouses. It has limitless possibilities to connect us and is a lifeline for many queer folk who are isolated or alone. I can only imagine how different my journey might have been if I had been able to Google "same sex attraction" at 13.

Down Low and Up Again

Living on the down low is related to self-esteem. I included this topic in the revised edition because it seemed like a natural fit for a book that talks a lot about challenging old, negative messages that have the capacity to stunt emotional growth and change. While many people have come out by living temporarily on the down low (and now live their lives more authentically), others have not yet found a way to confront their double lives and the pain that it may be causing them and the people they love.

Getting married or partnering up with someone of the opposite sex is what we're told we are supposed to do, at a certain age, often within a specific tradition. Understanding our true orientation may unfortunately come after we've followed the culture's expectations and created a life or a family based on what we thought were the relationships we wanted, but weren't really.

Society bears some of the responsibility for creating a world in which people don't always feel free to be themselves, and then are faced with enormous pressure to remain closeted and unhappy, or to face complex, and difficult decisions to risk breaking vows or hearts, in order to live more authentically.

In an ideal world, where variations of adult and responsible human sexuality are accepted from birth, people would not need to explore secret identities in covert ways. Children would be encouraged to ask lots of questions about budding sexual interests and in turn, be given accurate, responsible information about the variations in lifestyles and choices available to them.

Until that day, people must find their way through a myriad of challenges in order to understand sexual orientation and gender identity. It sometimes feels like parents, religious zealots, and society at large conspire to muddy the process and muddle our senses so that we have to peel away layers of conditioning and expectations before we can really see who we are.

To anyone reading this book that may be living on the down low, I hope that you are able to find a path to a life of peace and authenticity. I wish you courage and strength to face the challenges that lie ahead as you confront the double standards our society has created.

Resources

Bi Married Male Resources, www.bimarried.com

Bisexual Resource Center, www.biresource.org

Gay Married Men's Association (GAMMA), www.gay-married.com

Married Gay: Resources for gays or lesbians married to or partnered to someone of the opposite sex, www.marriedgay.org

Straight Spouse Network: Information and support for straight spouses of LGBTs, www.straightspouse.org

SEVENTEEN

Growth and Change

ONE OF THESE DAYS, I'M GONNA LOVE ME.
—*Kip Raines, Monty Powell, and Marcus Hummon,*
"One of These Days"

Although this book is not specifically about how to improve your relationships, your career, your sex life, your health, or your diet, as your self-esteem improves, all of these areas will begin to improve as well. In every area, you will place your best interests first, taking a long-term hedonist perspective that allows you to see yourself living happily for many years in the future, versus a short-term, impulse-driven perspective that can shorten your years and leave you feeling empty and alone. You will find yourself wanting to overcome self-destructive habits like smoking, using alcohol or meth, procrastinating, and either avoiding or becoming addicted to exercise. You will come to care more for yourself and want to be more loving and self-nurturing, which in turn will change the quality of your relationships with others. After all, healthy people attract other healthy people. And when unhealthy people or other crises come into your life, you will learn to appropriately deal with them and waste less emotional energy obsessing over things beyond your control. You will treat yourself more like a best friend and when you do slip up and say or do unhealthy things, you will take note and move on, promising yourself that you will work on having that happen less often without beating yourself into the ground.

Having healthy self-esteem will not make you selfish or demanding. It will not make you narcissistic, taking advantage of others for your own gain. Selfish behavior and attention seeking are in fact outward manifestations of inner insecurity and low self-esteem. It will help you experience life more authentically and use your natural intuition as a guide to healthier living. Good self-esteem involves developing a whole new perspective about yourself from one of feeling flawed, anxious, and undeserving to one of feeling okay with your human imperfections, feeling more peaceful and worthy of respect and affection.

I have encouraged you to feel your feelings at times in this book. You may have felt grief for old losses, like the ideal childhood or parents most of us longed for. Or, you may have felt angry, perhaps at people who feel entitled to judge you, your experiences, your feelings, and your behaviors, assuming that their way is correct and appropriate for you and everyone else.

As you become more comfortable with your spontaneous emotional life, it will be like getting to know a new friend, you will discover your true likes and dislikes, your preferences, and your positive and negative qualities. Building your self-esteem can be an exciting and incredibly freeing process. It can also be frightening and frustrating, requiring deeper work on your own or with a professional. You will likely have moments of both kinds of experiences. With practice, you will become more adept at navigating the ups and downs, accepting yourself as a human, and understanding that all humans are imperfect. Expect to have up days and down times since no one has all ups! It is okay to make mistakes, to relapse, to hear yourself say the very things over and over that you recognized as irrational and you thought you had overcome. But then remind yourself of the long-term, of having peaks and valleys from time to time, and see the bigger picture of your gradual progression toward becoming gentler, more compassionate, and more loving toward yourself.

As your self-esteem grows, you will find yourself becoming less tolerant of people stepping over appropriate boundaries. You will learn to set firm limits to protect yourself, but at the same time not shut everyone out. You are an important part of something big and beautiful. You must protect yourself but you must also open yourself up when it's safe and promising.

When your self-esteem grows, you will feel more empowered to take risks, some small—like showing your talents unabashedly at work—some big—like coming out to family or co-workers. This is not to say that everyone reading this book should take these same risks. You must gauge for yourself what is reasonable, what is in your own best self-interests, and what will maintain your livelihood.

One of the greatest missing pieces for people with low self-esteem is a well-developed spiritual life. People with low self-esteem often lack a sense of connectedness to the world and universe that they can rely on to help them through crises, emotional fatigue, and stagnation. Gays, lesbians, and our queer-identified kindred too often have been told that they are not a part of the world spiritually, that there is no room for them in religion (unless they change). Now is the time to take back your right to a healthy spiritual life, however you choose to define it—a belief in God or a higher power, or just an understanding of the valuable role you play in the organization of the world as a whole. You are a complex organism, capable of thinking about issues on multiple levels, not just right or wrong, yes or no. Push the limits of your thinking, weigh issues from several perspectives, find options and choices beyond the two most obvious. Live for the moments of joy you can find every day.

I find comfort sometimes in imagining myself as a part of a thin cotton fiber, twisted into a thread, braided into yarn, and woven into a huge tapestry that is the universe. I know that although my fiber may have tiny flaws or imperfections, it still provides some of the strength and color of the thread that holds together the yarn that colors and shapes the much larger tapestry. Someone looking at the tapestry from a distance sees only the great beauty, the completeness, the masterful design and genius behind it, not the tiny imperfections in each fiber underneath. In fact, it may just be the case that the imperfections are what give the piece texture and depth. This image is powerful to me because it reminds me to step back and take a new perspective, to see where I fit even if others cannot.

I hope this book has helped you to see yourself from this perspective and that as you grow, you will remember that *you are a part of the world, you have a right to exist,* and *you are worthy of love.* If you have read the book without doing the work, start the process now, today. Do the exercises, find a therapist, start a spiritual journey—do whatever you feel is necessary to start loving yourself.

REFERENCES AND RESOURCES

INTRODUCTION

Benotsch, E. G., Kalichman, S. C., & Kelly, J. A. 1999. "Sexual compulsivity and substance use in HIV seropositive men who have sex with men: Prevalence and predictors of high risk behaviors." *Addictive Behaviors*, 24(6), 857-868.

Gibson, P. 1989. "Gay male and lesbian youth suicide." In M. Feinleib, ed. *Prevention and Intervention in Youth Suicide* (Report to the Secretary's Task Force on Youth Suicide, 3:110-142). Washington, D.C. U.S. Department of Health and Human Services.

Nyamathi, A. 1991. "Relationship of resources to emotional distress, somatic complaints, and high-risk behaviors in drug recovery and homeless minority women." *Res Nurs Health* 14(4):269-277.

Proctor, C. D., and V. K. Groze. 1994. "Risk factors for suicide among gay, lesbian and bisexual youths." *Social Work* 39:505-513.

Remafedi, G., Farrow, J.A., & Deisher, R.W. 1991. "Risk Factors for attempted suicide in gay and bisexual youth." *Pediatrics* 87:869-875.

Rich, C. L., Fowler, R.C., Young, D. & Blenkush, M. 1986. San Diego suicide study: Comparison of gay to straight males. *Suicide and Life-Threatening Behavior* 16:448-457.

Saghir, M. T. & Robins, T. 1973. *Male and Female Homosexuality: A Comprehensive Investigation*. Baltimore: Williams & Wilkins.

Savin-Williams, R. C. 1994. "Verbal and physical abuse as stressors in the lives of lesbian, gay male, and bisexual youths: Associations with school problems, running away, substance abuse, prostitution, and suicide." *Journal of Consulting and Clinical Psychology* 62(2):251-269.

———. 1989a. "Parental influences on the self-esteem of gay and lesbian youths: A reflected appraisals model." *Journal of Homosexuality* 17: 93-109

———. 1989b. "Coming out to parents and self-esteem of gay and lesbian youths." *Journal of Homosexuality* 18:1-35.

Scheider, S. G., N. L. Farberow, and G. N. Kruks. 1989. "Suicidal behavior in adolescents and young adult gay men." *Suicide and Life-Threatening Behavior* 19:381-394.

Sears, J. T. 1991. *Growing Up Gay in the South: Race, Gender, and Journeys of the Spirit.* New York: Harrington Press.

CHAPTER 1

Beck, A. 1991. "Cognitive therapy: A 30-year retrospective." *American Psychologist* 46:368-375.

Ellis, A. 1975. *Guide to Rational Living.* New York: Wilshire Book Company.

CHAPTER 2

Adorno, T.W., Frenkel-Brunswick, E., Levinson, D.J. & Sanford, R.N. 1950. *The Authoritarian Personality.* New York: Harper.

Baumkind, D. 1968. "Authoritarian vs. authoritative parental control." Adolescence 3:255-272.

Bradshaw, J. 1988. *Healing the Shame That Binds You.* Deerfield Beach, Fla.: Health Communications, Inc.

Forward, S. 1989. *Toxic Parents: Overcoming Their Hurtful Legacy and Reclaiming Your Life.* New York: Bantam Books.

Isensee, R. 1991. *Growing Up Gay in a Dysfunctional Family: A Guide for Gay Men Reclaiming Their Lives.* New York: Prentice Hall.

Mehrabian, A. 1972. *Nonverbal Communication.* Chicago: Aldine-Atherton.

CHAPTER 3

Kinsey, A.C. et al. 1953. *Sexual Behavior in the Human Female.* Philadelphia: Saunders.

———. 1948. *Sexual Behavior in the Human Male.* Philadelphia: Saunders.

Miller, N. 1995. *Out of the Past: Gay and Lesbian History from 1869 to the Present.* New York: Vintage Books (Random House).

———. 1992. *Out in the World: Gay and Lesbian Life from Buenos Aires to Bangkok.* New York: Random House.

———. 1989. *In Search of Gay America.* New York: Atlantic Monthly Press.

Russo, V. 1987. *The Celluloid Closet: Homosexuality in the Movies* (Revised Edition). New York: Harper and Row.

Sullivan, A. 1995. *Virtually Normal: An Argument about Homosexuality.* New York: Alfred A. Knopf.

Tannen, D. 1998. *The Argument Culture: Moving from Dialogue to Debate.* New York: Random House.

CHAPTER 4

Berzon, B. 1996. *Setting Them Straight: You Can Do Something About Bigotry and Homophobia in Your Life*. New York: Plume.

Fox, M. 1983. *Original Blessing*. Santa Fe, N.M.: Bear & Company Publishing.

Helminiak, D. 1994. *What the Bible Really Says About Homosexuality*. San Francisco: Alamo Square Press.

Kertzer, M, and Hoffman, L. 1993. *What Is a Jew?: A Guide to the Beliefs, Traditions, and Practices of Judaism That Answers Questions for Both Jew and Non-Jew*. New York: Simon and Schuster.

Leyland, W., ed. 1998. *Queer Dharma: Voices of Gay Buddhists*. San Francisco: Gay Sunshine Press.

Murray, S., Roscoe, W., Allyn, E. & Crompton, L. 1997. *Islamic Homosexualities: Culture, History and Literature*. New York: New York University Press.

Spong, J. S. 1991. *Rescuing the Bible from Fundamentalism*. New York: HarperCollins. 1988.

Living in Sin: A Bishop Rethinks Human Sexuality. New York: HarperCollins.

Swidler, A., (ed.). 1993. *Homosexuality and World Religions*. Valley Forge, Penn.: Trinity Press International.

CHAPTER 5

Herek, G.M., and B. Greene. 1995. *AIDS, Identity, and Community: The HIV Epidemic and Lesbians and Gay Men*. Thousand Oaks, Calif.: Sage.

Jennings, K. 1998. *Telling Tales Out of School*. Los Angeles: Alyson Publications.

Kominars, S. & Kominars, K. 1996. *Accepting Ourselves: A Journey into Recovery from Addictive & Compulsive Behaviors for Gays, Lesbians & Bisexuals*. Center City, Minn.: Hazelden Publications.

Miller, N. 1995. *Out of the Past: Gay and Lesbian History from 1869 to the Present*. New York: Vintage Books.

Shilts, R. 1988. *And the Band Played On: Politics, People and the AIDS Epidemic*. New York: Viking Pen.

Sullivan, A. 1995. *Virtually Normal: An Argument about Homosexuality*. New York: Knopf.

Thompson, R. 1996. *Extraordinary Bodies: Figuring Physical Disability in American Literature and Culture*. New York: Columbia University Press.

Woog, D. 1998. Jocks: *True Stories of America's Gay Male Athletes*. Los Angeles: Alyson Publications.

———. 1995. *School's Out: The Impact of Gay and Lesbian Issues on America's Schools*. Los Angeles: Alyson Publications.

Young, P., & Duberman, M. 1996. *Lesbians and Gays and Sports: Issues in Lesbian and Gay Life*. New York: Chelsea House.

CHAPTER 6

O'Hara, Valerie. 1995. *Wellness at Work: Building Resilience to Job Stress.* Oakland, Calif.: New Harbinger Publications.

Rusi, Richard, and Lourdes Rodrigues-Nordes. 1995. *Out in the Workplace: The Pleasures and Perils of Coming Out on the Job.* Los Angeles: Alyson Publications.

CHAPTER 7

Berzon, Betty. 1997. *The Intimacy Dance: A Guide to Long-Term Success in Gay and Lesbian Relationships.* New York: Plume.

———. 1990. *Permanent Partners: Building Gay and Lesbian Relationships That Last.* New York: Plume.

Black, J., and Enns, G. 1997. *Better Boundaries: Owning and Treasuring Your Life.* Oakland, Calif.: New Harbinger Publications.

McKay, M, Davis, M. and Fanning. P. 1995. *Messages: The Communication Skills Workbook* (second edition). Oakland, Calif.: New Harbinger Publications.

McKay, M, Fanning, P. and Paleg, K. 1994. *Couple Skills: Making Your Relationship Work.* Oakland, Calif.: New Harbinger Publications.

CHAPTER 8

Cass, V.C. 1984. "Homosexual identity formation: testing a theoretical model." *Journal of Sex Research* 20(2):143-167.

———. 1990. "The implications of homosexual identity formation for the Kinsey model and scale of sexual preference." In *Homosexuality/Heterosexuality: Concepts of Sexual Orientation.* The Kinsey Institute Series, Vol. 2, edited by David P. McWhirter, Stephanie A. Sanders, and June M. Reinisch. New York: Oxford University Press.

Herek, G., and Beverly Greene. 1995. *AIDS, Identity, and Community: The HIV Epidemic and Lesbians and Gay Men.* Thousand Oaks, CA: Sage Publications.

Kramer, L. 2000. *Faggotts.* Grove Press.

Rodrigues, T. 1998. "UCSF study shows HIV risk tied to self-esteem issues." *Bay Area Reporter.* July 2, 33.

Sontag, S. 1990. *Illness As Metaphor and AIDS and Its Metaphors.* New York: Anchor.

Trimpey, J. 1996. *Rational Recovery: The New Cure for Substance Addiction.* New York: Pocket Books.

Waldo, C., S. Kegeles, and R. Hays. 1998. Paper presented at the June 29th, 1998, 12th International Conference of AIDS.

CHAPTER 9

Bourne, E. 1995. *The Anxiety and Phobia Workbook* (second edition). Oakland, Calif.: New Harbinger Publications.

Caplan, S. & Lang, G. 1995. *Grief's Courageous Journey: A Workbook*. Oakland, Calif.: New Harbinger Publications.

Copeland, M. E. 1992. *The Depression Workbook: A Guide for Living with Depression*. Oakland, Calif.: New Harbinger Publications.

Cornell, A. 1996. *The Power of Focusing: A Practical Guide to Emotional Self-Healing*. Oakland, Calif.: New Harbinger Publications.

Markway, B, Carmin, C., Pollard, A. & Flynn, T. 1992. *Dying of Embarrassment: Help for Social Anxiety and Social Phobia*. Oakland, Calif.: New Harbinger Publications.

Potter-Efron, R. & Potter-Efron, P. 1995. *Letting Go of Anger: The Ten Most Common Anger Styles and What to Do About Them*. Oakland, Calif.: New Harbinger Publications.

CHAPTER 10

Beck, J. 1995. *Cognitive Therapy: Basics and Beyond*. New York: The Guilford Press.

Burns, D. 1999. *Feeling Good: The New Mood Therapy Revised and Updated*. New York: Avon.

McKay, M., Davis, M. & Fanning. P. 1997. *Thoughts & Feelings: Taking Control of Your Moods and Your Life*. Oakland, Calif.: New Harbinger Publications.

McKay, M. & Fanning, P. 1992. *Self-Esteem* (second edition). Oakland, Calif.: New Harbinger Publications.

Greenberger, D. & Padesky, C. 1995. *Mind Over Mood: A Cognitive Therapy Treatment Manual for Clients*. New York: The Guilford Press.

CHAPTER 11

Alberti, R. & Emmons, M. 1995. *Your Perfect Right: A Guide to Assertive Living*. New York: Impact Publications.

Cash, T. 1997. *The Body Image Workbook: An 8-Step Program for Learning to Like Your Looks*. Oakland, Calif.: New Harbinger Publications.

Finney, L. 1997. *Clear Your Past, Change Your Future: Proven Techniques for Inner Exploration and Healing*. Oakland, Calif.: New Harbinger Publications.

Kort, J. 2006. *Ten Smart Things Gay Men Can Do to Find Real Love*. New York: Alyson.

Kort, J. 2003. *Ten Smart Things Gay Men Can Do to Improve Their Lives*. New York: Alyson.

McKay, M. & Fanning, P. 1992. *Self-Esteem: A Proven Program of Cognitive*

Techniques for Assessing, Improving, and Maintaining Your Self-Esteem. Oakland, Calif.: New Harbinger Publications.

——. 1991. *Prisoners of Belief: Exposing and Changing Beliefs That Control Your Life.* Oakland, Calif.: New Harbinger Publications.

Rutledge, T. 1997. *The Self-Forgiveness Handbook: A Practical and Empowering Guide.* Oakland, Calif.: New Harbinger Publications.

CHAPTER 12

De la Huerta, C. 1999. *Coming Out Spiritually: The Next Step.* New York: Tarcher.

Fabry, J. 1988. *Guideposts to Meaning: Discovering What Really Matters.* Oakland, Calif.: New Harbinger Publications.

Fox, M. 1991. *Creation Spirituality: Liberating Gifts for the Peoples of the Earth.* San Francisco: HarperCollins.

Hanh, T.N. 1991. *Peace Is Every Step: The Path of Mindfulness in Everyday Life.* New York: Bantam Books.

Kabat-Zinn, J. 1994. *Wherever You Go, There You Are: Mindfulness Meditation in Everyday Life.* New York: Hyperion.

——. 1990. *Full Catastrophe Living: Using the Wisdom of Your Body and Mind to Face Stress, Pain, and Illness.* New York: Bantam.

Kertzer, M & Hoffman, L. 1993. *What Is a Jew?: A Guide to the Beliefs, Traditions, and Practices of Judaism That Answers Questions for Both Jew and Non-Jew.* New York: Simon and Schuster.

Martin, M. 1992. *Atheism: A Philosophical Justification.* Philadelphia: Temple University Press.

O'Neill, C & Ritter, K. 1992. *Coming Out Within: Stages of Spiritual Awakening for Lesbians and Gay Men.* San Francisco: HarperCollins.

Taylor, S. 1995. *Lessons in Living.* New York: Doubleday.

Winell, M. 1994. *Leaving the Fold: A Guide for Former Fundamentalists and Others Leaving Their Religion.* Oakland, Calif.: New Harbinger Publications.

CHAPTER 13

Boenke, M. (ed.). 2003. *Transforming Families: Real Stories About Transgendered Loved Ones,* 2nd ed. California: Walter Trook Pub.

Boyd, H. 2004. *My Husband Betty: Love, Sex, and Life with a Crossdresser.* New York: Thunder's Mouth Press.

Brown, M.L. & Rounsley, C.A. 2003. *True Selves: Understanding Transsexualism—For Families, Friends, Co-workers, and Helping Professionals.* San Francisco: Jossey-Bass.

Burke, P. 1996. *Gender Shock: Exploding the Myths of Male and Female.* New York: Anchor.

Currah, P., Juang, R.M. & Minter, S.P. 2006. *Transgender Rights*, University of Minnesota Press.

Devor, A.H. 2003. "Witnessing and Mirroring: A Fourteen Stage Model of Transsexual Identity Formation," *Journal of Gay and Lesbian Psychotherapy*, 8 (1/2), 41-67.

Lev, A.I. 2004. *Transgender Emergence: Therapeutic Guidelines for Working with Gender Variant People and Their Families*. New York: Haworth Press.

MacKenzie, G.1994. *Transgender Nation*. Ohio: Popular Press.

Serrano, J. 2007. *Whipping Girl: A Transsexual Woman on Sexism and the Scapegoating of Femininity*. Emeryville, CA: Seal Press.

Teague, G. (ed.). 2006. *The New Goddess: Transgender Women in the Twenty-First Century*. Waterbury, CT: Fine Tooth Press.

CHAPTER 14

Adelman, M. 2000. *Midlife Lesbian Relationships: Friends, Lovers, Children, and Parents*. Binghamton, NY: Harrington Park Press.

Bergling, T. 2004. *Reeling in the Years: Gay Men's Perspectives on Age and Ageism*. Binghamton, NY: Southern Tier Editions.

Burda, J. 2004. *Estate Planning for Same Sex Couples*. Chicago: American Bar Association.

Claassen, C. 2005. *Whistling Women: A Study of the Lives of Older Lesbians*. New York: Haworth.

Clunis, D.M., Fredricksen-Goldsen, K.I., Freeman, P. & Nystrom, N.M. 2005. *Lives of Lesbian Elders: Looking Back, Looking Forward*. New York: Haworth Press.

Coleman, P. 2000. *Village Elders*. Chicago: University of Illinois Press.

Copper, B. 1987. *Ageism in the Lesbian Community*. Freedom, CA: The Crossing Press.

Curry, H., Clifford, D., & Hertz, F. 2005. *A Legal Guide For Lesbian & Gay Couples* (25th Anniversary Ed) 13th Edition. New York: Nolo.

Gershick, Z. 1998. *Gay Old Girls*. New York: Alyson Books.

Hertz, F. 1998. *Legal Affairs: Essential Advice for Same Sex Couples*. New York: Henry Holt & Co./Owl Books.

Jensen, K.L. 1999. *Lesbian Epiphanies: Women Coming Out Later in Life*. Binghamton, NY: Harrington Park Press.

Kooden, H. 2000. *Golden Men: The Power of Gay Midlife*. San Francisco: Harper.

Lockhart, J. 2002. *The Gay Men's Guide to Growing Older*. New York: Alyson Books.

Lustig, H.L. 1999. *4 Steps to Financial Security for Lesbian and Gay Couples*. New York: Ballantine.

Quam, J.K. 1997. *Social Services for Senior Gay Men and Lesbians*. Binghamton, NY: Harrington Park Press

Shernoff, M. (ed.) 1998. *Gay Widowers: Life After the Death of A Partner.* Binghamton, NY: Harrington Park Press.

CHAPTER 15

Lev, A.I. 2004. *The Complete Lesbian and Gay Parenting Guide.* Berkeley, CA: Berkley Trade
Paperbacks.
McGarry, K. 2003. *Fatherhood for Gay Men: An Emotional and Practical Guide to Becoming a Gay Dad.* San Francisco: Harrington Park Press.
Merilee, D. & Green, G. D. 1995. *The Lesbian Parenting Book: A Guide to Creating Families and Raising Children.* Seattle: Seal Press.
Priwer, S. & Phillips, C. 2006. *Gay Parenting: Complete Guide for Same-Sex Families.* Far Hills, NJ: New Horizon Press.
Sember, B.M. 2006. *Gay & Lesbian Parenting Choices: From Adopting or Using a Surrogate to Choosing the Perfect Father.* Franklin Lakes, NJ: Career Press.

CHAPTER 16

Abbot, D. & Famer, E. 1995. *From Wedded Wife to Lesbian Life: Stories of Transformation.* Berkeley, CA: Crossing Press.
Adams, H.E., Wright, L. W. & Lohr, B.A. 1996. "Is Homophobia Associated with Homosexual Arousal?", *Journal of Abnormal Psychology.* 105, 440-445.
Boykin, K. 2005. *Beyond the Down Low: Sex, Lies, and Denial in Black America.* New York: Carol & Graf.
Buxton, A.P. 1994. *The Other Side of the Closet: The Coming Out Crisis for Straight Spouses and Families.* New York: Wiley.
Grever, C. 2001. *My Husband is Gay: A Woman's Survival Guide.* Berkeley, CA: Crossing Press.
King, J.L. 2005. *On the Down Low: A Journey in the Lives of "Straight" Black Men Who Sleep with Men.* New York: Harlem Moon.
Klein, F. & Schwartz, T. (eds.). 2002. *Bisexual and Gay Husbands: Their Stories, Their Words.* New York: Haworth Press.
Leddick, D. 2003. *The Secret Lives of Married Men: Interviews with Gay Men Who Played It Straight.* New York: Alyson Books.
Ochas, R. 2001. *Bisexual Resource Guide* 4th Edition. Boston: Bisexual Resource Center.